TYPICAL GIRLS

STUDIES IN COMICS AND CARTOONS
Jared Gardner and Charles Hatfield, Series Editors

TYPICAL GIRLS

The Rhetoric of Womanhood in Comic Strips

SUSAN E. KIRTLEY

THE OHIO STATE UNIVERSITY PRESS

COLUMBUS

Library of Congress Cataloging-in-Publication Data

Names: Kirtley, Susan E., 1972– author.

Title: Typical girls : the rhetoric of womanhood in comic strips / Susan E. Kirtley.

Other titles: Studies in comics and cartoons.

Description: Columbus : The Ohio State University Press, [2021] | Series: Studies in comics and cartoons | Includes bibliographical references and index. | Summary: "Drawing from the work of Lynn Johnston (*For Better or For Worse*), Cathy Guisewite (*Cathy*), Nicole Hollander (*Sylvia*), Lynda Barry (*Ernie Pook's Comeek*), Barbara Brandon-Croft (*Where I'm Coming From*), Alison Bechdel (*Dykes to Watch Out For*), and Jan Eliot (*Stone Soup*), *Typical Girls* examines the development of womanhood and women's rights in popular comic strips"—Provided by publisher.

Identifiers: LCCN 2020052823 | ISBN 9780814214572 (cloth) | ISBN 0814214576 (cloth) | ISBN 9780814281222 (ebook) | ISBN 0814281222 (ebook)

Subjects: LCSH: Comic strip characters—Women. | Women in literature. | Women's rights in literature. | Comic books, strips, etc.—History and criticism.

Classification: LCC PN6714 .K47 2021 | DDC 741.5/3522—dc23

LC record available at https://lccn.loc.gov/2020052823

COVER DESIGN BY ANGELA MOODY
TEXT DESIGN BY JULIET WILLIAMS
TYPE SET IN PALATINO

For my favorite superhero team—Evelyn, Leone, and Tamasone

Castigat ridendo mores.
—Jean-Baptiste de Santeul

CONTENTS

ILLUSTRATIONS

ACKNOWLEDGMENTS

As a bookworm girl, I relished the friends I found in the pages of the comics. I felt a profound kinship with Charlie Brown and his longing to kick the football, although I must admit that, strangely enough, I identified most strongly with the quiet loyalty of Woodstock. I also adored Opus the Penguin and shared his love of odd infotainment devices. Later, I connected with the tragic melodrama of Rogue of the *X-Men,* imagining myself a similarly lonely spirit who was cursed to suck the energy from others. Over time I formed attachments to Grendel, Concrete, Tankgirl, and Dream, to name only a few. These fictional friends sustained and encouraged me, and, in ways I never could have imagined, led me to new friends and mentors, many of whom inspired this book.

It turns out that the creators behind the comics are just as amazing as their characters, and I'm grateful to Lynda Barry, Alison Bechdel, Barbara Brandon-Croft, Jan Eliot, Cathy Guisewite, Nicole Hollander, and Lynn Johnston for sharing their talents with the world.

Comics Studies is the most welcoming of fields, and I'm incredibly lucky to have such supportive friends and colleagues, particularly my fellow editors at *INKS,* the Comics Studies Society, and the MLA forum for Comics and Graphic Narratives. Thank you to friends and colleagues Jose Alaniz, Frederick Luis Aldama, Bart Beaty, Frank Bramlett, Peter Carlson, Brannon Costello, Brian Cremins, Lan Dong, Randy Duncan, Craig Fischer, Antero Garcia, Jared Gardner, Andréa Gilroy, Charles Hatfield, Gene Kannenberg, Andrew Kunka, Kathleen McClancy, Phil Nel, Ben Saunders, Diana Schutz, Nhora Serrano, Matt Smith, Nick Sousanis, Carol Tilley, Qiana Whitted, and the late, beloved Tom Spurgeon.

The research process for this book was supported by a Faculty Enhancement Grant from Portland State University and the Lucy Shelton Caswell Research Award. I would especially like to thank Jenny Robb and Susan Liberator from the Billy Ireland Cartoon Library and Museum for research assistance and support. I'm incredibly grateful to Ana Jimenez-Moreno, who has been a brilliant editor and superstar throughout the process, as well as the staff, anonymous reviewers, and the editorial board at The Ohio State University Press. Thanks, also, to my colleagues at Portland State University.

Finally, thank you to Bill Kirtley, Pat Kirtley, Kathy Brost, and Peter Brost for love, support, and care packages. And extra special thanks to Evelyn Kirtley Filipo, Leone Kirtley Filipo, and Tamasone Filipo.

I spent many years reading the comics and longing for the true friends I saw there, and today, I am ever-so-grateful that my wish came true.

THE WOMEN'S LIBERATION MOVEMENT IN COMIC STRIPS

By crystallizing an idea or an argument into a simple image, visual rhetoric permits the argument to be grasped in a flash and thus to reach an audience wider than that reached by verbal means, either spoken or written. Humor, irony, or satire allow the release of laughter, and thus ease communication to those who might otherwise find an idea uncomfortable or unacceptable.

—Elizabeth Israels Perry, "Introduction" in *Cartooning for Suffrage*

AS A CHILD, I began to read comic books because I was told, in no uncertain terms, that girls do not read comic books. In fact, I distinctly remember the day of this revelation. I was approximately nine years old, a shy and unassuming student at Jefferson Elementary School. As a precocious child, I didn't have all that many friends, but, in an awkward attempt at social interaction, I approached my classmate Sean, who was huddled against the brick wall of the school during recess on a crisp, sunny day, and asked what he was reading. The fact that Sean was willingly reading seemed to me highly suspicious behavior, but his reading material, which was bright and colorful and quite possibly naughty, intrigued me. However, my congenial attempt at bonding was rebuffed when Sean refused to even look up from what I realized was a comic book, stating emphatically, "Girls don't read comic books." After that sort of introduction, how could I resist? The next time I accompanied my mother grocery shopping I marched directly over to the spindly wire rack holding the comic books. They were sorely out of date and the selection was terrible, but it didn't matter. I pulled *The X-Men* off the rack and I was in love.

My adoration for newspaper comic strips was less fraught with
social anxiety and gender stereotypes, as my parents received not
one but two papers every day: the local town paper and the big-city
newspaper, which meant I could devour the comics in the comfort of
my own home without having to defend my reading practices. Reading the news was a highly ritualized endeavor in the Kirtley household, as the paper was first inspected by my parents and then handed
down to my sister and to me. The silent, reverent process of consuming the paper was the only exception to the "No reading at the table"
rule, when, as a family, we shared various sections of the paper, all
seated around the dining room table. While my parents began by
clucking over the inevitable and terrible news pages, I requested the
comics first and studied them intently, surrendering them only when
my mother wanted to do the crossword. Even the way I read the
comics was highly structured and hierarchical, beginning with my
favorites (which shifted over time from *The Far Side* to *Bloom County*
to *Calvin and Hobbes*), to my least favorites (such as the soap operas
like *Mary Worth,* which seemed well beyond my comprehension).

Reading the comics has been my morning ritual since childhood, a
tradition that continues to this day, even though I suspect I am one of
the few stubborn people who still insists on subscribing to the actual,
physical newspaper.[1] I am a Luddite outlier who relishes the walk
down the driveway each morning to receive my daily prize. Comic
strips hold a special place in my memory, for the comics pages were
another form of information for a curious and questioning girl, shaping and forming my notions of the world and culture around me.
Furthermore, over time as I became increasingly invested in feminist
concerns, the comics contributed to my understanding of what it was
to be female in America. Of course, I was watching movies and television and listening to music and reading books as well, but the comics pages were a quotidian pursuit, an everyday opportunity to sit
and study these small windows of domesticity and gender politics,
and ask my sister, "Do you get it? I don't get the joke."

It is perhaps not surprising, then, that as an adult I've returned
to the comics pages once more to better understand the impact and
import of the small snippets of wit and wisdom that I, along with so
many others, consumed daily, almost unconsciously, along with my

1. Of course, that's not entirely true, but according to the Pew Research Center,
US daily newspaper circulation declined from 63,340,000 in 1984 to 40,420,000 in
2014, a drop of approximately 36%.

Frosted Flakes (or more accurately cornflakes, as the sugary variety was a rare treat reserved for special occasions). Moreover, as a child who grew up enthralled by the Women's Rights movement, I am particularly intrigued by those comics created by women that rendered and reflected the history of feminism in the United States. Although they are, in the scheme of things, small in size and often considered ephemeral and disposable, comic strips serve as a reflection of society, larger in scope and significance than often acknowledged. Judith O'Sullivan argues:

> From its birth in 1892, the medium has entertained, interpreted, satirized, and shocked, holding an enchanted mirror to American society. At the same time, as the late communications historian Marshall McLuhan observed, comics have, by presenting characters who are at once the readers' beloved familiars and surrogates, provided "a sort of magically recurrent daily ritual . . . serving a very different function from equally popular art forms like the sports page and detective fictions." . . . The great strips are replete with significant issues and historical moments, including civil rights, feminism, and the constitutional guarantee of free expression. In short, a reading of American comics is a reading of twentieth-century social history. (9–10)

Both O'Sullivan and McLuhan point to the "magical" qualities of comics, in that they have an otherworldliness as mirrors or pictures that are consciously fashioned to delight and entertain on a daily basis, as they serially reproduce and reflect a particular image of society. Comic strips constitute an imagined reality which bears consequences for the real. For, as Ian Gordon points out in his book *Comic Strips and Consumer Culture: 1890–1945*, comic strips do more than simply reflect society, they help shape it. Gordon argues the fallacy of seeing "comic strips as a reflection of social attitudes rather than as a constituent element of the culture" (9). Furthermore, Gordon believes that by reading comics we can, as he aspired to do, "understand the audiences comics creators wished to appeal to and the context in which those audiences read comics" (10). Thus, in studying newspaper comics, the shape of a culture may be revealed, and the process also illuminates the audiences consuming the comics as well as the environment in which readers operated. Gordon posits, "Two histories are suppressed in comic strips: first the strip's relation to the history of the society in which it was created, and second the internal history of a particular comic strip. Recovering those histories allows us to better understand the dimensions of comic art's humor and its place in American culture" (10). This study works to uncover multiple histories: that of the comic strips themselves, the concomitant culture reflected by the strips, and the importance of these comics in arguing for changing perceptions of womanhood and women's rights in popular opinion.

David Carrier argues that comics "are read so casually that often their highly original features are taken for granted. A famous inaccessible painting readily inspires curiosity; comics, read over breakfast, seem to be 'just there'" (88), yet for their ordinary, unassuming presence, comic strips readily shape audience expectations and interests. Carrier continues on to posit that comic art acts as a reflection of society, "Comics are about their audience, we readers who project into them our desires" (92). Comic strips thus reflect the reader's hopes, beliefs, and expectations. This project explores a sampling of female-created comic strips from 1976 to the present through a rhetorical framework, filling a gap in current scholarship and giving these works extended scholarly examination, focusing on defining and exploring the ramifications of this multifarious expression of women's roles at a time of great change in history and in comic art.

Individually and collectively the scope of these strips has not yet been considered in academic writing, but comic strips are certainly, as scholar Tom Inge points out, "well loved" (xxi). However, these artists "should also be respected for what they have contributed to the visual and narrative arts of the world" ("Comics as Culture" 191). Though comic art has until recently been largely overlooked by scholars, when examined closely, the form demonstrates a highly sophisticated structure of its own, linking text and image in complex and intriguing ways, and building a story that could not be related by text or image alone. Joseph Witek argues that comic art demonstrates "a highly developed narrative grammar and vocabulary based on an inextricable combination of verbal and visual elements" (3). This study will explore how this intriguing pairing of words and pictures creates a rhetoric of womanhood specific to the form.

Thus, this project, while acknowledging its limited focus on a small sampling of female comic strip creators' work during a limited time period, seeks to offer a novel assessment of the historical moment during which the Women's Rights movement became a national conversation (focusing on the 1970s and 1980s, in particular), demonstrating the ways in which the most prominent and widely read comic strips created by women of the time bolster stereotypes of gender and domesticity even as they challenged them, presenting complicated women struggling to reconceive of success and fulfillment amidst competing visions of female identity, femininity, and domesticity. The comic strips of Lynn Johnston, Cathy Guisewite, Nicole Hollander, Lynda Barry, Barbara Brandon-Croft, Alison Bechdel, and Jan Eliot offer a nuanced understanding of females coming to terms with the many competing demands and opportunities for women. When considered as a group and even within the individual strips, complications and incongruities abound. Main character Cathy campaigns for Dukakis, the Family Medical Leave Act, and better childcare options for working families even as she obsesses over her weight and hairstyle. Elly from *For Better or For Worse* struggles with tedium and lack of recognition in her role as a stay-at-home mother, but basks in the male attention she garners when she dresses up for a night on the town. Brandon-Croft's characters worry about facial hair and police brutality. And Hollander's Sylvia soundly criticizes sexist double standards while reinforcing tropes of shrewish female behavior even as Barry's strip revels in the absurdity of courtship in a new landscape in which past rules and practices no longer apply. The protagonists of *Stone Soup* puzzle about the rituals of dating and double standards at the office.

How do we view these contradictions? What can be gleaned from reading newspaper comic strips created by women from the 1970s, 1980s, and 1990s? As these strips reveal a small accretion of daily truths, they can help develop a fuller understanding of the media's conception of a particularly turbulent moment in American history—the Women's Rights movement. Furthermore, this analysis focuses on comic strips, and thus both literally and more figuratively takes a "comic" point of view, the perspective that theorist Kenneth Burke argues is most "charitable" (*Attitudes* 107) and "most serviceable for the handling of human relationships" (106). Indeed, Burke's notion of the various "frames of reference," can prove a useful tool for interpreting and analyzing comic strips, as he argues that the frames specified in the analysis of literature can also usefully be applied to human relations, and that these assorted "attitudes" can shape the interpretation of experiences fictional and real. A. Cheree Carlson notes of Burke's position that "all human strategies for social coexistence may be categorized according to their parallels in literary form. He documents the 'curve of history' as it coheres to the patterns of tragedy, elegy, ode, burlesque, and several other 'frames'" (310), the most optimistic being the "comic" frame. Thus, the comic frame offers a "charitable" perspective, and "should enable people *to be observers of themselves, while acting. Its ultimate would not be passiveness, but maximum consciousness. One would 'transcend' himself by noting his own foibles*" (Burke, *Attitudes* 171). Apart from his unfortunate use of male pronouns to stand for all people, Burke's understanding of the comic "frame of reference" provides an especially useful tool for better understanding the potential of comic strips to reflect the culture of the time and to argue for a better future. Drawing from Burke's analysis, I assert that comic strips not only document the culture that creates them, but can inspire readers to turn their gaze from the strips onto their own lives, *observing* themselves and *acting* accordingly, and to do so in an optimistic and "charitable" way, for "the comic frame of acceptance but carries to completion the translative act. It considers human life as a project in 'composition,' where the poet works with the materials of social relationships. Composition, translation, also 'revision,' hence offering maximum opportunity for the resources of *criticism*" (Burke, *Attitudes* 173). The poet, or in this case, comics creator, composes art from the raw matter of human connections and invites readers as critics to recognize truths and transform these insights into actions. Comic strips, with their optimism and their capacity for delight, offer readers a way of seeing the world that critiques in the spirit of change, rather than resignation.

Furthermore, the strips are explored through a rhetorical lens, using theory to inform a reading of the strategies and approaches utilized by these comics in shaping their reception and, ultimately, the cultural context. Why take such an approach, utilizing classical rhetoric to examine a daily comic strip? In *The Name of the Rose*, Umberto Eco reasoned, "Perhaps the mission of those who love mankind is to make people laugh at the truth, to make truth laugh, because the only truth lies in learning to free ourselves from insane passion for the truth" (498). Comics and cartoons can, when in the hands of masters, "make truth laugh," revealing hard truths, and, for that matter, the impossibility of a singular truth, through humor, influencing the audience to see the world differently, and hopefully, prod them into action [I believe that reading comics through the lens of rhetoric helps us better understand and expand the theory in an increasingly multimodal world and, furthermore, offers useful tools for understanding this very public form of address.] Rhetoric, of course, began as an oral tradition before becoming stratified and applied primarily to literary texts. I believe that theories of rhetoric stand to gain a great deal, including increased relevance and significance when applied to hybrid, multimodal texts, just as rhetoric can offer a deeper understanding of the complex strategies employed by comics creators. However, before launching into a rhetorical analysis of these strips, this opening section provides context for representations of women in comic strips and an introduction to female comic strip artists before delving into a brief introduction to histories of feminism and a discussion of racism on the comics pages. Finally, a close examination of a typical day of newspaper comics pages helps set the stage for the analysis to follow.

(handwritten margin note: making an argument)

Funny Business: Women as Creators and Characters in Comic Strips

(handwritten margin note: study = narrow but discusses wider context)

While this study focuses narrowly on several strips over a period of time, it is important to acknowledge the wider context of these comic strips within the comics pages as well as within the history of female comic strip creators. These comics arose from a long tradition of comic strips that focused on families and domestic environments, and occasionally, on women. And although the majority of these comics strips were created by men, women also created comics, even though these accomplishments were often underplayed or ignored in historical accounts. Judith O'Sullivan explains:

> In the strip's infancy, isolated women cartoonists had occasionally carved a newspaper niche for themselves. The strips drawn by these women were usually domestic in nature, depicting, with various degrees of sentimentality, idealized children and animals. Chief among these early creators were Rose O'Neill, who is best remembered for her 1909 *Kewpies* ("Little Cupids"); Grace Gebbie Drayton, who depicted *The Terrible Tales of Kaptain Kiddo* (1909), and who lives on in the American imagination as the mother of the ever-popular

> *Campbell Kids* (1905); and Frances Edwina Dumm, the first female
> editorial cartoonist, famous for her dog strip, *Cap Stuffs and Tippie*
> (1917). (115)

In fact, even as Rose O'Neill and Frances Edwina Dumm were con-
juring sweet-faced children inhabiting idyllic domestic fantasies,
they were also arguing for women's suffrage. In her book *Cartooning for Suffrage,* Alice Sheppard explains that "cartooning as a men's
only domain had begun to change by the late nineteenth century.
Among the factors permitting women to enter the field were the rise
of training facilities, the rapid simplification of the process, and the
acceptance of women into positions of skilled employment" (28).
Thus, as more women created cartoons, many also entered the political arena, particularly campaigning for women's suffrage. Sheppard
identifies a number of prominent female cartoonists promoting the
right to vote for women, including "Nina Evans Allender, Blanche
Ames, Cornelia Barns, Edwina Dumm, Rose O'Neill, Frederikke
Schjoth Palmer, May Wilson Preston, Ida Sedgwick Proper, and
Alice Beach Winter" (96). These cartoonists were working to counter
numerous vicious attacks on female activists. Elizabeth Israels Perry
asserts, "Almost as soon as the American woman's rights movement
got underway in the mid-nineteenth century, negative visual images
of women activists began to appear in the popular press. Sometimes the image was of a lecturer on 'free thinking' portrayed as 'evil
temptress,' sometimes the reformer in bloomers smoking a cigar" (3),
yet, "as women prepared to renew their campaign in the early 1900s,
they began to harness the power of images to work for their side of
the argument" (3). Unfortunately, female cartoonists' contributions
to the campaign for women's suffrage are not often recognized, in
part because "the event they represented, the winning of the vote for
women, has not been central to political history" and "even scholars
who specialize in women's topics have not necessarily valued wom-
en's pictorial rhetoric" (Perry 4). Thus, the political contributions
of female cartoonists remain largely unappreciated, as the quest of
women's suffrage stays on the periphery of historical narratives, and
even most feminist scholars tend to overlook the impact of visual
rhetoric in early campaigns for women's rights.

As many turn-of-the-century female cartoonists set their sights
on swaying popular opinion on female suffrage, with women finally
gaining the right to vote in 1920, newspapers and in particular newspaper comics pages were also in the midst of an enormous trans-

formation. Judith O'Sullivan stresses, "The birth of this national art form, the comics, is closely connected with turn-of-the-century American urbanization and with the communications explosion that produced and revolutionized the American newspaper industry" (10). Numerous historiographies outline the importance of comic strips in the evolution of daily newspapers and point to the significance of Richard Outcault's *Hogan's Alley* (1895–1898), along with Rudolph Dirks's *The Katzenjammer Kids* (1897–2006), Frank King's *Gasoline Alley* (1918–present), George McManus's *Bringing Up Father* (1913–2000),Winsor McCay's *Little Nemo* (1905–1926), and Lyonel Feininger's *Kin-der-Kids* (1904–1905), among others, in contributing to the widespread appeal of the daily paper. Comic strips sold newspapers, and the extended relationship between comics and commerce is examined in great detail in Ian Gordon's aforementioned *Comic Strips and Consumer Culture: 1890–1945.*

In the earliest years of the comics, many strips focused on children, and what are now known as "kid strips" were particularly popular for their charm as well as their trenchant cultural critiques. O'Sullivan maintains that "Outcault established the archetype of the idiot savant as social commentator. Enormously popular, the strip's urban setting, crowded frames, expressive style, and slapstick humor reflected a country in transition, a land of burgeoning cities and immigrant populations," and, "many early comics pioneered as protagonist the visionary outsider. Mutes, madmen, children, and animals constitute the comics' early populations" (15), and "kid" strips have remained popular from the earliest days of newspaper strips.

Of course, some of the children featured in these early strips were female, but their representation may well have caused confusion for readers, particularly girls, as Lara Saguisag points out in *Incorrigibles and Innocents*:

> For girls growing up at the turn of the century, reading the comic supplement may have been a pleasurable yet bewildering experience. The supplement featured many series headlined by girls, which were presumably designed to appeal to young female readers. In these titles, the protagonists played boys' games, upset their parents, and did not behave like "proper" girls. Also, prominently featured in the comic supplements were images of troublemaking *women*; these fictional females challenged authority figures, rejected marriage and motherhood, sought to pursue education and professional careers, and demanded the right to vote. While the disorderly

girl was meant to elicit delightful, sentimental laughter, the "provoc-
ative" woman was created in the vein of derisive humor. (144–45)

Thus, the girls of these strips were allowed to follow along with
their male counterparts, rebelling and antagonizing the grown-ups.
However, with maturity came gendered restrictions for these young
women, as evidenced in the many family-focused strips that quickly
gained in popularity.

As Saguisag points out, females took on an even more prominent
role with the rise of several girl-centered strips, featuring girls and
young women finding their way in the working world (with varying
degrees of success and concomitant derision), reflecting a change in
public consciousness following the passage of the 19th Amendment.
Maurice Horn claims that

> 1920 was a momentous year in the history of women's rights in the
> United States: with the adoption of the 19th amendment to the Con-
> stitution women finally won the right to vote, after years of lobbying
> and agitation. The effect must have been electrifying on comic strip
> artists as it was on the country at large: in a matter of a few years
> women started populating the strips in ever-increasing numbers, as
> well as in more visible roles. (46)

And in that way the "girl" strips helped shape a new narrative of
women entering the workforce and, as in the case of Little Orphan
Annie, going on adventures of their own. Judith O'Sullivan found
that

> although the vast majority of "girl" strips created in the teens and
> twenties were drawn by men, they often provided exciting "role
> models." Such strips, designed to appeal to young ladies entering
> the work force, include *Polly and Her Pals*, begun in 1912 by Clifford
> Sterrett; *Winnie Winkle, the Breadwinner*, created in 1920 by Martin
> Branner; *Tillie the Toiler*, originated in 1921 by Russ Westover; and,
> of course, the indefatigable *Little Orphan Annie*, the 1924 brainchild
> of Harold Gray. (119)

Along with A. E. Hayward's *Somebody's Stenog* (1918–1941), these
strips showcased the new cultural landscape of women entering the
workforce. Guisewite's *Cathy* descends from these workplace-based

comics, as the main character seeks a successful career, a situation which is depicted as necessarily fraught, in that she is a woman, and her experience is represented as an anomaly or challenge rather than a commonplace. Interestingly enough, some of these "girl" strips evolved into domestic strips as the female characters were "tamed" and returned their attention, once again, to the home.

Chic Young's *Blondie*, which began in 1930 and continues in syndication to this day, is perhaps the most notable example, as it echoed shifting national sentiment. *Blondie* originally presented "the chronicle of a liberated working girl and her numerous suitors" (O'Sullivan 57), but eventually, "paralleling shifts in American economy from plenty to want, and in political ideology from left to right, the strip's focus changed from Blondie's alluring independence and sexuality to Dagwood's troubles at the office" (O'Sullivan 57), and the "formula that was to be maintained for fifty years was established—that is, the saga of the efficient wife and the well-meaning but bungling husband" (O'Sullivan 57). However, it should also be noted that in her earliest incarnation Blondie was perhaps more of a stereotypical "dumb blonde" character than a focused career woman or calm and competent homemaker. Young is said to have modeled Blondie's earliest iteration on flappers. In fact, an early ad campaign sought to titillate newspaper editors with sexual imagery, as a paper doll version of Blondie, clad in her lingerie, was delivered to newspaper editors with the note, "Here I am, just like I told you I'd be. Only, please, Mr. Editor, put some clothes on me quick. I sent them on ahead, you remember my pink bag. I'm *so* embarrassed! Blondie" (Harvey). Over time, though, Blondie left behind her career and her suitors and, apparently, her sexuality, transforming into a kindly mother who cared for her family and corralled her bumbling husband Dagwood in a thoroughly domesticated strip.

Domestic strips like *Blondie*, Sidney Smith's *The Gumps* (1917–1959), and George McManus's *Bringing Up Father* (1913–2000) all focused on home and family, and all did so from a distinctly male point of view. O'Sullivan notes that "domestic strips provide reassurance that the trivial tasks comprising day-to-day existence have cumulative meaning and that milestone events of courtship and marriage, as experienced by comic-strip characters who are the reader's beloved familiars, are meaningful experiences reflecting the purposeful nature of the universe" (58). Some of these domestic strips focused on children, such as *Barnaby* by Crockett Johnson (1942–1952) and

Peanuts by Charles Schulz (1950–2000), and these strips even offered strong girl characters, such as the wise Jane, who accompanied Barnaby on his many adventures, refusing the strictures of the adults with enviable self-possession, while remaining skeptical and grounded in regards to the mischievous antics of Barnaby's fairy godfather Mr. O'Malley. And *Peanuts* offered the strong-willed and influential figures of Lucy, Sally, Peppermint Patty, and Marcie. Yet these strips still revolved around the male characters, with females in supporting roles.

These family-focused strips render a familiar and intimate experience unfolding on a daily basis, thus reinforcing the significance of family bonds and community relationships. If these small, personal moments in the history of a household are worth celebrating, sharing, and archiving among the most important news stories of the day, this gives the readers' own everyday encounters weight and heft. Domestic strips argue for the import of the ordinary life. However, as previously discussed, comic strips both reflect and constitute popular opinion, and these early domestic strips often presented extremely stereotyped narratives of gendered behavior, particularly in regards to the adults, with forceful men transforming into submissive husbands after marriage to domineering wives. While Blondie is clearly the more capable partner and Dagwood much like another child, their amicable relationship was not the norm for many domestic comic strips. According to Monika Franzen and Nancy Ethiel in their book *Make Way: 200 Years of American Women in Cartoons*:

> The overwhelming majority of cartoonists, especially in the early years, were men. And their cartoons have generally reflected not women's view of themselves, but men's view of women—a view much affected by the feelings, both positive and negative, that women evoke in men. Rarely did early cartoonists concern themselves with women's own feelings and desires—especially for equality. They were far more concerned with the threat these desires posed to their own comfortable way of life. (13)

Moreover, women were frequently depicted as an especially potent "threat" to men in early comic strips. In *Women in the Comics*, Maurice Horn calls upon numerous studies, including those of Gerhart Saenger, which "found that while the male was traditionally the stronger sex, much more decisive, self-reliant and resourceful as long has he remained unmarried (and correspondingly aloof), it was the woman who held sway as soon as the matrimonial knot was tied" (3). Marriage, then, represented a trap that emasculated men and turned women into shrews. Horn further claims that "of all the leading cartoonists George McManus was undoubtedly the decade's greatest contributor to feminine iconography" (33), but he "was nothing if not a male chauvinist (albeit an inspired one): his female characters are either empty-headed sex objects or forbidding, repellant battleaxes" (34).

The trope of forceful female and submissive male recurred with a new twist as adventure strips gained in popularity, with women taking on a more dominant role outside of marriage, frequently rescuing their more bashful male counterparts. O'Sullivan notes that the "aggressive female and bashful male recurred in many adventure strips, from Al Capp's *Li'l Abner* to Jerome Siegel and Jerry Schuster's *Superman*" as well as in "Eisner and Iger's *Sheena, Queen of the Jungle*" (96). These adventure strips also featured numerous "exotic" female villains looking to ensnare the handsome heroes with feminine wiles. While women took on a more independent role in these early adventure strips, over time they were, for the most part, once again relegated to either a villain or a victim. Horn explains, "In the adventure strip women first appeared as the girl friend or companion of the hero," but over time "girls were depicted with increasing lasciviousness as ingenious plot devices allowed for their representation in strongly suggestive poses" (89), and "soon these female leads tired of their almost exclusively decorative roles and started stepping out of the 'damsel in distress' stereotype" (90). Ultimately, according to Horn, "girls were seen through the man's eye: flawed in the individual but perfect in the aggregate, they represented the wish-fulfillment of every man's fantasy; while the contradictions of man's sexual and affective desires were reflected in their symbolic trinity of opposites" (92).

One exception to the trend of male-created, female-centric strips was the infamous *Brenda Starr, Reporter,* created in 1940 by Dale Messick. O'Sullivan argues, "Chronicling the exploits of a daring female reporter, *Brenda Starr* transcended the restrictions of the domestic strip by incorporating elements of the adventure strip, then at the height of its popularity" (58). Dalia Messick, who took on the nom de plume "Dale," created a daring hero in Brenda Starr, who eventually married and had a child but never gave up her career or her adventures. In *Pretty in Ink,* comics historian Trina Robbins noted that "although the strip inspired a huge female following from the beginning . . . the artist never felt fully accepted by her male colleagues and she resisted joining the National Cartoonists Society" (63). Robbins argues that although women had been drawing comics previously, those women were focusing on "girl stuff," (64) while Messick "was trespassing on male territory" (64) with her foray into the adventure strip.

Robbins also notes the importance of the creation of Wonder Woman by William Moulton Marston in 1941 as a female action hero (although she appeared primarily in comic books rather than strips) and Miss Fury, created by Tarpe Mills in "April 1941, eight months before the birth of Marston's creation" (65). The strip features "Marla Drake, the socialite who becomes Miss Fury upon donning a form-fitting panther skin" (Robbins, *Great* 62) and took "the reader to from chic penthouses and nightclubs of New York to underground Nazi installations and anti-Nazi guerilla camps in Brazil" (62). The strip lasted until 1951, at which time Mills began working on romance comics.

Of course, with the institution of the Comics Code Authority in 1954, the comic book industry took a turn toward newly sanitized storylines, even as the Underground and Alternative movements pushed back against the constraints of mainstream publishing, exploring formally taboo subjects.[2] However, the Underground and Alternative comics movements were, for the most part, dominated by white men, and many felt the movements were misogynistic in both the culture of the creators and in the comics they created.

R. Crumb, one of the most prominent figures in the Underground comics movement, was well known for depicting women as mon-

---

2. This historical move has been well-documented in comics scholarship. See, for example, R. C. Harvey, *The Art of the Comic Book* (Jackson: U of Mississippi P, 1996) and *The Art of the Funnies: An Aesthetic History* (Jackson: U of Mississippi P, 1994); Charles Hatfield, *Alternative Comics: An Emerging Literature* (Jackson: U of Mississippi P, 2005); Jeet Heer and Kent Worcester, eds., *Arguing Comics: Literary Masters on a Popular Medium* (Jackson: U of Mississippi P, 2004) and *A Comics Studies Reader* (Jackson: U of Mississippi P, 2009); Thomas Inge, *Comics as Culture* (Jackson: U of Mississippi P, 1990); Trina Robbins, *A Century of Women Cartoonists* (San Francisco: Chronicle Books, 1993) and *From Girls to Grrlz: A History of Women's Comics from Teens to Zines* (San Francisco: Chronicle Books, 1999); and Joseph Witek, *Comic Books as History: The Narrative Art of Jack Jackson, Art Spiegelman, and Harvey Pekar* (Jackson: University Press of Mississippi, 1989).

strous creatures, objects of fascination and repulsion. His female characters were frequently depicted undergoing sexual assault and brutality with a sense of unrepentant glee. Claire Litton notes of Crumb's work, "Women were raped, dismembered, mutilated, and murdered, sometimes all at once." She continues:

> Ultimately, the underground comix movement was a squandered opportunity. Where there could have been an open forum for feminist art and collaborative, ground-breaking works, there was only hatred and sexism, often inspired by a man who admitted his fear and loathing of women.

Yet even as the Underground movement was, for the most part, a "No Girls Allowed" clubhouse, female creators were pushing back. Unfortunately, unlike the critical role feminist cartoonists played in the suffrage of women, their contributions were largely overlooked by the activities of the Women's Liberation era.

In *Graphic Women*, Hillary Chute argues that second-wave feminism drew from the energy of the Underground comix movement, gaining inspiration from the rebellious spirit of the creators, even encouraging women to create their own space apart from misogyny associated with the movement. Chute suggests:

> The growth of the underground comix movement was connected to second-wave feminism, which enabled a body of work that was explicitly political to sprout: if female activists complained of misogyny of the New Left, this was mirrored in underground comics, prompting women cartoonists to establish a space specifically for women's work. It is only in the comics underground that the U.S. first saw any substantial work by women allowed to explore their own artistic impulses, and further, women organizing collectives that undertook to articulate the challenges and goals of specifically female cartoonists. (20)

While I would argue that female cartoonists engaged in the fight for women's suffrage also created "substantial work" that examined their "artistic impulses" and created spaces that examined women's experiences as creators, it would seem that the Underground's turn toward introspective works that were not afraid to interrogate difficult, personal subjects resonated with many female comics creators, like Aline Kominsky-Crumb, Mary Fleener, Lee Marrs, Roberta Gregory, Joyce Farmer, Carol Lay, Melinda Gebbie, Lyn Chevli, and, of course, Trina Robbins. This group worked together and individually to create numerous significant works, including *It Ain't Me, Babe* (1970), *Wimmen's Comix* (1972–1992), and *Tits-n-Clits* (1975–1990).

Robbins, known both for her own comics and for her unwavering commitment to chronicling the "herstory" of female comics creators, remembers the challenges of creating comics in the 1960s and 1970s, when she felt isolated from male-dominated comics culture *and* the feminist movement. Robbins reflects:

> Most of the male underground cartoonists understood as little about the new women's movement as the newspapers did, and reacted to what they perceived as a threat by drawing commix filled with graphic violence directed mostly at women. People—especially women people—who criticized this misogyny were not especially welcome in this alternative version of the old boys' club, and were not invited into the commix being produced. (*From Girls* 85)

And, unfortunately, Robbins also failed to find support for her work in the mainstream feminist community of the time. In her article "Feminism Underground: The Comics Rhetoric of Lee Marrs and Roberta Gregory," Margaret Galvan asserts that "the feminist movement did not so easily support the comics medium that Wonder Woman called home" (204). Lee Marrs, creator of the notable work *Pudge, Girl Blimp,* shared in an interview that, in the moment, "the women's movement in the beginning didn't have any sense of humor in itself, which is sad but typical. . . . We got totally rejected by the women's movement for the most part" (Lipsky). According to Jessica Lipsky, "In a particularly hurtful example, feminist magazine *Ms.* refused to run *Wimmen's* ads." Robbins shared her disappointment with Bill Sherman of *The Comics Journal,* recalling that it was "really weird the way leftists and militant feminists don't seem to like comix. I think they're so hung up on their own intellect that somehow it isn't any good to them unless it's a sixteen-page tract of gray words" (54). It would seem that many of the leaders of the Women's Liberation movement of the time, at least according to the comics artists, failed to appreciate the power and possibilities of comics as rhetorical tools.

Crashing Waves: Failed Metaphors for Feminism

Of course, feminism and feminists are multifarious, as much as the terms are often understood as monolithic constructions. The term "feminist" didn't even arrive until the nineteenth century in France (Berkeley 6) and arrived much later in the United States. In *The Women's Liberation Movement in America,* Kathleen Berkeley notes that while feminism is frequently perceived as a homogeneous entity, the reality is far more complicated:

> Like almost all social movements, the feminist movement of the 1960s and 1970s was multifaceted. Feminists differed according to ideology, strategy, goals, and style. Unfortunately, however, the more liberationists pushed the radical button, the easier it became for the media and the public to assume incorrectly that there was a fixed and unalterable division between mainstream, liberal equality feminism (which emphasized political and legal reform) and avante garde, radical liberation feminism (which stressed revolutionary socioeconomic and cultural changes). (52)

differences

Christine Stansell makes the point that "feminism has encompassed a wide variety of social views and positions, sometimes antagonistic to one another" (xiv). Thus, multiple understandings of feminism and its goals as a political movement coexist, with the more mainstream wing working to bring about change within the system while the more radical element summarily eschews patriarchal organizations entirely.

Unfortunately, the heterogeneity of US feminisms gets obscured *waves* in frequent histories that rely on the metaphor of waves to describe the movement. Kathleen Laughlin and her colleagues[3] argue that "[using] the waves metaphor to delineate feminist activism in the United States is troublesome, to say the least. Despite its problems, the waves model has tremendous staying power when it comes to understanding, analyzing, writing about, and teaching the history of

---

3. The article "Is it Time to Jump Ship?: Feminist Historians Rethink the Waves Metaphor" from *Feminist Formations* (vol. 22, no. 1, 2010, pp. 76–135) is authored by Kathleen A. Laughlin, Julie Gallagher, Dorothy Sue Cobble, Eileen Boris, Premilla Nadasen, Stephanie Gilmore, and Leandra Zarnow. Within the piece, each historian authors a different section with different conclusions.

U.S. feminism" (76). In most chronicles, the first wave is seen as "dating from the first women's rights convention in the United States"
(Laughlin et al. 76) in 1848, while the second wave began "in the mid-
1960s" (77), with the third wave beginning with Rebecca Walker's
essay "I am the Third Wave" in 1992. The waves metaphor has been
ubiquitous for some time for a number of reasons, despite the obvious limitations, such as the fact that the comparison "entrenches the
perception of a 'singular' feminism in which gender is the predom-
inate category of analysis" (Laughlin et al. 77), and "has become a
crutch that obscures as much as it organizes the past into a neat pack-
age" (81). Premilla Nadasen explains:

> The waves metaphor privileges sectors of the movement that put
> gender at the center of their analysis. In this way, the metaphor re-
> inscribes race/class/sexuality biases and omissions within women's
> history; it obscures some of the local and low-key organizing in
> communities and masks the deep-running, seemingly still waters
> of everyday activism. What we miss when we highlight the wave is
> the nitty-gritty, day-to-day organizing: Women who stayed within
> the male-dominated institutions; women who could not separate
> out their identity as women from their involvement in race- or class-
> based struggles; women who did not come together in explicitly
> feminist organizations. (104)

positionality

I, along with many other scholars, acknowledge the faults of the
metaphor and search for other ways of discussing feminist history in
the United States. Dorothy Sue Cobble argues that academics should
"adjust the periodization" (87) beyond three simple, chronological
wave periods, while Eileen Boris suggests we consider a "braiding"
analogy (92), and Premilla Nadasen argues for "a river metaphor"
(105). Stephanie Gilmore posits that the waves still have merit, but
that "we need to trouble these waters a bit more" (106).

Still, as scholars look for new ways to talk about US feminist
history, the waves analogy continues to dominate the conversation
around feminism for numerous reasons. Julie Gallagher notes that
the waves metaphor "enables historians to explore change over time
and to compare one time to another" (84), "facilitates the inclusion of
women's activism into the complex narratives of U.S. history" (84),
and, frankly, "seems indispensable because it has become part of our
public discourse" (84). Thus, while I share the concerns about the

positionality

limitations of the waves metaphor to describe the history of US feminism, I also realize that, as a scholar, it is impossible to completely
ignore the metaphor, as it is frequently used in accounts of feminism.
Thus, I at times reference sources and critics who speak of the waves
of feminism, as Hillary Chute does elsewhere in this chapter. However, my own research and experience resonates strongly with the
notion that the distinct waves of feminism do not reflect the actual
history. In fact, studying these comic strips by women from the
1970s, 1980s, and 1990s speaks strongly to the notion that in everyday
"nitty-gritty" practice, feminism isn't easy or tidy or singular.

how own study may challenge wave metaphor

Rather, feminist history is messy and complicated, and essentializing experience diminishes the power of individuals and, in particular, the lived experiences of women of color. In fact, the concerns of
women of color have been noticeably absent from most histories of
the Women's Liberation movement and, in fact, the movement itself.
Kathleen Berkeley explains, "From its inception, NOW also sought
to attract prominent black women to its membership; but although
Pauli Murray and Aileen Hernandez were charter members, the organization was dominated by and reflected the interests of middle-class
white women" (31), and ultimately this insularity severely compro-
mised the successes of the movement. Berkeley continues, the "whiteness" of the Women's Liberation movement engendered in Black
women a deep mistrust: "They [black women] look at White women
and see the enemy—for racism is not confined to the White man"
(51). Christine Stansell argues that feminists are in the practice "of
universalizing extravagantly—making wild, improbable leaps across
chasms of class and race, poverty and affluence, leisured lives of toil
to draw basic similarities that stem from the shared condition of sex"
(xvii), yet "young black women would have none of the romance of
sisterhood" (267). Ultimately, this historic myopia eventually led to
an increased understanding of the situatedness of women and the
creation of "intersectional feminism," which recognizes the diverse
standpoints of individual women.

lead to inter-sectionality

Missing Pages: Racism and Comic Strips

While intersectional feminism is gaining traction in scholarly circles
and popular culture, during the 1960s and 1970s women of color were
not only discouraged from participating in the Women's Liberation

lack of diversity of feminism in comics &

movement but are also noticeably missing from the comics pages and ranks of comics creators, male or female. Diversity in the mainstream comics pages was virtually nonexistent, with no Latina/Latinx, South Asian, Southeast Asian, Arab Muslim, or LGBTQ+ recurring characters and very few Black ones. On the rare instances when people of color were represented, they were generally included as figures of villainy or comedy. According to Steven Loring Jones:

> In the comics section, Blacks were the principal comic figures, having surpassed the Irish at the turn of the century as the butt of America's jokes. Taking images from black-face minstrelsy, which was America's first national popular entertainment form and a mainstay of the American stage until the 1940's, many of the images of "Blacks" in the first half-century of the comics were not of Blacks at all.

Jones further explains that "newspapers published by the Afro-American press also entered into the fight against the negative depiction of Blacks. By the mid-1930's they were leading the struggle against any continuance of minstrelized representations." Jesse Ormes's comic strip, *Torchy Brown from Dixie to Harlem,* was one of those comic strips, debuting in 1937, and appearing in numerous Black newspapers before ending in 1938. Edward Brunner notes, "Not only was Torchy Brown almost certainly the first strip to be written and drawn by an African American woman, but its appearance in all editions of the *Pittsburgh Courier* (as many as fourteen) was as close to syndication as an African American strip could expect" (24). Ormes created other strips such as *Candy* and *Pattie Jo'-n-Ginger,* but it was *Torchy Brown* that truly triumphed. Brunner explains:

> In fifty-three weekly episodes that ran in the *Pittsburgh Courier* for exactly one year, from 1 May 1937, to 30 April 1938, Ormes sketched adventures of a young woman that were at once autobiographical and fantastic, presenting events from a distinctively female point of view (valuing interpersonal relations, affirming an aesthetic of taste and fashion, and using ingenuity and persistence to overcome traditional barriers to recognition). (25)

Alas, Ormes and her creation remained anomalous, with people of color appearing rarely in comic strips, particularly as female characters.

It wasn't until 1970 that a comic strip featuring a Black woman appeared in national syndication, when *Friday Foster* debuted. The strip featured the adventures of the eponymous Friday Foster, a bright and daring photographer's assistant, and ran until 1974, although it inspired one stand-alone comic book as well as a feature film starring Pam Grier. The strip was the creation of writer Jim Lawrence and artist Jorje Longeron, though in the final years it was also drawn by Howard Chaykin and Dick Giordano. Don Markstein maintains that while the strip "wasn't critically acclaimed, particularly prominent, or very popular," it was

> the first mainstream syndicated comic strip to star a black woman. In fact, other than a handful of broadly stereotyped caricatures from the industry's very early days (such as *Pore Lil Mose*, by *Yellow Kid* creator Richard F. Outcault) and a few series aimed solely at black newspapers (such as Jackie Ormes's pioneering *Torchy Brown*), no American comic strip had ever borne the name of a black lead character. Ted Shearer's *Quincy* arrived later the same year, and Brumsic Brandon Jr.'s *Luther* a year later, but *Friday Foster* was the first.

Steven Loring Jones notes:

> The Black activism of the 1960's also led to new individualized portrayals of Black characters in the mainstream press. . . . The Black characters since introduced in humorous strips like Franklin in "Peanuts" (1968), Lt. Flap in "Beetle Bailey" (1970), Clyde and Ginny in "Doonesbury" (1970–75), and Oliver Wendell Jones in "Bloom County" (1985) are Black caricatures drawn consistent with the manner in which the white figures are caricatured. Instead of huge lips and jet black faces to indicate Blackness, it is usually hair style, a goatee (for Black males), or dots or lines for shading. The focus of white cartoonists when portraying Black characters, has shifted from appearance to characterization.

Black female characters, and, for that matter, creators, continued to be even rarer, although Jones points to the editorial cartoons of Yaounde Olu, including "Slinky Ledbetter and Comp'ny" (1980) and "Jerri Kirl" (1983), as illustrating "a diversity of comic characters which were both stylized and non-traditional." Thus, the syndication of Barbara Brandon-Croft's *Where I'm Coming From* in 1989 holds particular historical weight. Brandon-Croft, an avowed Black feminist, provided an important and rarely represented perspective in the comics pages and illustrated Black women in all of their diversity.

Unfortunately, Brandon-Croft and other female comics creators of color were undoubtedly not well represented on the comics pages during the 1970s through the 1990s and perhaps this is not surprising, given that the newspaper comics pages have been extremely conservative. In 2001 Maurice Horn argued:

> The last 17 years have been marked by a series of social upheavals, and especially by what has come to be called "the sexual revolution," yet it would be difficult—indeed almost impossible—to find a reflection of these far-reaching events in the newspaper strips of the last decade and a half. In contrast to earlier times when the comics had held up a mirror to the society around them, the syndicated strips were now 15 to 20 years behind the times in social outlook. This flight from reality has been responsible, above anything else, for the rapidly shrinking newspaper strip readership in the 1960's and 1970's, especially among younger people. Instead of trying to update their comics in order to appeal to a more sophisticated audience, syndicate editors decided to hold on, at any cost, to the readership that was left. (188)

Horn suggests that newspaper comic strips largely ignored social and cultural trends, clinging to outdated ideals and a simulacrum of wholesome domesticity. This clinging to an imagined past, a past that is almost entirely white and middle-class, and bereft of Black Americans, not to mention people of Latinx, South Asian, Southeast Asian, Arab Muslim descent, or LGBTQ+, is little wonder, given that the audience for print newspapers has remained relatively stagnant and relatively conservative. According to Paula Berinstein in 2005, "newspapers are not serving everyone equally. Subscribership and readership are skewed toward older white people who own their homes," and "most weekday subscribers are over the age of 34, with just 17 percent in the 18 to 34 age groups. Eighty-seven percent of weekday subscribers are homeowners. Sixty percent are employed; 27 percent are retired. Ninety percent—90 percent!—are white. If these figures can be believed, young people, non-whites, and renters aren't subscribing" ("Black and White" 46). Interestingly enough, while age, education, race, and income all played key factors in newspaper readership, research found that men and women were represented fairly equally. And even though the study offers only a small window into the evolving demographics of print newspaper readership, it does present an impression of the intended audience. Yet, the comics frequently present a different sort of space and a contrasting perspective to the "hard news" even within the newspaper pages. Will a closer examination of newspaper strips from 1976 until the contemporary moment, particularly those created by women, offer challenges to dominant narratives of womanhood or will they simply reinforce received wisdom and common stereotypes? The following section provides a closer examination of a typical series of comics pages from 1984, helping to provide a larger context for considering individual strips over time and for studying the framework within which these particular strips operated.

[handwritten marginal note: key question?]

At Home in the Newspaper: The Comics Pages in 1984

Before isolating and studying several strips created by women from 1976 to the present, it is beneficial to gain an understanding of the context of the strips within the entirety of the newspaper comics pages. Thus, I chose a random selection of comics pages from my local paper, the *Oregonian,* on December 5, 1984, a date several years after the debut of *Cathy* and *For Better or For Worse,* and set out to survey the landscape of the newspaper comics pages. On December 5, 1984, the *Oregonian* newspaper featured thirty-six comic strips (four of the single-panel variety) over two pages, which also featured the "Wonderword," "Isaac Asimov's Super Quiz," the "Star Gazer" astrology guide," and "Jumble: That Scrambled Word Game." Thirty-three of the strips were created by men and three by women: *Sylvia* by Nicole Hollander, *Cathy* by Cathy Guisewite, and *For Better or For Worse* by Lynn Johnston. Six of the comics featured female characters in the title, such as *Winnie Winkle, Mary Worth, Hi and Lois,* and *Blondie.* None of the strips were authored by self-identified people of color, and, at least on this day, the only person of color depicted was one character on the bowling team of *Motley's Crew,* although some of the strips did have characters of color appearing on other days at that time, such as Franklin on *Peanuts.* Featured within the strips, there

[handwritten marginal note: context of example/ landscape]

are forty-nine male characters, thirty female characters, and ten animal or child characters of no identifiable gender.[4] A closer analysis of the behaviors of these characters reveals further patterns, suggestive of this particular time and place in American culture. The male characters in these strips primarily participate in active pursuits; they are depicted bowling, drawing, playing sports, putting up Christmas lights, skateboarding, and conducting an exorcism (*Bloom County*). The men serve in the military, both the contemporary army (*Beetle Bailey*) and the ancient French Foreign Legion (*Crock*). They are cowboys in the old West, (*Catfish*), Vikings (*Hagar the Horrible*), monks (*Fenton*), and "house-husbands" (*Adam*). The males drink and talk and work in offices.

Notably, two men actively care for children. In *Winnie Winkle*, William "Billy" Wright (aka "Mr. Right") is pictured in the first panel of a four-panel strip kneeling before a young boy and wondering, "What's a cute little fella doing all alone in a sleazy place like this?" The boy plaintively responds, "Da da?" In the second panel Billy responds, "I'm not your Daddy, but surely you belong to **someone**," before cuddling the boy closely in his arms. In the final panel Billy ushers the boy out the door, promising to find the boy's "person" and keep him "out of trouble." In subsequent daily strips it is revealed that the boy is Darren Sutton and his mother, Patricia, was abandoned while pregnant and is now working to take care of her son but is not, apparently, doing a good job of it. Billy warns Patricia to find more reliable care before stepping in himself. Although the context isn't apparent from this strip alone, it is clear from this example that the strapping, fair-haired man acts as the rescuer of lost children, swooping in protectively and comforting the boy in the absence of his mother. In her pointed nonappearance, the mother represents neglect. With women in the workforce and out of the home, the child suffers and must be rescued by the man.

Adam presents another contemporary development as women flooded the workplace, with Adam taking on the role of "house-husband" while his wife Laura works. In this particular daily strip, Adam walks outside and complains to a male friend who is pushing a stroller with a small child's head visible. Adam shares that his

---

4. The anthropormorphized birds of *Shoe* are counted as being clearly demarcated as male, while the bears of *Bears in Love* are not counted according to gender. Clearly, this rough count only provides a quick insight into the context of a representative comics page, rather than a strictly coded formal analysis.

wife feels that he's taking "the role of house-husband too lightly" and that he doesn't "keep the house clean." Adam's friend suggests that Laura "just wants you to be responsible. There's nothing wrong with that." Adam agrees, and the final panel depicts him home alone, with a telephone to his ear, the speech balloon indicating his call: "Hello: Dial-A-Maid?" Adam chooses to take on his cleaning responsibilities by outsourcing them to a maid, almost certainly female, rather than simply doing the work himself. While this strip jokingly critiques Adam's interpretation of his friend's call to "be responsible," it also, once again, suggests that it is the female's absence from the home environment that has caused this problem and created this friction by upending the traditional family dynamic. Furthermore, there is a sense that Laura is being unreasonable in her demands of Adam the "house-husband."

[handwritten margin note: absent / female / women / out of / place]

Although *Andy Capp* does not demonstrate a caring, masculine side, the strip similarly criticizes an absent female. In the four-panel strip, Andy is first seen in profile at a bar with an empty glass, his face resting in his hands and his plaid hat pulled low over his eyes. In the second panel, Andy rouses and points toward an unseen character, asking, "Are you going to buy me one, Suzie?" The third panel shifts to an image of the three taps, a large speech balloon dominating the top half of the frame. The absent female figure responds, "No! Y'Should be ashamed of yourself . . . scrounging off a woman?" The final panel shifts the focus once more to Andy, returned to his original position at the bar, although this time he turns his face to address the audience, commenting, "Great, isn't it? You give them equality and they throw it back in your face.' Andy argues that equality for women was a gift bestowed upon them by men, and that this benevolent gesture has been turned against males in a violent gesture, as shown by this particular man who fails to procure a drink from a female bartender. The absent woman stands for all women, ungrateful shrews resorting to hostility and utterly unappreciative of the male offering of equality.

[handwritten margin note: "ungrateful" / women / for equality / "given" to / them]

One very notable omission from this discussion is *Doonesbury*, which did not appear in the *Oregonian*, but did feature numerous female characters and directly supported Women's Liberation. In particular, the character Joanie Caucus came to stand as a symbol of the feminist movement since her first appearance in September 1972, when she argues with her husband regarding her feminist beliefs. Joanie leaves her husband and two children and enrolls in law school and remains an outspoken advocate for women's rights throughout the run of the strip. Kerry Soper argues that Joanie is "perhaps the most sympathetic female character" (*Garry Trudeau* 160) in *Doonesbury* and that "her dramatic character arc allowed her to represent a shifting zeitgeist" (160). Interestingly enough, Soper notes that Joanie's flaws and doubts encouraged the audience to sympathize with the character, making her feminist beliefs more palatable:

> It seems that Joanie would not have resonated so well with readers if she were less ridiculed with doubts, contradictions, and funny foibles. The fact that she radicalized herself and became a success in the world of law while still being self-deprecating and insecure, made her seem less strident in her feminism. Readers could thus identify with her struggles and see her as an individual first, and an icon of a movement second. (162)

Thus, Soper posits that it is Joanie's insecurity that endears her to the audience and renders her feminism "less strident," a generous perspective that did not seem to be applied to other female comic strip characters like Cathy, who was soundly criticized for her foibles. Regardless, Trudeau's explicit support of Women's Liberation in the early days of the strip, and feminism in general, marks it as a particularly noteworthy exception to the vast majority of comic strips from 1984 (and beyond), which rarely address feminist concerns, or do so with derision.[5]

However, unlike Joanie Caucus, the women represented on this day in these pages, when actually depicted, are usually crying, talking on the phone, gossiping, worrying about their appearance, and occasionally scheming. Their interactions swirl around relationships, emotions, and looks. There are very few professional women, and for the most part, the working women focus on fashion and sentiment rather than career. *On the Fastrack* presents an exception, with one woman standing amidst a group of coworkers—simply one of the gang rather than an anomaly—although in the context of the page, she is precisely that, the female character working alongside male colleagues without comment. The other career women represented on the page are largely place holders: in *Beetle Bailey*, the General's sec-

---

5. For a detailed analysis of Trudeau's rendering of Women's Liberation, see Valerie Voigt Olson's master's thesis, "Garry Trudeau's Treatment of Women's Liberation in *Doonesbury*" from 1982.

retary Miss Buxley and soldier (and office worker) Private Blips serve as foils for a gag between Lt. Fuzz and General Halftrack, and a nurse is praised for her caring in *Judge Parker*. While it is true that the "Fairy Godmother Dating Service" from *Sylvia* could loosely be deemed professional, the service still revolves around dating and relationships. Office workers Cathy and Charlene spend the strip fretting about their hair, makeup, dresses, and purses as they exit the bathroom before rushing back in, completely flustered by the fact that despite all of their primping, they "look exactly the same." The women of these pages are not strong and active agents of change—they are gossiping, conniving, self-centered, and riddled with doubt—if they are actually present. The women here are white and upper-class; this is certainly not a representation of intersectional identities. And while the pages from one randomly chosen day in 1984 cannot be said to represent a year or years of comic strips, it is, I think, significant that this random sampling suggests a snapshot of popular conceptions of men and women and, furthermore, I would argue, the daily comic pages such as these helped shaped the narrative of gender expectations.

The Strips Close Up

The following chapters focus on these narratives of gender as represented in a selection of comic strips created by women in the heyday of the Women's Liberation movement and shortly thereafter. It is well-known and well-documented that comic strips are traditionally a male-dominated medium, yet in the late 1970s and through the 1990s a small group of female-created comic strips came to national attention, rendering a rhetoric of womanhood that, influenced by feminism, informed national opinion, simultaneously reinforcing and rejecting popular stereotypes of women, children, and family while positing new roles for women inside and outside the home.

It should be noted that, while this study focuses on comic strips appearing in newspapers, the original publication contexts of the strips varied, and, consequently, the original experience of reading the comics differed as well. Syndicated daily newspaper strips like *Cathy, For Better or For Worse, Sylvia,* and *Stone Soup,* appeared every day in black and white on the comics pages and in color on Sundays. These strips were chosen by the syndicates and the local newspapers to appeal to the readership, and thus represented what the newspaper believed to be attractive to a largely white, middle-class audience. The strips reflected the paradigm of the readers and the newspaper leadership and did so every single day. This pressure to perform 365 times per year undoubtedly led to repetition and redundancy as the characters inched their way forward in small increments, but the frequency also established a comforting familiarity. When one sees characters every day, they become a fixture, a stable and reliable source of entertainment. The anticipation to see "what happens next" builds from day to day, but never lasts long enough to lose momentum or the narrative plot threads.

In contrast, *Where I'm Coming From* also appeared in syndication in mainstream newspapers, but did so only once a week, and furthermore, appeared on the editorial pages, thus marking it as a special offering—different in temporality and temperament, separated by placement and frequency. Regardless of its location, *Where I'm Coming From*'s placement within the mainstream papers represents a significant moment, particularly given that it featured Black characters and was created by a Black woman. However, readers would certainly note the position of the strip and ascertain that it did not represent a "normal," "everyday" comic, but rather, one with a political, editorial agenda. *Dykes to Watch Out For* also appeared less frequently, coming out every other week in alternative newspapers. *Dykes,* with its classical literary allusions and episodic delivery, appropriately emulates the serial nature of Charles Dickens's work, as both appealed to a devoted fan following who eagerly devoured the latest drama of their favorite characters. *DTWOF*'s publication in LGBTQ+ and alternative weeklies also influenced its reception, as such weeklies were largely available for free in larger cities and therefore reached a more urban audience with an interest in an "alternative" to the mainstream news. The strip's placement in left-leaning publications assured a largely receptive audience, and the melodramatic nature of the narrative helped maintain the audience's interest over the two-week intervals. *Ernie Pook's Comeek* also appeared in the alternative weeklies, albeit on a weekly basis, thus allowing it to address darker, more mature themes, appealing to the more radical readership.

Of course, the original experience of reading the strips serially in various newspapers isn't feasible today, and studying newspaper-based comic strips poses special challenges for the researcher. While

archives/access

many newspapers are archived in library databases, often only the stories are saved, rather than images. Locating scans of entire pages presents a much more difficult task and often requires funding to access the complete paper through sites such as newspapers.com, thus presenting serious financial roadblocks for scholars. Some of the more popular comic strips are available in anthologies, although these collections may also be expensive, out-of-print, or unavailable through library services. And, as previously indicated, even when the diligent researcher manages to obtain an anthology, they are often incomplete, collecting only bits and pieces from the strip's run, and these books are often organized by theme rather than chronologically. For those searching through scans of newspapers, the process is arduous at best, with the quality of the scans frequently questionable, and the hunt for the comics pages within the larger newspaper incredibly time-consuming. Some creators maintain online archives, which are an invaluable resource. Lynn Johnston, for example, offers a comprehensive online resource, archiving every strip from its initial publication in 1979 until its conclusion, with cross-referencing available. Alison Bechdel maintains a partial archive online, and other strips can be found beyond paywalls divorced from the larger context of the newspaper at sites such as UniversalUclick.com or GoComics.com.

In my research process, I relied on a combination of techniques to access the strips. Whenever possible, I tried to locate the comic strips within scans of the newspaper, which permitted me to consider the placement of the strip within the paper and on the page, as well as understanding the sequence from day to day. This, importantly, allowed me to see certain strips or arcs that are not represented in anthologies, such as Mr. Pinkley's assault on Cathy. However, I also relied on collections, which usually offered much clearer images. Furthermore, I was lucky enough to receive the Lucy Shelton Caswell Research Award in the summer of 2019, which supported my research in the archives of the Billy Ireland Cartoon Library and Museum at The Ohio State University, which allowed me to scrutinize original art from many of the creators. During my visit to the Billy Ireland, I was able to examine materials not available anywhere else, such as the personal papers of Nicole Hollander and Jan Eliot. The archives revealed Nicole Hollander's art notebooks from school (where she received a C), in addition to notes, sketches, and correspondence. Studying these artifacts, I came to understand Hollander's process from incipient idea to published piece, and the numerous

(margin note: archives)

(margin note: call-to-action)

(margin note: ch. outlines)

pieces revealed a fascinating hidden history as well, including a number of letters between Hollander and other creators, in particular female cartoonists. My research process reinforced my belief in the importance of archives such as that of the Billy Ireland, as well as a real need to make newspaper comic strips more available to the public, hopefully through high-quality collections as well as in online archives. Comic strips clearly deserve much more scholarly attention, and while I have done my best to provide as much original material as possible, using a combination of newspaper scans, book collections, and archival materials, I hope that future scholars will have more high-resolution materials available in order to replicate, as best we can, the original experience of reading the strips.

My research is presented in the chapters that follow, although I hope this is only the beginning of this particular conversation. Chapter One studies the importance of Cathy Guisewite's *Cathy*, which ran 1976–2010 and focused on the "new," single, career-woman, the eponymous "Cathy," who praised feminist principles and fought for equal rights, yet also illustrated female stereotypes, as Cathy longed for shoes, chocolate, and a marriage proposal. The next section shifts from a career-focused strip to a domestic one, as Chapter Two examines Lynn Johnston's *For Better or For Worse*, which ran from 1979 to 2008 and portrayed what appeared, on the surface, to be a traditional family, but that, on closer inspection, challenged readers to examine controversial issues such as child abuse, homosexuality, sexual harassment, and infidelity. Presenting a much more radical, punk perspective, Chapter Three explores the early years of Lynda Barry's strip *Ernie Pook's Comeek* (1979–2008), as it concentrated on the "Battle of the Sexes," particularly emphasizing the trials and tribulations of relationships and dating in the 1980s. Chapter Four focuses on Nicole Hollander's *Sylvia*, which ran 1981–2012 and depicted an alternative understanding of a more radical feminism, providing caustic commentary on the partisan landscape and gender politics. A few years later, Alison Bechdel's *Dykes to Watch Out For* (1983–2008) reflected the evolution of feminism, as many feminists moved to a more inclusive, intersectional movement, and this progression is documented in Chapter Five. The sixth chapter studies Barbara Brandon-Croft's *Where I'm Coming From*, syndicated from 1989–2005, as it represented a plurality of Black women on a weekly basis, challenging stereotypes and insisting on the presence of Black women's voices, albeit in the absence of their bodies. Chapter Seven follows the strip *Stone*

Soup, created by Jan Eliot in 1995 and concluding in 2020, offering an inductive argument for the ordinariness of feminism as a logical, everyday ideal enacted in the lives of a community. This concluding chapter further presents a reflection on the import of these comics from a certain time and place, exploring how they offer an evolving vision of gender.[6]

---

6. Comic strip titles have been abbreviated throughout the book, with *For Better or For Worse* abbreviated as *FBoFW, Dykes to Watch Out For* abbreviated as *DTWOF,* and *Where I'm Coming From* abbreviated as *WICF.*

CHAPTER 1

CROCODILITES **AND** *CATHY*

The Worst of Both Worlds

> Each of us wages a private battle each day between the grand fantasies we have for ourselves and what actually happens.
>
> —Cathy Guisewite, 1994 Commencement Address, University of Michigan

OVER THE COURSE of over thirty years, comic strip heroine Cathy Andrews inspired feelings of ardent devotion *and* passionate dislike in readers. While some individuals felt they'd found a kindred spirit who, like them, desperately struggled to find a balance between the demands of a career and maintaining relationships, others decried what they felt was Cathy's obsession with her appearance and her reliance on gender stereotypes. The blogger known as "Wandering Schmuck" saw the strip as

good summary of strip

a struggle by one woman growing up within the heart of the feminist movement of America (the seventies and eighties and early nineties). The main character, Cathy, is a sort of ego who fights between her superego (the superwoman "I can have it all!" feminist who makes 5 million dollars founding her own business while raising four bilingual-privately-educated children and knitting for charities in her spare time) and her id (the timid, "traditional" woman who just wants to curl up with a rich husband and have babies without thinking of the more complicated aspects of life) while trying to live on a day-to-day basis.

For Rina Piccolo, the creator of the strip *Tina's Groove, Cathy* was an inspiration. Piccolo explained:

> Newspaper comics in 1975 were all men, Beetle Bailey, Hagar the Horrible and Frank and Earnest. . . . All the female characters were like Blondie. They were either a housewife or a glamour girl. Cathy totally changed the page. Here's a young woman talking about, basically, her fat ass and how she couldn't fit into a swimsuit or that she had had it with her boyfriend and all the little neurotic things that a lot of women go through in day-to-day living. She was the first female character to really let loose and say what a lot of women were thinking at the time. (qtd. in Zerbisias)

For her part, Lucy Shelton Caswell, comics historian and former curator of The Billy Ireland Cartoon Library and Museum at The Ohio State University, noted of Cathy, "The character was ordinary. In some ways that made the strip extraordinary. . . . She isn't a supermom, she's no 'Brenda Starr' reporter with a glamorous job. She leads a life that is very familiar to women readers. That's what Cathy's women readers—and most are women—liked about it" (qtd. in McNulty). *Cathy* certainly struck a chord with readers, and, at the height of its popularity, the strip appeared in over 1,400 newspapers, in addition to spawning numerous anthologies and licensed products, including dolls, coffee mugs, and even Ben & Jerry's ice cream.

Given her pioneering place on the comics page and the focus on the tribulations of ordinary women, it is perhaps surprising that *Cathy* inspired such intense scorn and ridicule, particularly when the strip retired in 2010. In anticipation of the final strips, Lindsay Beyerstein complained of Cathy that "she's predictable, pathetic, and boring. She's the antithesis of funny. The sheer existential horror of 'Cathy' spurred my will to resist." In a column for the *New Yorker,* Meredith Blake noted that Cathy was "hopelessly out of fashion" and reproduced a Twitter Trend on "#WaysCathyShouldEnd," including, "Hoarding experts arrive too late to find Cathy flattened under a heap of diet aids, cats and dating books," and, "In a fit of self-loathing, Cathy performs at-home liposuction with a carving knife and a dustbuster; dies of sepsis." The popular feminist blog *Feministe* argued: "I've always gotten the impression that Cathy was meant as something for women to bond over, but for the most part it just reinforced a lot of wretched stereotypes about women" (qtd.

*both/
and
argument*

in Zerbisias), while Mary Elizabeth Williams reflected more evenly, "Empowerment is for her usually a fleeting state in an otherwise self-doubting existence. . . . She may be that nightmare, neurotic gal pal whose calls you screen, but girlfriend, admit it; sometimes she's also your own dark side." Was Cathy a feminist icon or self-loathing, misogynist stooge? This question represents something of a false dilemma, a bifurcation fallacy, and what ancient rhetoricians would call an example of *krokodeilites* or *crocodilites*[1] or, in plainer terms, the crocodile fallacy, in which either position does harm to the rhetor— an unsolvable dilemma. In *Cathy,* neither option, the empowered feminist nor the traditional housewife, is without harm, and when examined through a rhetorical lens, Cathy the character performs a delicate balance, making her case through personal experience. This example of *martyria,* a rhetorical form of evidence confirmed by experience, offers an alternative to either/or stereotypes of womanhood.

A strip from 1979 elegantly expresses Cathy's position as *crocodilites,* or caught in the jaws of the crocodile (see figure 1.1); in the strip Cathy laments her duality—a terrible, soul-crushing job and a horrible, draining relationship, ultimately declaring, "I am woman. I have it all. The worst of both worlds."[2] This example also demonstrates the common structure of the daily strips, marked by four repetitive panels with very little movement or variation. In the first and subsequent panels Cathy stands in the foreground with her desk, telephone, and

---

1. According to the *Oxford English Dictionary,* the classical sophism of *crocodilites* first appeared in T. Wilson's *Rule of Reason* in 1551, and was explained as "suche a kynde of subtiltie that when we haue graunted a thyng to our aduersarie. . the same turneth to our harme afterward." The origins of the concept were further elaborated by Thomas Stanley in *The History of Philosophy* in 1656: "The Crocodilite, so named from this Ægyptian Fable: A woman sitting by the side of Nilus, a Crocodile snatched away her child, promising to restore him, if she would answer truly to what he asked; which was, *Whether he meant to restore him or not.* She answered, *Not to restore him,* and challeng'd his promise, as having said the truth. He replyed, that *if he should let her have him, she had not told true.*" Nicola Glaubitz notes of the paradox: "The dilemma cannot be resolved: if the mother has correctly guessed the crocodile's intention, the crocodile cannot keep its promise because it will retrospectively contradict its own criterion for truth. Nor could the crocodile have kept its promise if she had lied because it had insisted on a true answer" (64). Crocodilites thus came to mean impossible situations, wherein all options result in self-harm.

2. Figures are taken from the newspaper whenever possible to get the closest approximation of the strips as originally published. However, at times the strips are taken from various anthologies, and are indicated as such.

FIGURE 1.1. Cathy Guisewite. *Cathy.* August 28, 1979.

papers situated behind her, clear evidence of her career, along with the briefcase in her hands. Yet her professional demeanor is softened by the small heart centered on her shirt, a romantic touch signifying her longing for love. Her stance and expression vary little, except for the addition of the childlike gesture of sticking out her tongue in the last panel, as she indicates her disgust with this trap.

To bear witness is a powerful logical tool for any argument, and *Cathy* testifies as to the experiences of ordinary women, providing small, daily snapshots of one woman's days, yet as a drawn and stylized creation, Cathy also represents a rendered portrayal of experience, one that rhetoricians would note is both invented and artistic. However, although Cathy is a character, she also shares a name with her creator, suggesting an authenticity or truthfulness by design. As a witness embodying women's lived experiences, I would argue that the importance of *Cathy* is more complicated than some false, Manichean notions of qualifying as a "true" feminist or laboring as a sexist stereotype. Clearly, in *Cathy* the title character struggles to find a balance between the ideas espoused by women's liberation and the more traditional, conventional women's roles advocated by mainstream American culture of the time. While loved and reviled, a close reading of the strip reveals a potent thread of feminism and a turn to a pattern of *epimone* of repetition, illustrating how little changes for women over time. The remainder of this chapter explores the ways in which *Cathy* exposes the trials of one woman's life, especially as she navigates the early years of the strip, providing context for the strip as well as analysis of key moments, which reveals a more complicated representation of feminism, challenging current thinking on the strip as a bifurcation fallacy that unfairly reduces the import and

argument

rhetorical term

legacy of *Cathy*'s complex perspective on an individual's experience of gender roles in the time of women's liberation, reflecting an important moment in American history, one page and one panel at a time.

The Origin of Ack!: *Cathy* in the Beginning

Given its frequent focus on fraught mother-daughter relationships, it is perhaps unsurprising that *Cathy* the comic strip began at the relentless urging of Cathy Guisewite's mother. Before her career as a cartoonist, Guisewite grew up in Midland, Michigan, graduating from the University of Michigan with a degree in English in 1972. After graduation, she worked at the W. B. Doner & Co. advertising agency, where she became its first female vice president. It was at this time that Guisewite found stress release by sketching rough doodles and sending them to her parents. Guisewite's mother urged her daughter to send her drawings out to publishers. In the *Cathy Twentieth Anniversary Collection,* Guisewite remembered, "I drew my first comic strip on the kitchen table in between bowls of fudge ripple ice cream. It wasn't a comic strip, really, just as explosion of frustration that wound up on paper instead of in my mouth" (7). In *The Cathy Chronicles,* Guisewite recalled that, "anxious to have me do even better, my parents researched comic strip syndicates, sought advice from Tom Wilson, the creator of *Ziggy,* and, finally, threatened to send my work to Universal Press Syndicate if I didn't" (18). Heeding her parents' warning/advice, Guisewite sent some work to the Universal Press Syndicate, who lauded the work's "honesty" despite the simple drawings and swiftly offered Guisewite a contract.

The pressure was intense. In *Fifteenth Anniversary Reflections,* Guisewite commented that she "quit taking art class when I was seven years old because I was planning a career as a cowboy and felt it would be a waste of time to learn how to draw" (vii). Therefore, upon receiving the deal from Universal Press, Guisewite "spent every night that followed frantically trying to learn how to draw on a drawing board under the stairway in my apartment" (*Cathy Twentieth Anniversary Collection* 7). It was a steep learning curve, though Guisewite found support from Lee Salem and Jim Andrews, as she explained in an interview with Tom Heintjes:

> Lee told me how big to make the boxes. I was just drawing on paper with a ball-point pen, so Lee told me that some people use

Rapidograph pens on Bristol board. I bought those. Everything about the next couple of months was a constant panic and fun of learning to do everything completely from zero. . . . I bought a book called *Backstage at the Strips* by Mort Walker, and that book was my bible of how to physically do a comic strip. I got great inspiration from that. I bought tracing paper, and I developed a system of drawing the same picture on tracing paper over and over. Somebody told me about lightboxes, so I got a lightbox and developed a system that when I would get four frames that were decently drawn on tracing paper, I would use the lightbox to trace them in ink onto Bristol board. I never drew in pencil at all. That was the system I used to put together the first six weeks of strips, and that is the exact same system I used 34 years later when I drew the last strip.

Guisewite's efforts came to fruition when *Cathy* the comic strip officially launched on November 22, 1976. The creator, however, suffered a bout of nerves, and for her part, "hid in my office in the advertising agency where I worked as a writer, praying that no one would read the comics that day" (*Cathy Twentieth Anniversary Collection* 5).

[margin note: Struggled to gain footing b/c...]

Guisewite points out the pioneering nature of the strip, for, at the time of *Cathy*'s debut, "Pursuing a career was a new phase for women," and "Except for Brenda Starr and Nancy, all the comic strips starred men" (*Cathy Twentieth Anniversary Collection* 5). In the early days, the strip struggled to find its footing. Guisewite posited that "the art was extremely primitive, and the comic strip editors were not used to seeing that kind of primitive-looking art. The second problem was that almost all of the features editors at that time were men, and it was a very different voice to be in the comics page" (Heintjes "Cathy"). However, over time the strip gained a wider following, eventually appearing in over 1,400 newspapers, and numerous merchandising deals and an Emmy-winning animated special followed. Guisewite continued working at the advertising agency full-time while working on the strip until 1980, when she decided to move to Los Angeles to devote her full attention into what was becoming a pop culture phenomenon. Guisewite also gained notoriety as a public figure, appearing regularly on *The Tonight Show with Johnny Carson*.

[margin note: ① style; ② men in charge; eventually very successful]

Interestingly enough, profiles of Guisewite from the early days of the strip seemed to miss the strip's critique of the media promoting unattainable and unhealthy beauty standards for women, and instead, chose to focus on the creator's appearance, such as the 1980 piece by Louise Sweeney for *The Christian Science Monitor,* which described Guisewite as a "leggy brunette who has not yet had to cope with a 30th birthday" and argued that "the Cathy you see in the comic strip, although named for her creator, doesn't look much like her. Cathy Guisewite in person looks like a young doe, with large brown hair. She is 5 foot 2 inches, small-boned, slender, agile, not the lovable klutz that Cathy is" (Sweeney). Not only was Guisewite the creator likened to a small woodland creature, even her voice was scrutinized, for Sweeney noted that Guisewite sounded different than she had expected, for her voice "is not the breathy, little girl, early-Jackie Kennedy voice you might expect of 'Cathy.' It is the voice of an older woman." Somehow, the author seems to feel it important to point out that the "real" Cathy is thin and attractive with a strong voice, and not at all like her creation, thus playing out the sexist obsession with stereotypes of female beauty that Cathy the cartoon figure lamented on a daily basis.

Over the years *Cathy*'s popularity grew, spawning greeting cards, dolls, and other licensed products along with numerous anthologies. Yet over time, as the women's liberation moment faded into the background of national consciousness, admiration for *Cathy* also waned. Rather than the purveyor of humorous quips, *Cathy* had become the butt of the joke, appearing as the punch line in various venues, including Tina Fey's television program *30 Rock* and various skits on *Saturday Night Live.* In 2010 Guisewite decided to end the strip to spend more time with her daughter, and the wave of scorn that met this decision surprised many, including Rosalind Warren, the editor of *The Best Contemporary Women's Humor,* who exclaimed, "The reaction has been venomous . . . I was surprised myself" (qtd. in Zerbisias). While fellow creator Rina Piccolo recognized *Cathy*'s historical significance for female creators, she was also quoted in "Was Cathy a Voice of Female Progress or Stereotyped Neurosis?: Character was No Blondie, But Feminists are Happy to See Her Go" as arguing that the comic was stuck in a time warp: "She did it in the '70s, and in the '80s, and in the '90s, and in the 2000s, and, at this point, women's lives have changed quite a bit. She ran the gag into the ground. The crowd that says good riddance just got sick of it" (*Toronto Star* IN 1). In contrast, Guisewite maintained that the struggles of women in 2010 were, in fact, very similar to those of thirty years ago, declaring, "I don't know, as women, what are we past? . . . When I write about dieting, I feel like I am writing as truthfully to women's pressures and concerns today as I was 34 years ago. The daily battle with self-image, self-consciousness and will power is exactly the same to me" (*Toronto Star* IN 1). Today *Cathy*'s legacy is unclear. Was she the embodiment of detrimental stereotypes of female neuroses or a feminist trailblazer? Is it possible to be both? Neither?

In Good Company: *Cathy* in Context

Beginning in November 1976, *Cathy* appeared in syndication in newspapers across the country. While Guisewite was something of an accidental cartoonist who never seriously studied art, she found inspiration in her favorite childhood comics, as she explained in an interview with Tom Heintjes:

not an artist but influenced by other comics

> I loved reading the comic strips. I usually read them with my dad. The ones I remember reading the most were *Peanuts, Nancy, Henry* and *Blondie*. It never would have occurred to me to put my thoughts into a comic strip if it weren't for *Peanuts*. That strip was absolutely, 100 percent the guiding influence on my comic strip. I grew up reading Sparky's strip about real anxieties and frustrations and humiliations and all those real human emotions, and he gave a voice to all those emotions on the comics pages. ("Cathy")

While focusing on "real human emotions," *Cathy* was never lauded for the quality of the art. In fact, *Doonesbury* cartoonist Gary Trudeau commented, "I've always thought that my main contribution to the comics page was that I made it safe for bad drawing, that *Cathy* and *Bloom County* and particularly *Dilbert* would have been unthinkable had I not challenged the assumption that competent draftsmanship was prerequisite to a career in cartooning" (qtd. in Soper, *Gary Trudeau* 130). Guisewite's creation process, utilizing tracing paper, pens, and lightboxes, remained much the same throughout the entire run of the strip, although a closer look at the first few years of the cartoon reveal the artist's development from a rougher, shakier style, to a more practiced and solid line—still simple, but definitely more polished. In his essay, "Storylines," Jared Gardner expresses the importance of the creator's linework in understanding comics, noting, "the physical labor of storytelling is always visible in graphic narrative, whether the visible marks themselves remain, in a way unique to

importance of style

any mechanically reproduced narrative medium" (65), and *Cathy* as comic undeniably calls attention to its eponymous creator, encouraging the audience to believe we are coming "face to face with a graphiateur" (64), creating our own idealized author figure for Guisewite, so much so that interviewers frequently expressed surprise that the actual Guisewite was so unlike her creation. And while Guisewite did utilize assistants as the strip gained in popularity, they worked primarily on the licensed products, suggesting that the vast majority of her strips were drawn by her own hand. And these strips, from a self-professed writer and drawing autodidact, rather than trained artist, suggest a humble, accessible aesthetic, with the rounded edges, thick, frumpy bodies, and simplified facial expressions positing a cutesy or sweet aesthetic one might associate with children doodling in notebooks and diaries.

Cathy appeared as a black and white daily strip, usually comprised of four panels, as well as a larger color strip on Sundays, usually featuring seven to ten panels following a larger initial panel featuring a stylized, decorated *Cathy* logo that changed from week to week. The art style is decidedly simple, with rounded, abstract figures and minimalist features. The backgrounds are sparse, and the bodies of the figures do little move the story forward, remaining, for the most part, static and inactive. Rather, movement is conveyed by the use of supporting details, such as sweat droplets or movement lines. While there are moments of physical comedy, particularly when Cathy falls or screams, the strip is typically not one that relies on broad bodily gags, but rather one that utilizes situational humor and wordplay as the basis for the joke. While the daily strips, as previously mentioned, generally have four panels, there are occasional exceptions, and apart from a rare explanatory caption, there is no narrative text box or heterodiegetic narrator, with the language coming directly from the characters, written in slightly stylized but highly readable font and surrounded by straightforward speech balloons. *Cathy* is a loquacious strip; the characters chatter incessantly, often to themselves, for Cathy frequently engages in long-winded monologues, as well as engaging with other characters. The audience acts as a heterodiegetic focalizer, watching the scenes as they unfold, but always removed from the actions of the diegesis. The characters age extremely slowly, but they do reference current events, even as they are divorced from real time, evolving incrementally. Over this leisurely evolution, the humor of *Cathy* reflects the artistic style— the wit displays a soft touch as embodied in the gentle curves of the characters' rounded bodies. The comedy primarily emerges from character-driven misunderstandings, witty dialogue, and situational humor. This is not a strip of grand guffaws or scathing take-downs, but of small, knowing smiles of recognition and sympathy.

The strip followed the daily trials and tribulations of its main character, Cathy, as she navigated what the creator called the "four major guilt groups," "food, love, career, and mothers," surrounded by a cast of several recurring characters, including Cathy's domineering mother, her agreeable (and often absent) father, primary suitor Irving, best friend Andrea, and several years later, her rescue dog Electra. Cathy's age is indeterminate, particularly as time moved so slowly, but she appears to be in her late twenties or early thirties for over thirty years. Cathy spends much of the strip working at Product Testing Incorporated, although she is eventually laid off and then rehired. Throughout her career, Cathy strives to find an appropriate work/life balance, often lamenting the impossibility of adhering to unattainable standards of beauty, decrying the fashion industry and media pressure to remain thin. In the first renderings, Cathy's silhouette is shaky and insecure, something of an agitated scrawl rather than practiced illustration. Over time Guisewite settled into her style, drafting main character Cathy with a thick, solid outline that formed a sloping, oval shape for her body. The rendering evokes the smooth, comforting silhouette of a Russian nesting doll. Cathy's head is round and full, and she is known for the long strings of hair, parted in the center, that frame her face, apart from regular hairstyle disasters. Cathy has large, wide, conjoined eyes, diminutive eyebrows, and a mouth that transforms to evoke a variety of emotions. Fans and critics frequently commented on Cathy's missing nose, which appeared very rarely in profile. (The other characters in the strip do have simple noses.) Cathy's eyebrows and mouth are her most expressive features, with her mouth transforming from a simple sweep of a smile to a wide-open scream and her eyebrows frequently tilting to convey a range of emotions from exasperation to shame. While Cathy's outfits change and are the frequent topic of discussion, she is most frequently depicted wearing pants and a red sweater (when in color) with a small pink heart in the center, and it is this look which is frequently parodied in other popular culture renditions of the character.

The other key players in the strip share a similarly simple aesthetic, with soft, rounded bodies but marginally different hairstyles, noses, and accessories. Cathy's neighborhood is decidedly *not* diverse, and fails to feature people of color, a range of economic backgrounds, or the LGBTQ+ community. Cathy exists in a small, homogenous bubble and if she represents any version of feminism, it is a strand associated with middle-class white women, situated apart from diversity or difference.

The most dominant (and domineering) character other than Cathy is her mother, Anne Andrews, clearly identified by her glasses and frilly apron. Anne is an ever-present force in her daughter's life, worrying about her daughter, offering her advice, and encouraging her to settle down and get married. The two women represent two distinct generations affected by the Women's Liberation movement of the 1970s. While Cathy vocally embraces many of the tenets of Women's Lib, particularly in reference to her career and the notion of "having it all," Anne hearkens back to an earlier image of ideal womanhood, stressing domesticity and family, in spite of a brief interest in Women's Liberation after forming a "Consciousness Raising" group that ultimately failed and cemented her commitment to more traditional notions of women as homemakers. As Christine Stansell argues, at the time, motherhood and feminism were frequently pictured as incompatible: "Motherhood seemed to be about concessions to others, not revolution. It was most certainly the state that feminists wanted to escape, not that which they wanted to become" (262). Thus, in many ways Cathy and Anne played out a humorous enactment of a contemporary conflict over women's evolving roles in society, a tableau unfolding in many American homes.

Other characters contributed to the diegesis, fulfilling various functions, although none held the import of Cathy's mother. Cathy's father, Bill, is a generically pleasant man, who remained in the background much of the time, both literally and figuratively, although he provides a solid and supportive counterpart to the officious Anne. Two other characters, Irving and Andrea, form the core of the cast, and represent vastly different worldviews. While Cathy dated a rotating cast of swains over many, many years, she returned time and again to Irving Hillman, eventually marrying him in 2005. Irving, a sturdy man with thick, dark hair and a somewhat bulbous nose, changed his look over the years and very slowly evolved from a cheating, chauvinistic philanderer to an ever-so-slightly more mature partner. Cathy's friend Andrea, however, presented a staunchly feminist point-of-view, attempting to bolster a dithering Cathy. Andrea, easily identified by her dark, bob haircut and jaunty scarves, eventually embraced the nuclear family, marrying and having two children, Zenith and Gus, but maintained her fight for equality while struggling to reenter the workplace after her job was given away. As the overt political struggle over women's equality as represented in the strip waned, Andrea disappeared from the daily pages, appearing only in the final years when Cathy found her old friend and asked her to be a part of her wedding. Cathy was also supported by her close friend Charlene, the receptionist at Product Testing Inc., and was bedeviled by Mabel, a returning character who appeared in a variety of service positions, including as a server, a salesperson, and a bank teller. Mabel, who always positioned a pencil in her dark, curly hair, could be counted on to hassle Cathy at any given institution. Over the years the characters formed a community, addressing new trends but continually circling the same themes.

[margin note: Community]

As Cathy and her community visited and revisited the "four major guilt groups" of food, career, love, and mothers, they also reflected the historical moment. Many readers and critics critiqued *Cathy*'s repetition, particularly in the later years, as a distinct breakdown and lack of imagination on the part of the creator, who failed, in their eyes, to find new ideas and keep the strip fresh. However, Guisewite indicates that, while the trends, fads, and technology changed a great deal since the beginning of the strip, for women, ultimately, very little changed in their status or positions of power. Could it be, that, rather than a failure, this repetition represents a choice to exhibit the rhetorical strategy of *epimone,* or the repetition of an image that speaks to its enduring relevance? Sister Miriam Joseph claims that, "because of its insistent repetition of an idea in the same words" (or in this case very similar images), "epimone is an effective figure in swaying the opinions of a crowd" (220). And *Cathy,* which appeared in so many newspapers and on so many refrigerators, was certainly influencing its readers. Furthermore, as Kerry Soper argues in his analysis of *Doonesbury,* "the identities, habits, even politics of the characters remain somewhat static. They are like sitcom characters that can never learn from their experiences; the same story, with minor variations, is told again and again" (*Gary Trudeau* 126). We cannot, as readers, expect fictional characters in comic strips to exhibit the same growth and development as real-world counterparts. Part of the charm of the serial strip is the comfort of the famil-

[margin note: Counter-argument to "outdated"]
[margin note: × repetition]

iar. Furthermore, the audience learns from the foibles arising from the inertia of the characters. Soper, once again, studies the lessons of Gary Trudeau's *Doonesbury*, concluding:

> While Chaplin's Little Tramp or Trudeau's Zonker persists from episode to episode as an unchanging, unintentionally wise fool—never abandoning delusions, obsessions, and a selfish engagement with the world—the reader can spot the lessons that need to be learned and thus can use the repetitive motifs as prompts to overcome their own delusions or political naiveté, in effect, we learn from their experiences because they cannot. (*Gary Trudeau* 127)

repetition

Although Cathy doesn't "learn her lesson," but rather continues to struggle with the pressures of unattainable beauty ideals, with balancing her desire for a fulfilling career and her wish for a successful romantic relationship, and with her weight on a daily basis, the reader can learn from Cathy's mistakes, understanding the lessons she fails to grasp.

The Life Lessons of Cathy

What, then, should readers take away from the many days and many years of *Cathy*? While it is important to look closely at the many story arcs that developed over the years (many of which have been forgotten or are rarely discussed), it is also useful to study the strip's beginning and ending. The comic strip first appeared on November 22, 1976, with a phone call, for the very first strip featured Cathy waiting, impatiently, for Irving to phone her (see figure 1.2). In the first panel, Cathy stands, arms folded, next to a simple side table, frowning. Her thought balloon indicates her thoughts: "Cathy, he's hurt you too many times! Next time he calls, just **bite your tongue** and give him your answer!!" In the next frame the phone rings and quavering movement lines surrounding her as well as the wobbly lines comprising the body indicate Cathy's overall instability once the long-awaited call has finally happened. Although she's been waiting and preparing for it, the call has still managed to rattle her. In the final panel, Cathy grips the phone to her head with a wavering smile, her small tongue sticking out. A speech balloon indicates her answer, "Yeth!" In a bit of comical wordplay, Cathy has, in fact, bitten her tongue, but her playful smile and the jubilant tilt of her eyes

begins & ends w/ a phone call

FIGURE 1.2. Cathy Guisewite. *Cathy.* November 22, 1976.

indicate that rather than remembering the ills and hurt he's done to her as outlined in her pep-talk monologue of the previous panel, she chooses to quite literally bite her tongue and repress the past, and instead her response is an enthusiastic, though garbled, affirmation of "Yeth!"

It is, perhaps, fitting that many years later the final strip ends with another reference to Cathy's relationship status and to another telephone, for the concluding strip of *Cathy*, published October 3, 2010, features Cathy's revelation that, having finally married the caller from her first appearance, Irving, she is pregnant with a girl (see figure 1.3). The strip differs from the first in that it is a Sunday, and thus is in color and enjoys a full nine panels and three rows, rather than the smaller daily format. The first two panels introduce the eponymous title (as was traditional for the Sunday strips), encased in a purple heart, but they also present the full cast of important characters from the run of the strip, all with heart symbols hovering above their heads in fluffy thought balloons. Cathy's dog Electra holds a banner reading, "thank you," while a box of tissues is positioned just to Cathy's side, indicating love for the audience as well as the sadness of the final goodbye. In the third panel (and the first of the second row), Cathy and Irving are depicted entering into the home of Cathy's parents, where Anne rushes to her daughter, quickly eclipsing Cathy's truncated statement, "Mom, I . . . I . . ." with a diatribe that continues for five panels:

> Whatever it is, sweetie, Dad and I are here for you! Unless we're suffocating! Then we'll stand over there! Or Dad could stand there and I could stand here! Or we could hop around trading places! Or

> . . . What am I saying?? You don't need us to fix anything! You're an incredible woman from an incredible time for women! Your generation opened doors, demanded chances, raised expectations, transformed society and exceeded the dreams of every generation before you! You **have** to know anything's possible!

During this dialogue, Bill Andrews gently ushers Irving off to the side and out of the panel, and the fifth, sixth, and seventh panels show only Cathy and her mother. The central relationship of mother and daughter occupies the bulk of the strip in word and image, with Anne stressing both her support and her pride in her daughter and in all women of her generation, recalling the earliest discussions of Women's Lib as presented in the strip and recognizing the long journey that Cathy, as symbolic of a generation of women following the advent of Women's Liberation, has experienced. Anne shouts her approval and joy in her daughter and the accomplishments of her generation, while indicating that despite her desire to support her child, she realizes her daughter doesn't need her. The eighth panel, placed in the third row and almost centered, features Cathy alone, her face and torso visible and surrounded by an actual frame, which borders the bottom of her face and her stomach, emphasizing the upcoming revelation of the next generation of women. Cathy states, "I **do** know anything's possible, Mom." In the ninth and final frame Cathy, patting her stomach, declares, "There's going to be another girl in the world." In this definitive panel, all four of the primary characters are featured, with the baby encased in Cathy's stomach thinking trademark statement, "aack," written in pink letters and emerging from yet another swirling thought balloon drifting away from Cathy's abdomen.

At this point Anne has fallen to her knees, her arms and face lifted skyward in joy and supplication, as she exclaims, "I'm going to be a Grandma??!" in a speech balloon surrounded by hearts. Off to the side, their figures appropriately framed by the couch they both frequent regularly as supporting characters with relatively little to do, the two men converse. Bill pats Irving, encouraging him to "Buckle up, son," while Irving holds his phone to his father-in-law, asking, "Want to see the ultrasound on my Iphone?" A simple, awkward side table, reminiscent of the table from that first strip in 1976, divides the panel and the men and women, but this time the phone is held not by Cathy, waiting for a call from a man, but by the man himself, demon-

FIGURE 1.3. Cathy Guisewite. *Cathy*. October 3, 2010.

strating that now, the woman is not waiting but moving ahead, while the man documents the proof of her creative power.

Cathy, as evidenced by her position in the doorway, has finally crossed the threshold and arrived, fulfilled in her relationship and ready to take on the role of mother, which Anne bequeathed to her daughter. The strip comes to a close with the finality of Cathy's "happily ever after," as demonstrated by her marriage and new baby. Notably, it is not independence or a new promotion that signals a happy end, or even a reference to balancing work and family, but rather wedlock and motherhood coming full circle with the love of new parents and grandparents. Does this conclusion signal what the many critics argue—that *Cathy* bolsters stereotypes for women, positing that happiness resides in domestic bliss rather than professional success? The choice to end the strip with Cathy finally married and on the verge of motherhood is significant, but the power of Anne's speech regarding the accomplishments of women should not be diminished.

As Guisewite has suggested, Cathy was a product of the times, an ordinary woman experiencing an extraordinary historical moment; she was a comforting, reassuring character living through a period of tremendous change, rather than an aspirational figure to emulate. Cathy represents a friend one might share dating nightmares with, a confidante who will keep secrets. It is through the many strips over many years and days that one can read a narrative of this one (fictionalized) woman's experience of the Women's Liberation movement and the years that followed. And once more, it is notable that

[handwritten margin notes: "Cathy happily ever after", "domestic bliss vs mom's speech"]

Cathy's experience of feminism reflects that of the white, educated, middle-class woman and does not engage with intersectional identities or concerns.

In her book *When Everything Changed: The Amazing Journey of American Women from 1960 to the Present,* writer Gail Collins explained of the 1970s and 1980s:

> American women were about to experience an extraordinary period of change that would undo virtually every assumption about the natural limitations of their sex. It was going to be a profound journey of many parts—terrifying and exhilarating, silly and profound, a path to half-realized dreams, unexpected disappointments, and unimaginable opportunities. (182)

Furthermore, according to Collins, one can "look back on a decade as fraught with change as the 1970s, and you can pick your own vision. Best of times or worse of times. Women who wanted to work often found it easier to get a job than men did, but the jobs they found still tended to pay much less" (259). In *The Feminist Promise: 1792 to the Present,* Christine Stansell notes of the Women's Liberation movement of the 1970s, "Feminism is an argument, not received truth; it is an entrée into a fuller engagement with America and the world, not an exit visa out of a male-dominated society into utopia. It cannot end all the afflictions that women suffer, nor find a remedy for all the problems that arise between women and men" (xix). Through its daily frames, Cathy provides a window into one woman's struggle to make sense of this moment and this movement in her daily life. In *Reflections: A Fifteenth Anniversary Collection,* Guisewite maintains:

middle ground

> A lot of us found ourselves floundering between two ideals—the "liberated woman" and the "traditional woman"—with absolutely no idea how to integrate the two. These were exhilarating, but trying, times for middle America. So much of what is taken for granted today was brand new to many of us then, and the role models were all such extremes. You could either be a "women's libber" or be "just like your mother." There was a support group for everything but the middle ground; those lost souls who, like me, were in complete agreement with both sides of the argument at once. (45)

cathy "middle ground" role model

Cathy offers a vision of the "support group," defined as she is by her challenge to make sense of herself and this new realm of possibility, navigating traditional notions of normative gendered behavior and roles. She exists in this liminal, in-between space, buffeting between what she interprets as two, divided ends of a single spectrum. These opposing poles of "women's libber" and "just like your mother" are represented as characters in the strip, although this, too, is a simplification that requires additional exploration. Anne embodies the traditional female role of wife and mother, while Andrea symbolizes the new, "liberated" woman, although even these strict binaries begin to break down upon more rigorous inspection.

Generations of Change

For the most part, Anne represents a strong and central force in the strip, and one drawn largely from Guisewite's actual relationship with her own mother. In *Reflections*, Guisewite explains of her mother/daughter dynamic, "none of the relationships in the strip are as intense, or as closely quoted from real life" (153) and that

Cathy 2 mom (Anne)

> if the women's movement made those of us who were twenty years old in 1970 confused, it made our mothers berserk. . . . It wasn't that Mom didn't agree with the "liberated woman" concept . . . more that she had a whole life and ten thousand mother/daughter speeches in the other system. As a result, every single new idea both inspired and offended my mother to the exact same degree. She became a bundle of contradictions; a woman who sent me a subscription to *Ms.* magazine in the same envelope as a six-part series she had clipped and laminated from *Woman's Day* on "The Perfect Bride." (154)

Anne supports her daughter by feeding her and nagging her in equal measure, reducing her to a child in most of their interactions, as seen in this strip from 1978 (see figure 1.4), in which Cathy walks down the street in three separate panels, exclaiming, "I am woman! I am self-confident and self-assured! I am woman! I am independent and alive! I am strong!! I am in control!! I am woman!!!" (*Cathy Chronicles* 133). In the final panel Cathy arrives on her mother's doorstep and is

FIGURE 1.4. Cathy Guisewite. *The Cathy Chronicles.* Kansas City: Sheed Andrews and McMeel, 1978, p. 133.

greeted by her mother, resplendent in a frilly, polka dot apron and heels, who welcomes her daughter, "Hi, sweetie. How's Mommy's little girl?" Cathy walks through the first three panels with her arms raised in triumph, and, in an unusual focalizing technique rarely seen in the strip, the point of view shifts around her figure, emphasizing her victorious stance, reminiscent of a boxer celebrating a win. But in the final panel Cathy is defeated, her arms, eyes, and face slumped downward, while her mother pats her hair and face. She has lost her independence and her mantra of empowerment once confronted by the powerful simulacrum of domestic perfection as embodied by Anne.

Anne contradictions However, as Guisewite indicated, Anne is marked by contradictions, even reading feminist literature and dabbling with a consciousness-raising group in 1979, with the results ultimately unraveling, yet again, in favor of traditional gender roles. In a story arc from 1979, Anne inadvertently reads Marilyn French's 1977 novel *The Women's Room* with her book group. Many of the themes of the book, including women's empowerment, resonate with Anne, although these ideas are quickly squelched by ingrained dominant narratives of female behavior. Anne fails to recognize these incongruities, resulting in a comical disconnect for the reader, as in this example from 1979 (see figure 1.5), in which Anne explains that she thought *The Women's Room* was a "cute little romance," but after reading it came to realize, "I'm a victim in a man's world! An unpaid slave! My life is a waste!" Cathy attempts to comfort her mother, stating "Mom . . . Mom . . . Let's talk about this!," but Anne is cheered by the final panel, as if awakening from a trance or dream of inequity, responding, "Not now, dear. I have to fix dinner before your father gets home." This trend of representing the humorous disconnect between a realization of feminist ideals and Anne's real life of acting out gendered stereo-

FIGURE 1.5. Cathy Guisewite. *Cathy: Twentieth Anniversary Collection.* Kansas City: Andrews and McMeel, 1996, p. 21.

types is repeated numerous times in reference to the consciousness-raising group—every realization quickly unravels, becoming an affirmation of traditional, pre-Women's Liberation archetypes of female roles, with the humor residing in the reader's identification of the divergence between recognizing sexism in theory and practicing it in one's own life. This is not surprising, perhaps, given that Anne learned the "10 Steps to a Raised Consciousness" from "the back of a beef stroganoff recipe."

Anne's counterpoint resides in Cathy's friend Andrea, a staunch feminist who attempts to educate Cathy in female empowerment. In an interview with *Makers,* Guisewite explained:

> The character Andrea was very much my feminist side and the side of me that embraced all of feminism and all of being enlightened and being strong and on my own. She represented a woman who didn't doubt herself and that was, that had great vision and great energy and great commitment to her dreams, and her life was not complicated by a relationships or insecurities. She was confident, and proud, and smart and not ambivalent.

Andrea appears in the earliest strips as a contrast to Cathy's uncertainty. She wears her hair in a dark bob and usually sports a dashing scarf tied around her neck—a cosmopolitan touch that contrasts with Cathy's cutesy heart sweater. In the early years of the strip, Andrea drags Cathy to transcendental meditation, a "Woman of Today" club, a "New Horizons for Women" seminar, and "Assertiveness Training," all of which fail to inspire Cathy to wholeheartedly embrace Andrea's feminist fervor. And although Andrea played a prominent role in a story line that tackled maternity leave and childcare for workers, she provided only a small measure of support during one of the most interesting and rarely discussed flashpoint moments in the strip, a storyline in which Cathy was sexually harassed by her superior, Mr. Pinkley.

Cathy's #MeToo Moment

In a series of strips that ran from October 22 to November 11, 1980, Cathy is sexually assaulted by her boss, Mr. Pinkley. Strangely, this story arc is rarely anthologized or discussed, although it stands *importance* as a fascinating example of *Cathy* exploring topical, relevant, and *of Cathy* extremely important issues from a female perspective and doing so within the context of the daily comics page. As the story begins, Cathy's car is in the shop and her ex-boyfriend refuses to give her a ride home. On October 23, 1980, Mr. Pinkley, overhearing her predicament, offers Cathy a ride and brings her back home to her apartment, arguing that, as a gentleman, he must "show a lady to her door." Cathy realizes that there is "no point in arguing with your whole upbringing," when Mr. Pinkley reveals he is, in fact, no gentleman and asks whether Cathy will invite him in for a drink. While critics are quick to disparage the draftsmanship of *Cathy*, it is very clear from the details in the final panel of the strip that Cathy is decidedly uncomfortable and Mr. Pinkley is assuming a dominant, lecherous posture (see figure 1.6). In the fourth panel the two figures stand outside her doorway, and Mr. Pinkley leans in, one arm spread wide, touching the door, while his legs are crossed in a casual stance. His lopsided smirk and lifted eyebrows indicate his lascivious intentions. While Cathy stands close to Mr. Pinkley, as she is also framed in the doorway, her expression in one of absolute distress. Her quavering frown conveys her anxiety. These small details clearly communicate the anxiety of the situation.

In the October 24, 1980, strip, Cathy stands outside her own door, and questions whether inviting her boss in is a good idea, stating, "I appreciate the ride home, Mr. Pinkley, but you're my **boss**." Mr. Pinkley, his face expressing concern, questions, "You can't invite your boss in for a drink? All my other business associates have me in for a drink now and then. I'd be hurt if you thought so little of our professional relationship that you couldn't have me in for a drink, Cathy." And thus Mr. Pinkley challenges Cathy to ask him in for an "innocent" drink, contrasting her behavior with that of other, undoubtedly

FIGURE 1.6. Cathy Guisewite. *Cathy.* October 23, 1980.

male, colleagues. If she wants to be treated like her male counterparts in the working world, shouldn't she, too, have a drink with her boss, especially after he indicates that he is "hurt" that she doubts their "professional relationship"? Cathy relents, entering her apartment with an "Oh, okay. Come on in, Mr. Pinkley." At this point Mr. Pinkley has transformed from the wounded colleague to the libidinous creep, his wide smirk returning as he leans into her apartment, asking her to call him "Earl."

On October 25, 1980, Mr. Pinkley is seen racing around Cathy's apartment with a wide smile, loosening his tie as he exclaims, "I've never seen a single woman's apartment before, Cathy. So this is what it's really like! So this is how you live. So this is where it all happens. Ha Hah! Let's drink a toast to the emancipated woman!" The use of *anaphora,* repeating the word "So," emphasizes the mundane nature of Cathy's ordinary domicile, which Mr. Pinkley seems to think revelatory as he careens through the panels and her apartment. The final panel depicts Cathy emerging from the kitchen and disrupting Mr. Pinkley's fantasy, asking, "Do you want Diet Pepsi or Fresca?" Mr. Pinkley's smile falls into a small frown as Cathy punctures his fantasy, which contrasts widely with his explanation from the previous day that this was a purely professional interaction. These are extremely pedestrian beverage choices. There are no martinis, no wine, simply soda.

The dramatic storyline is interrupted by a curiously banal Sunday comic on October 26, in which Cathy attempts to order a sandwich at a restaurant and is overwhelmed by customization options, but the thread continues on October 27 as Cathy prepares a Diet Pepsi for her boss. On October 28, Cathy sits on the couch facing Mr. Pinkley's chair (see figure 1.7). In the first panel as she wonders, "Maybe Mr. Pinkley always looks like that when he's drinking," but the second panel shows that Mr. Pinkley has moved to the couch and is seated very close to Cathy, as her thought balloon tries to explain away her discomfort, "Maybe he just moved to the couch because the chair is uncomfortable. . . . Maybe his hand just happened to brush my arm when he sat down." In the third panel, Mr. Pinkley swoops in for a kiss. In this panel both faces are obscured; the audience cannot see Cathy's reaction to this violation as only their backs are visible. Motion lines indicate that Mr. Pinkley has moved his arm around Cathy's shoulder, and his larger body dominates the pair, covering hers. The back of Mr. Pinkley's head, with a small smattering of hair surrounding his bald spot, eclipses Cathy's as he kisses her. We do not see their lips or faces, only the back of his head and her stringy hair. Her face has been subsumed by his. The background, once filled with Cathy's thoughts, is noticeably empty, except for the single word, "KISS!" hanging in the air, not encompassed by a balloon. The final panel presents a tight shot of Cathy and Mr. Pinkley sitting on the couch in the aftermath of the kiss, Mr. Pinkley smiling widely with his arm around her, seemingly at ease and in a good humor, while Cathy's wide but downturned mouth and worried eyebrows indicate disgust and shame, a thought balloon rationalizing, "Maybe he was reaching for a pretzel and his mouth just hit my face by accident." Despite Cathy's loquacious inner monologue represented in her thought balloons, this is a comic in which no words are verbalized by the characters, only thoughts emanating from Cathy, and the only actual noise coming from the kiss. Cathy says nothing, nor does Mr. Pinkley. The entire encounter plays out quietly and devastatingly, with Cathy making excuses for her boss and trying to rationalize his behavior.

In the strip from October 29, (see figure 1.8), Cathy stands up and confronts her boss, "Mr. Pinkley, you kissed me! You said you came here to talk business!" Pinkley responds by leaping off the couch, arms outstretched, shouting, "Yahoo! Let's get down to business!!" In the third frame, Cathy punches Mr. Pinkley in the nose, with the loud and humorous textual onomatopoeia "BONK!" hanging in the air, undermining the drama and turning an act of self-defense into an amusing moment. In the final panel, Mr. Pinkley is laid out on the ground in front of Cathy, as she asks, "So . . . What did you think of my work on the Baker project?" This daily strip represents yet another remarkable moment for the series; when Cathy tries to call

FIGURE 1.7. Cathy Guisewite. *Cathy.* October 28, 1980.

FIGURE 1.8. Cathy Guisewite. *Cathy.* October 29, 1980.

out her superior on his claims of furthering a work conversation, Mr. Pinkley engages in wordplay, calling on the double meaning of getting down to "business." A physical retaliation in this scene seems the only response, after which Cathy, rising above her passed-out boss, finally, and sadly, returns the conversation to work. This strip is significant for its physical humor. *Cathy* is not an action strip and usually doesn't rely on slapstick shenanigans. However, on this day and in this encounter, an attempted assault is met with a fist, as it almost appears that Mr. Pinkley runs into Cathy's punch. Sexual assault represents an incredibly frightening and dramatic moment, but here it is played for laughs. While some might criticize this choice, it is notable that Cathy emerges as the survivor, the victor in the scene, while her boss is vanquished and unconscious on the ground as she literally rises above his attack.

On subsequent days, Cathy tries to rouse Mr. Pinkley and is delighted when the doorbell rings, thinking help has arrived, only to be shocked to realize it is only trick-or-treaters. Cathy telephones Mrs. Pinkley and explains that she has punched her husband and he is unconscious, but Mrs. Pinkley does not hear Cathy, instead continuing a monologue about redecorating, suggesting a willful resistance and lack of support from a female who stands to gain more by supporting her husband and the patriarchal system than by helping another woman. Once again, the storyline is interrupted by a superficial Sunday strip in which Cathy gives Irving a tour of her office, but the story arc returns on November 3, when Cathy worries she'll be fired for punching her boss, but also wonders whether "he'll respect me for rejecting his advances! Maybe I finally knocked some sense into him! Maybe he'll rediscover love with Mrs. Pinkley and I'll be made president of the company." But in the final panel Cathy doubts this fanciful monologue, stating, "Maybe chocolate fudge brownies don't make your face break out." This sequence outlines the best possible scenario, which Cathy knows will not happen, and recalls Cathy's frequent obsession with fattening snack foods and her appearance, all within the context of a sexual assault.

Mr. Pinkley finally awakens on November 4 and is immediately frantic that he is late for work. Clearly his concern is for his professional life, and he registers no dismay or shame at his situation or his actions. When Cathy confronts him, angrily calling out to a rapidly departing Pinkley, "Shouldn't you say something besides, 'I'm late for work'?," Mr. Pinkley responds, "Of course . . . What was I thinking? You're late for work." And, in that moment, Mr. Pinkley upends Cathy's previous position as a strong female fighting back against assault and reasserts himself as the dominant male power, the superior figure in the professional relationship with the power to fire her and to silence her for his attack. Cathy is once again his inferior in work and in life.

Initially it is Mr. Pinkley who controls the narrative surrounding the attack, for when Cathy arrives back at work on November 5, 1980, she is met with whispers from her coworkers. Again, she attempts to confront Pinkley, not about his misconduct, but this time about the office gossip, asking, "Mr. Pinkley, did you say something to the people in our office?," to which he replies, "Oh, I may have mentioned to Charlene that I spent the night at your place." Cathy must wait until November 6 to respond, arguing, "Mr. Pinkley, first you talked your way into my apartment. . . . Then you put the moves on me. . . . Now you're punishing me for rejecting you by spreading stories around the office that aren't true. I won't take this, Mr. Pinkley." Her boss ignores Cathy's outrage, wondering, "Say, Cathy, did I leave my sportcoat at your place?" As Cathy replies in the affirmative, a female figure is seen lurking in the background, before running off to

FIGURE 1.9. Cathy Guisewite. *Cathy.* November 8, 1980.

announce another juicy piece of gossip to the staff, as Cathy laments, "The hotline always listens to the wrong parts of the speech." Thus, while Cathy tries to confront Mr. Pinkley about his behavior, particularly his efforts to spread false, malicious, and damaging gossip, her boss is nonplussed and her coworkers, instead of supporting Cathy, continue to slander their colleague.

Cathy turns to her feminist friend Andrea for guidance and support on November 7, but after explaining the predicament to Andrea, Cathy's mother arrives, at which point she clams up, saying "nothing" is new. Is Cathy ashamed of what happened? Or does she view her mother as a part of another generation unable to process such a situation? The answer is unclear, but the issue is never revisited with her family. On November 8, Cathy's mother has disappeared (see figure 1.9), and Andrea counsels her friend, arguing, "Cathy, do you realize that sexual harassment is power play of the worst kind. . . . Do you think it's right that millions of women suffer because they're too afraid for their jobs to take a stand against it??" Cathy agrees with her friend, but when Andrea asks, "Then what are you going to do about Mr. Pinkley??" Cathy responds, "I'll show him! I'll quit my job!!" In the final panel Andrea throws up her arms and runs around screaming, "AAAA! Wrong! Wrong! Wrong!" but Cathy is flummoxed, reflecting, "I do better on the 'yes' or 'no' questions." Here is an example when one hopes that the reader is able to, as Soper notes of *Doonesbury,* "spot the lessons that need to be learned." Cathy, perhaps mirroring the panic and confusion of many women in such a situation, wants to leave her job, but Andrea acts as the voice of reason, arguing that Cathy must make a stand.

After a brief digression for yet another unrelated Sunday comic in which Cathy tries to take the perfect autumn picture of Irving, the harassment story arc comes to a close on November 10 and 11,

1980. In the November 10 strip, Andrea is once again pictured in the confines of Cathy's apartment, sitting on the very same couch where the attack occurred, advising her friend, "Quitting your job because of sexual harassment is the worst thing you could do, Cathy! Don't you read any of these women's magazines you get??" When Cathy responds in the affirmative, Andrea demands, "Well, what is the one thing that every one of these magazines tells you do do??!" Cathy hands Andrea a magazine and retorts, "Go buy a sweater dress." It would seem that either Cathy and Andrea are reading very different women's magazines (one might imagine *Ms.* versus *Cosmopolitan*), or that these publications are not, in fact, offering concrete, practical advice for women faced with real-world issues such as harassment, but rather fashion tips and style advice. Regardless, Cathy's comment suggests that, by and large, society is silent on the issue of sexual harassment in the workplace and does not issue any sort of useful information for women when faced with an assault from a coworker or boss, preferring to focus on less contentious topics such as sartorial choices.

In the conclusion to the storyline on November 11, Cathy and Andrea are depicted having a conversation in a restaurant, as evidenced by the two women seated side-by-side at a table covered with a checkered cloth, eating bowls of what appears to be salad (see figure 1.10). Cathy, now smiling, gestures with her hands and asserts, "I told Charlene exactly what happened with Mr. Pinkley and she spread the news around the office like wildfire. I don't think we'll ever have that kind of problem again! I really learned a lot from all of this, Andrea." Andrea suggests, "Life is easier if you tackle your problems head on," but Cathy explains, "Life is easier if you have the receptionist on your side." The first three panels of the strip focus on various shots of the two women sitting side-by-side facing the reader. This positionality feels forced for the focalizer's pleasure in viewing the women straight-on, as a real-world situation would dictate the pair face one another. The arrangement is awkward, as is the conversation. The final panel closes in on a tight shot of Cathy alone, her fork raised and her face, eyes, and eyebrows raised in a quavering smile, indicating that though she's pleased with the outcome, she is also uneasy. Cathy's hard-won lesson forces her to go through backchannels to subvert her boss's narrative, and the ultimate outcome is not a reckoning for her attacker, but rather a murmured sharing

FIGURE 1.10. Cathy Guisewite. *Cathy*. November 11, 1980.

of her counter account through the gossip network. She has learned not to be decisive and confront sexual assault directly, but rather, to outwardly pretend that nothing has happened, not challenging her boss and reporting the abuse to the authorities or the higher administration in her workplace. Instead, Cathy's found that her best way forward is to rely on the women behind the scenes to share her story, and hopefully, protect themselves.

However, the result of Cathy's behind-the-scenes campaign represents an interesting shift; for the bulk of the story arc, Mr. Pinkley was in control of the situation and the narrative by virtue of his power and position, but ultimately Cathy is able to reach out to a sisterhood and reclaim control of the story and its perception with the help of receptionist Charlene. Once Charlene disrupts Pinkley's narrative, Cathy feels confident the problem has been resolved and praises her coworker for saving her from humiliation. But has anything really changed? Again, Cathy chooses to go through an informal "whisper network" rather than filing a grievance through established channels of the organization, and Mr. Pinkley suffers no consequences for his action. This is, of course, in addition to the intimidation and fear Cathy would have to suffer, both for her position and her person, if she chose to keep working with Pinkley. Yet, strangely enough, on the next day, November 12, the storyline is forgotten and in the daily strip Cathy details her new diet, completely forgetting about the assault. The storyline is dropped. There are no repercussions for Mr. Pinkley, and he remains her boss for the remainder of the run of the strip, except when Cathy is laid off. He even appears as one of the beaming characters featured on the masthead of the final strip in 2010. In a 2010 interview, Tom Heintjes asked Guisewite about the story arc, and she responded:

Yeah, at that time, that was a specific thing of wanting to have Cathy go through what I was starting to hear about in the workplace. It's hard to believe now, but everything was new about the concept of women in the workplace. Many women were treated poorly, and sexual harassment was a big new topic. In that case, I was simply writing about what I was hearing, what was going on, not something that was happening to me specifically. ("Cathy")

importance of strip

This story arc is an important one in the history of the strip. While *Cathy* is largely remembered for Cathy's focus on food, romance, and fashion, it also presented topical issues, and did so in a messy, complicated way. In this example of *martyria*, Cathy bears witness to the act of sexual harassment, offering evidence based in experience. Studying this narrative arc from 1980 feels very relevant forty years later, as the news reports that women are assaulted and harassed in the workplace every day, and the recent #metoo movement in social media revealed widespread and widely underreported sexual harassment.

rhetoric

connection to current moment

Despite the difficult subject matter, *Cathy* critiques through humor. While sexual harassment is certainly serious business, the comic strip ridicules Mr. Pinkley as absurd and impotent. Nancy Walker argues that there are two forms of feminist humor, and the most common type "makes use of a double text to pose a subtle challenge to the stereotype or the circumstance that the writer appears superficially to merely describe" (13). And while Walker notes that "by no means is *women's* humor synonymous with *feminist* humor" (13) in this case I would argue that although this representation of one woman's experience of harassment from a work superior does not offer tidy solutions or easy lessons, it does offer a subtle challenge by simply calling out the issue and representing it on the comics pages as something that happens and needs to be addressed and discussed. While one can critique Cathy's response, the strip makes it very clear that Mr. Pinkley is in the wrong in all his actions, while Cathy, bewildered as she is, stands in the right. Furthermore, the sequence negates the argument that women who dress a certain way or behave a certain way are "asking for" an assault. Cathy, with her round, generic figure and plain face could be any and every woman. While the dominant narratives of popular culture and comics often reduce females to damsels to be rescued by the more active male characters or triumphant Amazonian warriors, Cathy presents another vision, one

importance of strip
challenges issues
representation

Cathy doing her best / not a "feminist icon"

which shatters this fallacy, this argument about womanhood, and performs a complicated image of a woman who experiences harassment, stands her ground and defends herself, and chooses to rely on an informal network of female support to move through the event, never challenging the patriarchal system at large, but doing her best. Yet this experience is largely lost in *Cathy* collections and in comics history, swept away as an unsavory episode that unfortunately replicates the real-world experiences of so many women.

Cathy on the Campaign Trail

While Mr. Pinkley's attack on Cathy has disappeared, by and large, from anthologies and discussions of the strip, Cathy's foray into politics in the form of the 1986 election did cause something of a stir at the time, and this particular storyline presents a fascinating example of what Nancy Walker argues is the second, more overt, form of feminist humor, which "confronts the sources of discrimination, and has tended to emerge during periods of organized agitation for women's rights" (13). Cathy's unabashedly feminist friend Andrea married Luke and, in 1986, gave birth to baby girl Zenith. Andrea, always organized, had planned everything, except, according to Guisewite, "the fact that there was no maternity leave offered at the company where she worked" (*Reflections* 262). Andrea was laid off after taking more than two weeks off for maternity leave and, in the 1988 election, Andrea actively campaigned for Dukakis. Guisewite explained:

issue of maternity leave / Andrea

> Between Andrea's history of being vocal on women's issues and her own experience of being fired for taking a maternity leave, I felt it was only natural for her to actively campaign for Dukakis, the candidate who supported the same national day-care and parental leave legislation she did, in the 1988 election. Since none of the many strips I'd done in the past two years on the same subjects had gotten even one negative response, I was a little surprised at the fury that resulted from nine election-related strips. Cathy was dropped for a time from some papers and moved to the editorial page in others. (*Reflections* 265)

The series of controversial strips centers around Andrea and her daughter Zenith as they attempt to campaign for Dukakis, but are frequently sidetracked by more domestic concerns. On a strip from October 26, 1988, Andrea is pictured on her couch with her daughter facing the television, only the back of which is visible. The scene is dominated by text emanating from the television, which explains, "Senate Republicans killed a day care subsidy plan this month, preferring to back Bush's plan to give families a $1,000 tax credit for each child under age 4." Andrea grimaces as the television monologue continues, devolving into a comical rant: "The Bush plan comes to $2.74 per day per child. While no one could offer decent day care for $2.74 a day, his plan would allow each impoverished family to buy a decent VCR. Not only would children have something to watch while mommy rips her hair out, but each VCR purchase would further boost the Japanese economy so they could keep boosting our economy by buying up all our buildings and businesses." In the final panel, Andrea rises from the couch, "Get your bottle, honey. Mommy has to go to bed for four years." This strip offers a text-based diatribe on the President's plan for childcare, which purports to be the unbiased reporting emanating from the television news, but quickly devolves into a pointed, humorous slippery slope logical fallacy suggesting that this terrible childcare plan will lead to "the Japanese" buying up American businesses and buildings. Text dominates the strip, with Andrea and Zenith overwhelmed by the lettering, and their figures are crushed by the bad news until the final panel, at which point Andrea decides to avoid the situation by leaving the panel and heading "to bed for the next four years."

The following day represents one of the more poignant and political moments in the history of the strip (see figure 1.11). The panels feature Andrea facing the reader while feeding Zenith in her high chair. Each panel is dominated by a loquacious thought balloon. In the first panel, a chubby, happy Zenith with a sweet bow perched on her head reaches for the jar of food clutched in her mother's hand, as Andrea thinks, "I lost my job when I had a baby because Republicans believe maternity leaves should be decided on by individual companies, and my company decided not to give them." The background is sparse, focusing attention on the mother/daughter pair, bringing them into sharp relief. This *should* be a sweet, uncomplicated domestic scene of a mother bonding with her baby. The second panel features a tighter shot of the twosome, as Andrea spoons food onto her daughter's tray table, but Zenith's smile has transformed into a wail and tears fly off her as she reaches for the food. Andrea con-

Cathy

FIGURE 1.11. Cathy Guisewite. *Cathy*. October 27, 1988.

tinues, "I can't afford to get another job because Republicans believe day care help should be the choice of individual companies, and the 10,000 companies I've applied to have chosen not to offer it." By the third panel, Zenith has devolved into a full-on tantrum, tears flying and her tongue out as she screams and flails. Andrea, her face impassive, reflects, "This would all make me sick except Republicans believe health care should be a personal matter, and I am a person who's unemployed, uninsured and ineligible for aid." The final panel moves back slightly to a wider shot, with Andrea facing the audience, as if speaking to the reader directly. Zenith now has the jar of food and her smile is wide as she dumps the contents everywhere. Andrea concludes, "It was easier to support the concept of giving power to the individual when I was an individual who had some." Andrea has relinquished control of the food and her personhood to her tyrannical daughter, just as she's lost her worth in the eyes of the government. She lost her job for being a mother. She cannot get childcare. She cannot get sick. The strip disrupts idyllic notions of motherhood by focusing on Andrea's lack of control. In becoming a mother, she has lost her rights and her identity.

The following day, October 28, Andrea continues her diatribe, confiding in Cathy as they walk through what appears to be a park. Once again this is a wordy strip, with the figures positioned peripheral to the text. As they walk, Andrea explains her situation to a silent Cathy:

The Reagan-Bush administration has done nothing about the fact that 44% of the work force is women, but we still have no national equity law requiring equal pay. It's done nothing about the fact that

[handwritten marginalia:] Motherhood childcare a Hack on Republicans

67% of the women who have preschool children work full time and need day care help . . . nothing about the fact that almost 90% of the families on welfare are single mothers with no way out. Yet, incredibly, many people look at the current government and think things are going pretty well. The government is like a baby. It looks like a little angel when it's sleeping.

baby as tyrant

baby as government

In this strip Andrea directly attacks the current administration and calls into question the failure of the ERA amendment (although it isn't named outright) and protection for equal pay. She questions the lack of daycare and support for single mothers as well as complacency within the populous, making a fascinating parallel between the sweet baby as pictured in the previous day's strip and the government: both appear sweet and angelic when asleep. Of course, this clever wordplay resonates with the idea that the government is asleep, unperturbed by its numerous failings, while a child rests innocently and without responsibility. The joke astutely hearkens back to the notion of the baby as tyrant, in control yet irresponsible, and needing the direction and care of a mother.

On subsequent days Andrea decides to canvas the neighborhood, urging people, particularly women, to vote. She organizes her daughter's play group into something more than a "grass roots campaign," but rather a "grass stain campaign." On November 2, 1988, Andrea sits cross-legged in front of her couch preparing fliers for the neighborhood as Zenith plays with the handout (see figure 1.12). In the first panel Andrea holds up the flier and addresses her daughter, "Look what Mommy wrote, '25% of the children in the country today live with a single parent. We need Dukakis because he supports a national daycare plan and laws to raise day-care standards.'" Andrea

rhetoric

continues her speech and her reliance on logos marshalling facts to make a case for Dukakis in the subsequent panels as Zenith runs off, carrying a wad of fliers. The final panel depicts a toilet clogged with pamphlets, flanked by a downcast Andrea and a mischievous Zenith, smiling and sucking her thumb. Andrea finishes her diatribe, ". . . And 99% of all children under age 3 will stuff political fliers down the toilet before Mommy has a chance to hand them out." Andrea's political intentions have, once again been quite literally cast into the toilet. The first three panels emphasize the candidate's name, Dukakis, repeating the name each time and explaining why he is needed, focusing on statistics relating to issues for women, including equal

FIGURE 1.12. Cathy Guisewite. *Cathy*. November 2, 1988.

pay, daycare, and maternity leave, but her speech is returned to the reality of mothers in the home, quite literally cleaning up the waste and refuse, with her laborious thinking shoved into the toilet by her child. Although Andrea is aware of what she has lost and what must be done on the national level, her duties thwart her ambitions to agitate for change. Her daughter, the evidence of her femaleness and her motherhood, holds her hostage, scuttling her dreams, equating her thinking with feces.

The strip continues to evoke motherhood as political fodder in the November 4, 1988, strip, which features another wordy and largely static comic in which an intergenerational group of women share a meal. Andrea sits with Cathy and Anne holding a smiling Zenith at her lap. The three are drawn from the chest up, facing the audience, eating at a table as Andrea launches into another monologue. Andrea explains:

> When Republicans talk about the thriving economy they've built, they don't mention that their economy requires most mothers to work outside the home to try to help pay the bills. When they talk about family values, they don't mention that they've consistently voted against any legislation that would help struggling working mothers out of the hole. When women have no choice but to work more and spend less time with their children, what do Republicans think all those children are going to do?

Cathy's mother responds, "Children will do what they've always done, Andrea. Grow up and blame their mothers." Once again this is a largely static comic. The figures don't move much, simply gesticulating a bit, and the point of view shifts slightly to accommodate the long speeches. The joke is a bit clumsy, relying primarily on text, but the meaning is very clear: The Republicans evoke "family values" but fail to support families. Anne points out that the Republicans will not bear any of the burden of the blame for women spending less time with their children, who instead will misdirect their anger, as they've always done, at mothers. This strip offers a rueful chuckle at best, with the two mother/daughter pairs lined up together, for long-time readers know that Cathy frequently blames her mother for her anxieties and Zenith is now positioned to do the same. A painful cycle of culpability acted out in yet another domestic scene. It seems that Andrea's knowledge of the truly guilty party makes no difference in the end.

The Sunday strip a few days later on November 6, 1988 continues to call upon mothers to vote and shape the election, in a rare Sunday strip devoted entirely to a character other than Cathy (see figure 1.13). The strip includes the traditional first panel, including the heart-shaped "Cathy" title, but features Andrea trying to calm a crying Zenith, surrounded by dirty dishes, a distinctly domestic reminder of her labors. The nine-panel strip also evokes *Sylvia,* both in its scene and its tone, for it features a conversation between a clueless television news program and the exasperated voice of reason—this time Andrea rather than Sylvia. The first two panels depict Andrea soothing her daughter and begging her to be quiet so she can "hear the news," but the third panel shows an empty living room, a couch littered with discarded clothing and toys, an overflowing laundry basket in the forefront, and the back of the television in the left-side of the panel. The scene suggests the contrast between the idealized notion of home and family and the reality. This is no tender, mother-daughter bonding moment. Instead, the detritus of domesticity covers every surface, preventing Andrea from engaging with the politics of the outside world. The voice of society at large enters through the jagged edges of the word balloon emanating from the television, which imply the words of the newscaster, stating, "One of the key differences between Republicans and Democrats is how they'll handle childcare. . . . Yet surprisingly few women have been heard on this important point." The emptiness of the rooms underscores the lack of female voices, but Andrea rushes into the room in the fourth panel. She carries her daughter and a broom, sweat droplets flying as she shouts, "Women who work full time and do all the shopping,

FIGURE 1.13. Cathy Guisewite. *Cathy.* November 6, 1988.

cooking and cleaning for a husband and children do not have time to write editorials for their tv stations!" Andrea, surrounded by the work to be done, embodies this statement, her labors clearly in evidence. The images underscore this rupture between the disembodied voice of authority, pondering the absence of women in the national conversation on childcare and the messy, embodied reality that women charged with caring for children and working outside the home simply do not have the time to engage in political discussions.

reality vs portrayal of motherhood & politics

But the television poses another question in the fifth panel, wondering, "Does this mean the Republican program is adequate?" to which Andrea, arms stuffed in the laundry basket responds, "What program?? 67% of mothers with children under age three work full time. We don't have time to send telegrams begging for help to the White House!" Andrea is once again responding to the theoretical query with *logos*, marshalling statistics to support her assertion. But the sixth panel emphasizes *pathos*, emotion clearly evident in a tight shot of Andrea's face, as she grimaces, with worry lines around her eyes, her visage juxtaposed next to the back of the television. The television responds, "Maybe the Democrats' plan for government-sponsored day care isn't necessary. . . . Maybe we don't need the Democrats' program for guaranteed maternity leave," and Andrea reacts, screaming with rage, her arms raised, her mouth and tongue wide. In her flailing, she knocks a bowl of what appears to be popcorn off the top of the television. She cries, "Women who can't afford to feed their children, or who could be fired for taking more than two weeks off to give birth, can't fly to Washington to support rallies!" In another case of *martyria*, Andrea's words and deeds provide evidence to prove that a Democratic national childcare initiative is necessary.

rhetoric

The voice from the television makes its final case, pondering, "Well, I guess we'll find out on election day. Are working moms content with the status quo . . . or has a whole new force started to sweep the nation?" In the penultimate panel, the shot widens to show Andrea, quietly clutching her broom, the visual embodiment of this angry force of women, a dark squiggle over her head, paired with her grimacing face and angry eyebrows evoking disgust. She is clearly not content with the way things are and is ready to make a change. In contrast with her evident rage of the preceding panels, the final image feels more hopeful, with a now-smiling Andrea sweeping her broom, a symbolically domestic tool, as she and Zenith stride out of the frame and into a new future. In hindsight, this final, more optimistic panel is rather melancholy, for in the real world Dukakis loses and this "whole new force" of female solidarity does not, in fact, "sweep the nation," but the argument of the strip is clear: mothers must channel their rage and band together to vote to counter the detached, ignorant dominant narrative to improve the lives of women and families.

[margin handwriting: strip encouraged voting]

After this strip *Cathy* spends a few days discussing voting in more general terms before turning to a new storyline featuring housetraining Cathy's new puppy, Electra. It's another domestic story arc, but an anodyne one, for the politically motivated storyline enraged many readers and caused some papers to replace *Cathy* or move it to the editorial section. Reporter Beverly Beyette covered the controversy:

[margin handwriting: controversy of political storyline]

> A series of strips by Los Angeles cartoonist Cathy Guisewite, whose "Cathy" cartoon normally confines itself to baby boomer concerns about dating and child-rearing, has re-ignited the debate over just how argumentative the funnies page should be. At least 20 papers of the 500-plus carrying "Cathy" have pulled or moved to the Op-Ed pages strips for this week and last, in which one cartoon character not only urges women to vote in Tuesday's election but also takes on Republicans on issues ranging from child care to the environment.

The strips even drew the attention of Judy Hughes, the president of the National Federation of Republican Women, who, in a November 5 letter to the *Washington Post*, wrote:

> I can honestly say that in my 26 years as a political activist, I never thought I'd be waging war against something on the funny pages.

However, in the past two weeks "Cathy" has completely distorted the Republican stand on so-called "women's issues." . . . The comic pages are designed for mindless amusement, not mindless distortion. They are not meant to be a forum for political endorsements, which is why most newspapers have the good sense to place political cartoons on the editorial pages. Until Guisewite changes the tone of her comic, I suggest your paper move "Cathy" to a more suitable section. (A21)

Guisewite told Beyette she didn't regret the controversy, stating, "I'm glad I did it. I knew going in that I ran the risk of alienating some readers (but) it was important enough . . . to weather the alienation." While *Cathy* is largely remembered as a strip about chocolate and shoes, and these were certainly frequent subjects, *Cathy* also took a stand for women's rights, particularly as evidenced during the 1988 election. Rather than a more covert critique of the absurdity of the fashion industry or fad diets, the strip attempted to martial *logos*, bringing in numerous statistics, and *pathos* stirring up sympathy for the plight of a young mother. This potent form of humorous argument should, I believe, be considered feminist.

Cathy was political at times

rhetoric

Over time Andrea faded out of the comic, disappearing for many years, as did these more overt political declarations. In fact, the strip fell into what many felt was a repetitive cycle; Steve Murray wrote, "The newer strips, however, serve to highlight how trapped in a cycle Cathy has become. The comic pioneered a new area of women as cartoonists and cartoon subjects, but eventually Cathy became as anachronistic as the strips it ran alongside back in the '70s." It was not until Cathy finally married Irving in 2005 that her feminist friend Andrea reappeared, her children grown. Five years after the wedding, *Cathy* ended with the announcement that Cathy was pregnant with a daughter. The cycle of motherhood had been fulfilled. Did Cathy ever find a balance between work and family? The finale implies that joy resides in marital bliss and procreation, rather than professional acclaim. But I would argue that while it is essential to consider the ramifications of the beginning and the ending of any text, one should not ignore what comes between, particularly when Cathy's journey has been so long and varied. Kerry Soper argues of *Doonesbury*, "The strip as a whole is like a massive, sprawling, comic-satiric, verbal/visual novel that chronicles and critically comments upon the cultural experience of Americans for close to four decades" (*Gary*

importance of considering Cathy as a whole

Trudeau 146 47), and though there are certainly differences between the strips, I believe much the same argument can be made for *Cathy,* for, as Susan Shimanoff argues, it is "true that Cathy presented exaggerated portrayals of everyday interactions, but for cartoons to be effective the 'exaggeration must first be based on a collective perception that the cartoon reflects some inner truth'" (804). In an essay for *The Comics Journal* titled, "On Hating Cathy," Juliet Kahn argues:

> *Cathy* is important. And beyond all of that? *Cathy* is good. Yeah. *Cathy* is incisive and funny and clever. *Cathy* takes the slop of my life, the shame and the pain and the work of it, and manages to find it funny without diminishing it. All those women who taped up *Cathy* comics to their refrigerators and cubicle walls? Their appreciation is just as meaningful, multidimensional, and significant as your love for *Calvin & Hobbes, Pogo,* and *Life in Hell. Cathy* managed to make women laugh about the circumstances of their lives without blaming them *for* those circumstances. *Cathy* doesn't make you feel like a shitty feminist for hating your thighs, *Cathy* just wants you to know that you're not alone in feeling that way. . . . And if you're not personally into it? If *Cathy* still doesn't make you laugh, make you sigh, make you sit down and appreciate its charms? That's fine. You don't have to like it. But you can respect it the way you respect the myriad of work by men you do not personally enjoy but understand mattered. *not a "perfect feminist" & that's why she was relatable*

While Cathy's reactions are marked by excess, as Kahn points out, within Cathy's encounters there resides some kernel of verisimilitude, of identification with readers.

Nancy Walker maintains that "the use of common female stereotypes as either a means for writing a cautionary tale . . . or an expression of frustration with an assigned subordinate role is a dominant technique in women's humorous writing" (62), and Cathy both invokes and pokes holes in gender stereotypes, playfully and pointedly chipping away at notions of "The Woman Who Does Everything More Beautifully than You," a common target of Hollander's *Sylvia.* At times *Cathy* is more obvious in challenging patriarchy, as in her plea for Dukakis, and at other times her argument fades away, overwhelmed by the weight of the daily strips lamenting the newest diet craze, but this does not lessen *Cathy's* impact. Nancy Walker stresses, "To assume that humor in which a female figure acknowledges injustice but does not act to change it is nonfeminist is to define feminism in terms of activism, and to ignore the very constraints that have effectively prevented women from acting on their own behalf for most of human history" (152–53). For her part, Guisewite explained to Tom Heintjes:

> I feel like a lot of the time, my strip made sort of political comments about the state of women, their expectations, the state of women in the office, being harassed, being held back, being utterly confused by the mixed messages we get from everything from what size to be, how to feel about ourselves, how to look. To me, that's all sort of political. A lot of what I wrote about was the woman's place in the world and the pressure we're under to be a certain way, to think certain things, to have or not have certain opportunities. ("Cathy")

In her book on *The Feminist Promise,* Christine Stansell reflects, "The American obsession with a single life—can women who work outside the home sustain a satisfying family life?—looks disturbingly static" (398). Rachel Syme concurs, explaining, "It would be easy to dismiss Guisewite from across the generational chasm, as simply a by-product of her time, but Cathy's struggles aren't quite as far from our own as we'd often like to think. Women may have more nuanced language for how they talk about the distance between what they choose to project and how they feel on the inside, but two minutes on Instagram is enough to prove that generating authentic confidence is still a confounding process." Cathy struggled with her identity for over thirty years, asking herself whether working women can also balance family, repeating the question until she finally, depending on one's interpretation, succeeds or fails by marrying and becoming a mother. While some critics and readers mark this as a disappointment on the part of the creator to find new ideas, I would argue for that other interpretation—that the strip exhibits *epimone*, circling the same issues because these issues remain relevant.

After deciding to retire the strip in 2010, Guisewite reflected, "I am not stopping the strip because I think anything has been resolved," she said. "When I see my daughter and her generation, I see that a lot of the games between men and women, the fixation on fashion—'I'll die if my hair doesn't look right.' And I really thought we could have lost that in the last 30 years. But we haven't" (qtd. in Kahn). Thus, I would contend that through this strategy, this circling back, time

overall argument [handwritten margin note]

and again, *Cathy* offers a critique of ongoing societal standards and double standards, day after day, panel after panel. Cathy disrupts the false dichotomy of either being a feminist or not, of being for traditional values or against them. When Guisewite announced her retirement, *Stone Soup* creator Jan Eliot reflected on *Cathy's* import in a blog post titled "The Amazing Cathy Guisewite":

> *Cathy* brought the cares and concerns of young women to the comics pages in a new way. Her character spoke for everyone who was starting out in life, in a new career, in an office, in the often bewildering world of dating. Cathy was a feminist, and brought feminism to the funnies in a very real, down to earth way. Read through an early (or more recent) Cathy collection and you'll find some very fine diatribes about the perceptions of women and their relationship to men. A stroll through any workplace during the last 35 years would reveal walls and doors and break room cupboards plastered with *Cathy* cartoons.

Cathy was flawed, but she was always a friend. She floundered her way through life, not as an aspirational figure but rather as a friendly confidante with whom one might commiserate, and who found a life beyond the confines of the newspaper. As Eliot indicates, Cathy entered into the lives of readers in a very real way, taped to cubicle walls and stuck to refrigerators. Cathy was emblematic, not for a heroic victory but for the struggle. She was not a role model to be lauded, nor did she argue for a return to the simulacrum of a nuclear, Beaver Cleaver style family, and she was never able to please all the critics. Rather, *Cathy* walked a tightrope between false binaries, and did so successfully, even with the crocodiles waiting for her to fail.

overall argument [handwritten margin note]

CHAPTER 2

VISUALIZING MOTHERHOOD IN THE COMIC FRAME

For Better or For Worse

> Motherhood may appear to be timeless, but it actually bears a date; instead of emanating from nature, it is the product of specific cultural and historical contexts.

—Lindal Buchanan

LYNN JOHNSTON'S incredibly popular daily comic strip *For Better or For Worse* began in 1979 and ran through 2008 before "rebooting" with a mix of old and new cartoons, an experiment which lasted until 2010. For almost thirty years the strip acted as a serial soap opera and as social commentary, exploring issues of child abuse, adultery, sexism, racism, and homophobia through the everyday lives of the fictional Patterson family and their Canadian community. *For Better or For Worse* reflected readers' hopes, beliefs, and expectations as it rendered the quotidian trials and tribulations of a suburban family, and, additionally, it sometimes challenged and sometimes reinforced traditions, biases, and prejudices. Since 1979 an eager readership has watched the Pattersons age in (almost) real time, and on August 30, 2008, Elizabeth, who began the strip as a precocious toddler, married her great love, Anthony. During the wedding, Elizabeth's grandfather was admitted to the hospital in serious condition, and as the newlyweds rushed to his side, Iris, Elizabeth's grandmother explained that a marriage is a "promise that should last a lifetime. It defines you as a person and describes your soul. It's a promise to be there, one for the other, no matter what happens, no

73

matter who falls . . . for better or for worse, my dears . . . for better or for worse." And with those words, the strip was brought full circle.

While the strip and the characters evolved and changed over the years, in the earliest days the focus was very much on motherhood as rendered through the experiences of main character Elly Patterson, and a close examination reveals that the strip utilized Kenneth Burke's "comic frame," a way of representing human experience through a gentle, comical structure to argue for another understanding of the maternal experience, in addition to positing notions of identification through consubstantiality, to dismantle dominant narratives of an idealized motherhood. Yet, even as it argued for a more complicated conception of motherhood, the strip simultaneously maintained stereotypes of gender-normative behavior and domestic relations. This chapter explores *For Better or For Worse*'s representation of motherhood through the comic frame, outlining the shifting perspective on motherhood at the time, as well as the rhetorical argument signified by the strip.

Motherhood and "Women's Lip"

In *Perfect Madness: Motherhood in the Age of Anxiety,* Judith Warner wonders, "Where did feminism fail mothers?" (19). This is a polarizing question, and one that bears additional exploration. Of course, motherhood has long been valorized in literature and society; in *Rhetorics of Motherhood* Lindal Buchanan asserts, "The Mother, I maintain, operates as a god term within public discourse and connotes a myriad of positive associations, including children, love, protection, home, nourishment, altruism, morality, religion, self-sacrifice, strength, the reproductive body, the private sphere, and the nation" (8). Of course, these mythic associations come with a price— unrealistic expectations as well as a sense of invisibility, as mothers are generally expected to remain sheltered within the home, rather than participating in public forums. In "The Rhetoric of Mom Blogs: A Study of Mothering Made Public," Madeline Yonker argues, "The invisibility of motherhood can be linked to the historic invisibility of women in general" (38), and "a cause (or effect?) of the invisibility of motherhood is its relegation to the privacy of the home or personal life" (38–39). The Women's Liberation movement encouraged women to step outside the home and voice their experiences, reconsidering the social constructions of motherhood. As Madeline Yonker notes, "Betty Friedan's *The Feminine Mystique* (1963) and Adrienne Rich's *Of Woman Born: Motherhood as Experience and Institution* (1976) . . . began to uncover the contradictions and problems inherent in public expectations of motherhood" (21). In *Of Woman Born,* Rich crafted an incredibly personal and intensely scholarly text, weaving her own experiences with a historical genealogy of motherhood, reflecting, "Motherhood—unmentioned in the histories of conquest and serfdom, wars and treaties, exploration and imperialism—has a history, it has an ideology, it is more fundamental than tribalism or nationalism" (15). She further argued, "Motherhood, in the sense of an intense, reciprocal relationship with a particular child, or children, is *one part* of the female process; it is not an identity for all time" (17). Rich thus disputes the conflation of a mother's relationship with her child with the entirety of her identity. Rich contends that motherhood stands as an aspect of experience rather than the totality of it.

While Rich and Friedan were critical of cultural representations of motherhood, other, more radical factions of the feminist movement of the time were critical of mothers themselves. Christine Stansell observes of the time, "Mothers, too, came in for disdain, for their capitulation to a soul-crushing system, their timidity before male power, their compulsion to conscript their daughters into the same circumstances that crippled them. This was a politics with the habit of lashing out at intimates rather than august authority" (221). In *Right Wing Women* (1983), Andrea Dworkin went so far as to argue, "Mothers are the immediate enforcers of male will, the guards at the cell door, the flunkies who administer the electric shocks to punish rebellion" (15). For some feminists, mothers were the enemy, not an ally. And it was in this environment that *For Better or For Worse,* a comic strip revolving around mother Elly Patterson, launched.

[margin annotation: enemy: represent. vs mothers themselves]

[margin annotation: how strip came about]

Origins in Ontario

While Lynn Johnston always knew she wanted to be an artist, she hadn't originally considered a career as a cartoonist. Born Lynn Ridgway on May 28, 1947, in Collingwood, Ontario, her mother worked as a calligrapher and bookkeeper, and her father found employment as a jeweler. Early on, Johnston's grandfather encouraged her interest in comics. While her grandfather favored Walt Kelly's *Pogo,* from her earliest days Johnston enjoyed Charles Schulz's *Peanuts,* foreshadowing her eventual close friendship with the creator. In *A Look Inside,* Johnston recalls:

> Until *Peanuts* appeared, I tended to agree with all of my grandfather's pronouncements, but about this one strip, he was dead wrong. No other strip, except for perhaps *Miss Peach,* featured children as intuitive, articulate people, with all of the thoughts and responsibilities we knew we had! *Peanuts* not only made kids worth listening to, it featured women as strong, dominant characters. Women were equals. This new strip was as refreshing to us as it was to the free-spirited adults who embraced its honesty with open arms. *Peanuts* became my favorite, and although our work differs in many ways, it is surely the model on which I've based my style of writing and timing. (29–30)

For Johnston, the comics were a necessity, a balm for a difficult childhood. In *A Look Inside,* she reflected, "Comic books in general were a real *need* for me; a key to survival in what I perceived to be a lonely world. When my mother made us give up comic books for Lent, it was the longest penance I've ever done" (30). In recent years Johnston has opened up about the abuse she suffered at the hands of her mother and how drawing provided a refuge as well as a point of connection with her younger brother, Alan, with whom she was often at odds otherwise.

In a blog for GoComics, Johnston remembered:

> I was first inspired to draw funny pictures when I was in elementary school. My brother (two years my junior) and I shared a room. With television still an unaffordable miracle, we had to entertain each other. Alan loved to laugh, and when I drew cartoons of people with enormous mouths, eyes and nostrils, he would laugh till he cried. The drug was then well into my veins.

In her adolescence Johnston discovered *Mad Magazine* and more subversive comics, and by high school her "drawing style was beginning to jell" (*A Look Inside* 32). After graduating from high school, Johnston attended the Vancouver School of Art. She studied there for three years before leaving for a position at Canawest Films, an animation studio, where she worked on coloring the Abbott and

Costello series, among other jobs. At the age of twenty, Johnston married Doug Franks, a television cameraman for the CBC. In 1969 they decided to relocate to Hamilton, Ontario, where she worked as a medical illustrator at McMaster University for five years, before deciding to work from home as a freelance illustrator. Johnston gave birth to son Aaron in 1972, and six months later her husband left. However, Johnston found a champion in her obstetrician, Dr. Elkin, who encouraged her to draw cartoons on parenting and pregnancy. She published three book collections of these cartoons, the first being *David We're Pregnant* (1973), the second book, *Hi Mom, Hi Dad* (1975), and the third, *Do They Ever Grow Up?* (1980). As her career profile increased, Johnston met and began dating Rod Johnston, a dental student. They married and moved to Lake Manitoba where Rod Johnston took up a position as a traveling dentist, and Lynn was expecting their daughter Katie in 1977. It was at that time that Johnston's career took a precipitous turn.

While pregnant with her second child, Johnston received word that Universal Press Syndicate was interested in hiring her for a daily comic strip. Johnston recalls, "My three little books had found their way to the desk of Jim Andrews, who, with the success of Cathy Guisewite's *Cathy*, was looking for a cartoonist to do a strip on family life from a woman's point of view. He wanted something contemporary, a little controversial perhaps" (*A Look Inside* 56–57). Johnston worked up a selection of twenty sample strips and received back "a critique from the editor, Lee Salem, and a twenty-year contract" (*A Look Inside* 57). Johnston traveled to Kansas City to finalize the details and the first daily strip debuted on September 9, 1979.

The first few years of *For Better or For Worse* were created from Lake Manitoba, but the family moved to a farm near North Bay, Ontario in 1984. At both properties Johnston was happy to be able to work from home and remain close to her children. With advice from Cathy Guisewite, Johnston developed a process that helped her meet her deadlines:

> When I have several weeks written, I draw my panels in pencil. I can draw two to three weeks of panels in an eight-hour day. The next day, I'll ink them in and erase the pencil lines, then I apply a textures film to add some visual interest. I wear animator's gloves while I work because—well, to be truthful, I can't seem to keep from smudging things. I use a flexible, Speedball C-6 nib for all of the

actual "drawing"; for straight and ruled lines, I use Rapidographs; 32 nibs for lettering. Pelican Tusche brand India ink for acetate sheets seems to work best for me. . . . I like #2 ply, smooth surface Strathmore paper—but, right now, I'm using #3. (*A Look Inside* 61)

This process would guide Johnston through roughly thirty years of daily strips, although much later she took on assistants to help with coloring, lettering, and the administrative details.

Cartooning had become Johnston's career and it was one that helped sustain her financially and mentally. In *I've Got the One-More-Washload Blues,* Johnston commented, "People ask me when I started drawing—and I have to say that I've always drawn. They ask me why I draw cartoons and the only answer is that it feels good. It feels great, in fact" (5). And Johnston's passion did not go unnoticed; her strip was a huge success, carried in over 2000 newspapers and resulting in over thirty book collections. Johnston was showered with popular appeal and critical acclaim, including Reuben and Inkpot awards and a Gemini award (1987). Johnston was made a Member of the Order of Canada (1992) and was nominated for a Pulitzer prize for Lawrence's coming out storyline (1993).

why strip successful

The strip was lauded for its frankness in depicting family life and addressing difficult topics such as sibling rivalry, dementia, alcoholism, child abuse, and homophobia. Johnston set off a firestorm of controversy when Lawrence Poirier, son Michael's good friend, came out in a storyline that ran from March 26 to April 24, 1993. While many papers pulled the series and some readers responded with angry attacks, overall, Johnston's sensitive treatment of the subject was praised. Johnston argued:

> If the Pattersons were an average family in an average neighborhood, they would at some time be aware of the diversity in the people around them and would have to accept and try to understand those differences. I felt that I was being true to life and to my work if I gave Lawrence the courage to tell Michael he was gay. I wanted to challenge myself, to see if I could broach a sensitive subject and write it into the strip with care and compassion. I included a bit of laughter, too. (*It's the Thought* 106)

For Johnston, the storyline was inductive, rising out of her belief that the diegesis of *For Better or For Worse* was in every way average, an ordinary community. Consequently, there would be LGBTQ+ people in the neighborhood, and it was important to incorporate these individuals into the narrative through a character the readers knew well. Johnston acknowledged:

> *For Better or For Worse* has always been a sort of real-life chronicle, a look into the workings of a family and a neighborhood—an average neighborhood that could be in any town, anywhere. Although I have focused on the lighter side, it has been important for me to explore those things in life that are not necessarily laughable, but, things that pose a challenge, things that must be dealt with seriously and worked through. (*It's the Thought* 106)

Johnston provided a warning about the storyline to editors, along with alternate strips should they not feel comfortable with Lawrence's coming out storyline. While some declined the story arc and a few even canceled the strip entirely, many published Lawrence's story. The narrative garnered a huge reaction, and Johnston received 25,000 personal letters, all of which were answered (*It's the Thought* 108). Ultimately, Johnston concluded it was the right choice to run the story:

backlash for gay character

> I learned a great deal when we ran the Lawrence story. I learned that the comics page is a powerful communicator. I learned that people read our work and care about what we say. We all look forward every day to that one page in the paper where the small truths lie, hoping for a laugh, or a little sarcasm, and despite the reduction in numbers and size, the comics matter a great deal. Those of us who produce these panels have a responsibility to ourselves, our syndicates, our publishers, and our audience to use this space with conscience and with care. I believe I did that with this story. I believe I made a difference. My syndicate and many editors allowed me to take a risk . . . and, yes, without question, it was the right thing to do! (*It's the Thought* 108)

But Lawrence's story wasn't the only challenging topic Johnston tackled. She also addressed child abuse, alcoholism, dementia, and disability. While the majority of characters in the strip were white, Johnston created a fictional First Nation of "Mtigwaki," where Elizabeth taught school, and did extensive research in order to portray the

diversity

Native culture accurately. For her efforts she received the Debwewin Citation for excellence in Aboriginal-issues journalism in 2004. Johnston also featured Shannon Lake, a character with intellectual disabilities, modeled after her own niece. Thus, Johnston stretched the perspective beyond the white, middle-class Pattersons. However, the focus always circled back to the decent and kind Pattersons, and readers came to feel that the Pattersons weren't just any family, they were *their* family.

Early Years and Training

For Better or For Worse features the Patterson family and is loosely based on Johnston's own home life, with family members aging over the years. Main character Elly Patterson is a stay-at-home mother for much of the strip's run; she later works in and eventually owns a bookstore. Father, John Patterson, is a dentist and was patterned on Rod Johnston. Children, Michael and Elizabeth Patterson, were inspired by Johnston's own children, taking the middle names and many characteristics from their real-world counterparts. However, in order to separate the fictional children from her actual children, Johnston decided to "pause" the development of Michael and Elizabeth for three years "to allow separation to occur" (*Suddenly Silver* 5), thus allowing some distance between the fictional and factual families. Daughter, April, appeared in 1991 and was the direct result of Johnston's longing for another child, a wish that could be fulfilled within the comic, although not in real life. The strip takes place in the fictional town of Milborough, located about an hour's drive from Toronto, Canada.

art training background + style

Readers and critics often comment on Johnston's storytelling abilities as well as her distinctive, elevated aesthetic. The characters are rendered in a style that is centered between realistic and cartoon-like, a middle ground which showcases her artistic training as well as just enough abstraction to soften the edges of the strip and its storyline. While not photo-realistic or as detailed as *Prince Valiant,* the style is more detailed and representative than *Zits* or *Cathy.* Johnston's extensive art training in college as well as her experience as a medical illustrator is very much in evidence in the extremely expressive facial expressions and body language of her characters, and when appropriate, specifics such as clothing and household debris are carefully executed. Johnston clearly has the skill to use her art to tell her story, and she often does just that, relying on the wrinkles around the eyes or the twist of a mouth to interact with and sometimes undermine the text, landing the joke with ease.

The text is carried in speech balloons, sound effects, and intradiegetic objects, but never in captions. There is no narrator outside the diegesis, and the reader appears to be looking directly into the narrative, a heterodiegetic focalizer viewing the unfolding story from a distance. The strip is lettered with clear, bold capitals, and Johnston seems to take a special delight in drawing evocative sound effects with special lettering chosen specifically to conjure the appropriate response in the reader. The language is accessible and familiar— a vernacular marked by family life and friendships. The two parents are college educated and intelligent, and the children speak in the dialect of the schoolyard. They are a pleasant, polite lot, with occasional exclamations of frustration, which are usually played for fun. Johnston notes that there were sporadic Canadian terms that her syndicate objected to, such as "cheque" rather than "check," but for the most part, the language was accessible across North America, and the communication was welcoming and approachable to the reader. In the piece "Crossovers and Changeovers: Reading Lynn Johnston through Margaret Mahy," Sam Hester suggests, "The fact that much of Johnston's readership is in the United States has almost certainly contributed to her efforts to create a 'universal' story that would be just as compelling to readers south of the border and elsewhere," but that "through both her text and artwork, we receive strong impressions of Canadian scenery." On a day to day basis, however, the most important landscape is that of the home.

Framing the Family

For Better or For Worse offers a distinctive perspective on domesticity and mothering that was quite remarkable at the time—rather than elevating and essentializing mothers, as has often been the case in popular culture, or demonizing them, as was the trend of some feminists of the time, Johnston gently and sympathetically depicted the often invisible pressures and disappointments of motherhood, creating a compassionate, insightful lens that executed an experience

representation of motherhood not essentializing or demonizing

"comic frame" [margin note]

seldom discussed in actuality rather than simulacrum. This truth is particularly powerful when understood within what Kenneth Burke suggests is the "comic frame," a narrative that reaches out to the audience to persuade through gentle humor.

In *Attitudes Toward History,* Kenneth Burke discusses "frames of reference," narratives individuals invoke in order to contextualize experience. Burke contends that "out of such frames we derive our vocabularies for the charting of human motives. And implicit in our theory of motives is a program of action, since we form ourselves and judge others (collaborating with them or against them) in accordance with our attitudes" (92). In "Ghandi and the Comic Frame," A. Cheree Carlson claims, "Frames are the symbolic structures by which human beings impose order upon their personal and social experiences. Frames serve as perspectives from which all interpretations of experience are made" (447). Thus, narratives can productively be understood as either frames of acceptance or rejection, a stance of approval or denial in consuming and interpreting human experience. According to Burke, in the comic frame "the element of *acceptance* is uppermost" (*Attitudes* 43); the comic frame exhibits a stance marked by belief. While the reader may not agree with the supposition of the comic narrative, he or she recognizes the argument and responds from a place of willingness to receive the idea. The comic frame, as outlined in *Attitudes Toward History,* "requires the maximum of forensic complexity. . . . Comedy deals with *man in society,* tragedy with the *cosmic man* (42), and the frame is "essentially *humane,* leading in periods of comparative stability to the comedy of manners, the dramatization of quirks and foibles" (42). This humanizing, humane construction is "charitable, but at the same time it is not gullible" (107). Unlike the tragic frame, no villains are required for a comic plot to function (41), only ordinary people making foolish, and relatable, choices. Burke explains:

[margin note: *frames of acceptance vs rejection*]

[margin note: *ordinary people*]

> The progress of humane enlightenment can go no further than in picturing people not as *vicious,* but as *mistaken.* When you add that people are necessarily mistaken, that all people are exposed to situations in which they must act as fools, that every insight contains its own special kind of blindness, you complete the comic circle, returning again to the lesson of humility that underlies great tragedy. (*Attitudes* 41)

✻ comics frame

The comic frame thus educates the audience about humility, just as a tragedy might, but does so within a more common, ordinary setting, one familiar to the audience. A. Cheree Carlson notes that the comic frame agitates for change, for improvement, but does so without ever losing sight of a shared humanity:

> A movement arising from a comic frame would not accept naively the flaws in the present system; it would change or even overthrow the system if necessary. But it would also have a regard for social order as a human creation and respect the fact that some order must exist for humans to function. The social order can be changed, but never at the cost of the humanity of those on the other side. (448)

Comic frame as rhetorical

Therefore, the comic frame operates in gentle affirmation, guiding readers to relate to the characters, sharing their frustrations and encouraging identification, another important means of rhetorical strategy outlined by Burke.

In *A Rhetoric of Motives*, Burke clarifies the importance of the listener or viewer identifying with the rhetor in such cases: "In being identified with B, A is 'substantially one' with a person other than himself. Yet at the same time he remains unique, an individual locus of motives. Thus he is both joined and separate, at once a distinct substance and consubstantial with another . . . in acting-together, men have common sensations, concepts, images, ideas, attitudes that make them *consubstantial*" (Burke 21). Brooke and Hogg argue that

> identification between persons is the fundamental act in rhetoric, at both foundational and persuasive levels. Foundationally, we make the effort to listen or read, Burke says, only when we already believe the speaker or writer is engaged with us in a common project of some sort (no matter how far apart their approach to that project may be). We are persuaded when we come to believe that the speaker or writer speaks for us in some way. (118)

Thus, through the positive act of opening oneself up to identifying with the experiences of another, we can accept that, however removed we might be, we can act together toward a common goal. While Kenneth Burke's rhetorical treatises might seem removed from the comics pages of the daily newspaper, the audience reading *For*

identification as rhetoric & part of the comics frame

connected to Johnston strip

Better or For Worse enters into a gentle, humane, yet educational diegesis, identifying with the characters and being guided toward a more nuanced understanding of the pains and pleasures of motherhood.

Misogyny in Millborough

The fight for Women's Liberation was, not surprisingly, not met with widespread public celebration and support. In fact, the movement garnered a great deal of criticism and backlash in political circles and public conversations. For some, feminist ideas represented a serious assault on long-ingrained notions of family and ideals of womanhood, and many scoffed or joked about the absurdity of challenging gender stereotypes. In a strip from January 31, 1981, the strip pokes fun at "Women's Lip," as Michael questions his father on his mother's whereabouts (see figure 2.1). In the first panel, John is positioned in profile to the right of the frame, mowing the lawn with daughter Lizzy in a carrier on his back. Michael, on the left side of the frame, asks for lunch and the opportunity to "do something." In the second panel, John is depicted wearing an apron and stirring a pan while Michael sits beside him on the stove, wondering, "How come Mom went out by herself, Dad?" The third panel illustrates John's answer as he's seen changing Lizzy's diaper with Michael in the background, his face covered in food. John replies, "Your mother gets the urge, now & then, to get away from the house. She says she needs to be by herself. To be free, I guess" These first three panels show very clearly precisely what it is Elly wishes to escape, the unceasing demands of children and the unending domestic chores, which John shoulders with a grimace and, as evidenced by Michael's face and the dripping baby, some degree of difficulty. In the final panel, John awkwardly holds the oozing baby in one arm and the bottle in the other as Michael queries, "Is that what they call Women's Lip?" John smirks in response, equating, as the audience must, the idea of women "escaping" domestic roles as a silly act of rebellion, parallel to "giving some lip," or acting in a disrespectful or insouciant manner, in effect rudely talking back to tradition. The wordplay takes place in the context of two males talking, with one having to assume the traditional female duties, playing on "women's lib" and "women's lip," equating the two for comedy and essentially trivializing women's

FIGURE 2.1. Lynn Johnston. *For Better or For Worse.* January 31, 1981.

liberation as petty and insolent. Johnston noted that this strip drew a mixed response, with some praising it and others condemning it. And, just as many were conflicted about the necessity and practicality of women's liberation, *For Better or For Worse* reflected inconsistency in addressing feminist ideals. While the main character, Elly, directly indicated indifference to women's liberation, her daily struggles represent a woman grappling with romanticized tropes of motherhood and striving to move beyond a narrow role consigned to her as a woman and maternal figure.

At times in her career, creator Lynn Johnston found gender stereotypes worked to her advantage. During an interview for a position as a medical illustrator at McMaster University, Johnston indicated that her appearance and her gender worked to her advantage. While sharing her portfolio, Johnston noticed of the interviewer:

> His eyes, though open and receptive, were focused not on my artistic qualifications but on the miniskirt I wore. This was the shortest of the short skirts era and the dress I had chosen, through far from improper, was evidently revealing enough. I sat. His eyes sat. I crossed and uncrossed my legs. His eyes crossed and uncrossed. "Can you draw graphs?" he finally asked. "Yes," I replied confidently. "Good. Be at the hospital at nine of Monday." At a time when Erica Jong, Germaine Greer, and Jane Fonda were all pressuring women to reject male chauvinist porkdom, I rejoiced in the inequality of the sexes, did up my zipper (the one on the art case), and demurely thanked him for his confidence in my ability to draw. (*A Look Inside* 41–42).

In an interview with Chris Mautner, Johnston declared that she, like her character Elly, did not take part in the feminist movement:

> I know that I relate to Elly in this one area, in that I didn't person-
> ally take part in a lot of the early feminist campaigns and work for
> equality and a lot of other things, but I stood back and gladly ben-
> efited from it and became stronger because of it. . . . We didn't see
> women rise to the top of the cartooning industry. It was a wonderful
> time for many of us who didn't realize how much we were benefit-
> ing. And often we would make jokes about the feminists who were
> adamant about their [sic] being unisex washrooms for example.

As Johnston notes, her character Elly exhibits similar ambivalence about feminism as a movement. In a strip from 1980, Elly rests alone in bed while John is at a conference (see figure 2.2). In the first panel, Elly is pictured resting in the center of a bed, her arms behind her head, the covers pulled up to her chin. Her face is pensive as she ponders, "John sure takes up a lot of room. When he's away the bed feels huge." In the second and third panels, Elly's eyes widen and worry lines surround her face as she pulls the covers up higher; the darkness of the room becomes darker and more evident without the whiteness of the thought balloons. Stylized text indicates "squeaks" and "drips." In the final panel, Elly is completely covered by the blankets, with the pillow over her head. Only her frightened eyes are visible, peeking out, as the thought balloon queries, "I wonder how many feminists are afraid of the dark?" The strip suggests Elly's ambivalence with feminism, deliberating on how a feminist, who is ostensibly alone at night and without a partner, contends with fear.

A few weeks later, on May 11, 1980, Elly makes an even more pointed statement about feminism in a Sunday strip in which she and John go out for a romantic dinner (see figure 2.3). In the first, largest panel, Elly tells the babysitter, who holds the two children, that she is "meeting John at Chez Louis." In the second panel, a smil-ing man opens the door for a dressed-up Elly, her hair in an upswept style. In the third panel, another smiling man holds the door of Chez Louis open for Elly, declaring, "Oh, pardon us . . . Ladies first!" Elly and the gentleman are flanked by two other men, with the elegantly attired and coiffed Elly pictured in the center of the panel, domi-nating the frame and standing as the central point of the tableau. In the fourth panel, John gallantly takes Elly's coat, stating, "Your

FIGURE 2.2. Lynn Johnston. *For Better or For Worse.* April 22, 1980.

FIGURE 2.3. Lynn Johnston. *For Better or For Worse.* May 11, 1980.

coat, Madame," while a waiter gently pulls out her chair. The final four panels feature tight, narrow close-ups of Elly and John seated at the table. In panel five, John and Elly smile at one another; John holds the menu and the waiter's dark midsection is visible behind the table. Elly beams as a thought balloon explains, "All evening, men have been giving me this 'lady' treatment." Panel six tightens on Elly's thoughtful face, her eyebrows now pulled into in a flat line and her mouth turned down as she stares at her wine glass. John's face is a black silhouette as she continues, "A woman fighting for equality would object to their sexist attitude." John's darkened silhouette takes a drink in panel seven as Elly looks down, her eyebrows arching in worry, her pupils tiny dots as she thinks, "There must be something wrong with me" The final panel continues the thought, with Elly now grinning up at the waiter who is filling her wine glass, as she concludes, "I <u>love</u> it!" In this strip Elly steps out of her mother role, and, freed from the chores and childrearing (duties displaced on another woman), she assumes a more glamorous, more attractive feminine persona, apart from her children. Based on her perceived beauty, she receives preferential treatment from various men and is afforded the courtesies of opened doors and first entry. Elly suggests that "a woman fighting for equality" would object to such sexism, but she "loves" it, arguing that a feminist stance is incompatible with polite manners and means not only renouncing opened doors, but objecting to such misogyny. Elly's charmed scene makes the women "fighting for equality" seem petty and foolish, as she revels in the enchanted behavior of the men around her, not acknowledging the feminists' true battle against discrimination and harassment, rather than polite gestures. The strip minimizes feminist concerns as a childish protest against good manners and chivalry, instead arguing for the benefits of superficial attention based on appearances. Yet this claim would most likely carry weight with readers that felt that women's liberation was an assault on the home and family, a position argued very publicly by Phyllis Schlafly in her 1972 essay, "What's Wrong with Equal Rights for Women."

> The second reason why American women are a privileged group is that we are the beneficiaries of a tradition of special respect for women which dates from the Christian Age of Chivalry. The honor and respect paid to Mary, the Mother of Christ, resulted in all women, in effect, being put on a pedestal. This respect for women is not just the lip service that politicians pay to "God, Motherhood, and the Flag." It is not—as some youthful agitators seem to think—just a matter of opening doors for women, seeing that they are seated first, carrying their bundles, and helping them in and out of automobiles. Such good manners are merely the superficial evidences of a total attitude toward women which expresses itself in many more tangible ways, such as money. In other civilizations, such as the African and the American Indian, the men strut around wearing feathers and beads and hunting and fishing (great sport for men!), while the women do all the hard, tiresome drudgery including the tilling of

the soil (if any is done), the hewing of wood, the making of fires, the carrying of water, as well as the cooking, sewing and caring for babies. This is not the American way because we were lucky enough to inherit the traditions of the Age of Chivalry.

Schlafly equates these "good manners" as proof of an utter devotion to women, cherishing their wellbeing through small gestures and financial responsibility. Schlafly argues that this is a distinctly (white) American value, and in a stunningly racist contention, reasons that "African and American Indian" men "strut around" and force the women to do the "drudgery," without reward, but because of their great providence, American women benefit from the "Age of Chivalry," which is apparently a distinctly Christian attribute, and are gifted with diamonds and goodwill as a result of the "honor and respect paid to Mary, the Mother of Christ."

Schlafly continues this disturbing line of reasoning, suggesting that, just as she suspected, the feminists protesting such acts of chivalry are, in fact, waging an all-out attack on families: "The women's libbers are radicals who are waging a total assault on the family, on marriage, and on children." This Sunday edition of *FBoFW* lightheartedly (and much less stridently) supports Schlafly's position, positing Elly as a family woman who cherishes male gallantry and decries the foolishness of women who reject such courtly treatment. Elly recognizes the "privilege" of white, Christian, American (in this case "North American") women, snubbing feminists as missing out and misunderstanding the honors afforded to women as demonstrated by small pleasantries and kind attentions.

And, although not regularly chastened for it in the press like her comic strip colleague Cathy, Elly also decries her body, criticizing beauty double-standards for men and women, as is seen in a strip from August 5, 1980 (see figure 2.4). In this rather static strip, Elly asks her friend, "Why is it that we are expected to retain our figures while our men can go to pot? We spend years in the kitchen, we get pregnant, and yet we're still supposed to look like sylphs. Why is it that a paunch is fine on a man, but is ugly on a girl who's had two kids?" Elly's friend responds, "Right—if anyone deserves to be fat, we do." Over the years Elly tries various diets and frequently laments her matronly figure. Unlike Cathy, however, Elly's dismay over her body is directly linked to motherhood. The strip points out the unfair expectations while simultaneously revealing Elly's vain attempts to

FIGURE 2.4. Lynn Johnston. *For Better or For Worse.* August 5, 1980.

be thin. There are no conclusions here about body acceptance or, alternately, determinations about a woman's obligation to maintain a certain body type, but rather a representation of an unfair physical ideal that one woman nevertheless tries to achieve.

Gender Roles and Expectations

John and Elly both struggle to reconcile themselves to shifting expectations and understandings of their domestic roles as husband and wife, mother and father, which frequently leads to comical misunderstandings. Rather than portraying domestic bliss, in which each spouse values and appreciates the work of the partner, they often look with envy at the other's role, as in a strip from September 24, 1979 (see figure 2.5). The daily strip is divided into only two panels, an infrequent choice for this particular comics, which ultimately underscores the duality of the two images, and the "flip-side" imagery of two sides of a coin, never reconciling or understanding the other. In the first image, Elly is pictured in a kitchen, carrying an enormous stack of laundry as a pot boils over. Dirty dishes crowd a counter on the foreground, and son Michael sits in a high chair, covering his nose and pointing at the baby on the ground, small emanata indicating a smelly diaper. In the upper right-hand corner, another figure pulls at a hanging plant, which swings and spills dirt. Surrounded by chaos, Elly's thought balloon indicates, "I really envy John his job— escaping to an air conditioned office—meeting new people—accomplishing things—lunches out . . . adult conversations—the freedom."

FIGURE 2.5. Lynn Johnston. *For Better or For Worse.* September 24, 1979.

In the facing panel John is depicted in his dental office, leaning over a reclining patient, who is drooling in the exam chair. An assistant hovers nearby, tools at the ready, while another assistant peeks through a doorway in the background, pointing to an official-looking piece of paper, which might be a bill or notice requiring John's attention. John's thought balloon explains, "I really envy Elly's easy life, the luxury of home . . . comfortable surroundings . . . fun with the kids . . . time to relax . . . the freedom." In both cases the background is blank, but the immediately pressing concerns overwhelm the two primary figures. They are both responsible to other people, and other, unpleasant tasks, yet the text expresses their envious and utterly inaccurate visions of their counterpart's daily experience.

The duality plays out in image and text, with the two panels facing one another like a double-page spread, depicting the dreary reality as opposed to the dreams as expressed in text. The repetition of the two captions underscores their parallel misunderstanding. Both "really envy" the other's days. Elly imagines John relaxing in a clean, secure office; chatting with friends, enjoying delicious, social lunches; and actually "accomplishing things," as opposed to her domestic chores, which are unrecognized as true accomplishments. John, however, imagines Elly romping with the children in a cozy home, resting at her leisure. Both poignantly perceive the other's days as "freedom," but the reader observes the fallacy of the daydreams. Neither is free; both are trapped by convention, necessity, and even their erroneous beliefs, which cast them, individually, as the victim, the aggrieved party in the partnership.

John, in particular, seems especially clueless about domestic labor, perhaps not surprising given that his wage-earning and prestigious

FIGURE 2.6. Lynn Johnston. *For Better or For Worse.* April 5, 1981.

position as a dentist immediately garners respect. In a daily from October 26, 1979, John praises Elly, arguing, "I do appreciate what you do around here! I come home to a clean house, good food, well-managed finances, & happy kids. But I admit that I find it hard to see how the house & kids can occupy your every waking minute. What do you **do** all day, Elly?" Elly's daily chores are depicted in great detail in a Sunday strip from April 5, 1981, yet John once again remains oblivious (see figure 2.6).

The first four panels are silent, showing Elly cleaning up after a spill as Elizabeth and Farley look on, carrying an enormous pile of folded laundry, serving a meal to her smiling family, and cleaning up the dishes as John lifts his arms wide and stretches, yawning. John has turned away from Elly, his back literally turned to her labor, and she confronts him in the fifth panel, asking, "Aren't you going to help me clean up?" John turns toward her, newspaper in hand, his expression puzzled. He responds in the sixth and final panel, reclining on a large couch that takes up the entire panel, holding the paper during his respite: "Are you kidding? I *worked* all day!" Elly gawks at

FIGURE 2.7. Lynn Johnston. *For Better or For Worse.* August 20, 1980.

him, squeezed into the left side of the panel, her eyes wide, round, and goggling. John ignores all of Elly's efforts throughout the entire sequence, and then chooses to take up all of the space of the final panel while resting on the couch. Elly must stand, snubbed and squeezed out of the picture. John's work, though unseen, dwarfs his wife's, and his needs and wants occupy the superior position.

At times John does acknowledge Elly's efforts, as in a strip from August 20, 1980, when he equates her to a paid laborer. In this strip, it is implied that Elly is as one of his female dental assistants: another worker, another "girl" in his employ (see figure 2.7). In the four-panel strip, Elly appears to be serving chips to John and a guest from a bowl, most likely at a party. In the first panel, John addresses the friend pictured in the foreground, smiling as Elly serves him. "You don't know what hassles are, Ted," John explains. John's statement is belied by the fact that he is being waited on by Elly. In the second panel, John continues with his pampered rant, messily enjoying the snacks and turning to his left to address Ted, "Altogether I've got 9 girls working for me." Elly's occupies the entire right side of the panel, wearing a patterned dress and hoop earrings. Her eyebrows are lifted, questioningly, her mouth a tiny dot of concentration and, most likely exasperation. The third panel features a closeup of Elly's face and hands as she counts, "4. .5. .6. .7. .8. ." Elly's face dominates the fourth panel, situated in the right side of the box. She reels back in anger, her mouth open grotesquely wide and her eyes squinting with rage as she shouts with text that cannot be contained by a speech balloon, but rather takes up the entire top of the panel, "You FINK!!! You counted ME!" On the left side of the panel, a much smaller John

FIGURE 2.8. Lynn Johnston. *For Better or For Worse.* August 21, 1980.

is hunched over, smiling smugly, his drink and snack flying out of his hands, obviously laughing at his joke. John has made a witticism about "the girls" working for him, including his wife, in the context of the party, showing off for his friend as Elly serves them. He further belittles her and his own colleagues by calling them "girls" rather than women.

The following day John doubles down on his sexism, once again dominating the relationship and, in this case, the conversation (see figure 2.8). If one reads daily, it is logical that the conversation immediately follows Elly's enraged outburst. However, Elly is no longer screaming, rather, she remains completely silent for the entire four-panel strip. John lectures his wife as they stand, facing one another in profile. Their positions vary little over the four panels as John explicates, "Elly, you are far too sensitive. If I kid you about your role, you're immediately on the defensive. Contrary to popular belief, I am not a **chauvinist** pig!" In the final panel John smiles a bit, the lines around his eyes softening as he delivers the punch line: "I just bring home the bacon." In the monologue, John diminishes Elly, claiming that her response to his quip about her role as another "girl" working for him marks her as "too sensitive," "too defensive," and, furthermore, that he is not to blame, nor is he a sexist "pig." Instead, he plays on the common vernacular phrase, "bringing home the bacon," arguing that he provides for the family. Thus, rather than acting as an animal, John functions as a provider and caretaker, the superior hunter of animals and wage-earner. Elly is completely silenced throughout the exchange, her worried and downcast expression maintained throughout the sequence, and John takes on the dominant position, dispelling any claim that he is a "chauvinist pig" and suppressing

dominant vs
submissive ; imagery

his wife's rage and her voice. In subsequent years, Elly goes back to school and back to work, finding her voice and a role outside of the home, but in these early years John certainly espoused machismo while Elly struggled to find an identity beyond homemaker.

Ambivalent Motherhood

Adrienne Rich argued that mothers "are also, often to our amazement, flooded with feelings of both love and violence intenser [sic] and fiercer than we had every known" (19), and *FBoFW* provides a particularly unvarnished record of one mother's experience. For her part, creator Lynn Johnston suffered abuse from her mother, which, in turn, made it difficult for Johnston to be a mother herself. In an extremely candid interview with Tom Heintjes in 1994, Johnston opened up about her family life—both as a child and parent—and explained her protective stance toward her parents, shielding them from criticism and even praising them in her books until after they had passed away. After their deaths, Johnston revealed:

> My mother's philosophy was, the harder you beat them, the more they'll realize that what they've done is wrong. She would hit me until she was exhausted. She would use brushes, broomsticks, anything she could wield. I could look at the different bruises and tell what she had hit me with. If it was a black bruise with a red stripe down the middle, it was a piece of kindling. If it was a brown bruise with a certain shape to it, it was a hairbrush. If it was perfectly round, it was a wooden spoon. I used to go to school with bruises from the middle of my back to my heels. (Heintjes "Lynn")

Johnston linked her mother's aggression to her frustration about the narrow paths open to her: "My mother was so full of anger and hate. She was a brilliant woman. She could have done anything. She was a writer, she was an artist, she was a calligrapher, just a brilliant, talented lady with potential beyond belief. Right after the war, she married a man and had a family. But she wanted a career. She wanted to be a doctor. . . . But at that time it was not appropriate for a woman to go to work. Her work was in the home." Thus, Johnston's mother's brilliance and ambition were thwarted by conventions that contained her, and her bitterness manifested in the abuse of her children. John-

mother's reason for abuse

ston confided to Heintjes that this burden carried a heavy weight, and when she became a mother to son Aaron, she "didn't know how to raise a child. And I wasn't close to my parents, and because I was too proud to go to my parents for help, I mistreated that little baby. I didn't want a baby. I wanted the stability that a family was supposed to represent" ("Lynn"). Johnston had been abandoned by her first husband and could find no help or any kind of role model in her own mother or her father, and wrestled with parenting alone. On one dark occasion, Johnston told Heintjes that her son

[handwritten margin note: Johnston didn't know how to parent]

> was very unhappy and he was screaming and screaming, and I threw him out into a snow bank in his pajamas. This was in Ontario, and it was not warm here. And he put his hands against the window of the front door, pleading to be let in. And I was inside, screaming at him, "If you don't want to sleep all night, you can friggin' sleep outside!" And this was a teeny baby. And I don't know what it was—it was almost like at that moment, my guardian angel put his hand on my shoulder and said, "Open the door." The next morning, I called a very good friend of mine who was working at the hospital. I had also been doing some work for this hospital on a freelance basis. And I said to my friend, "I need some help. I don't know how to parent." ("Lynn")

Johnston explained that she had to learn to be a mother, and she did so with time and friends and help from her new husband, Rod, but it was not a golden, glorious epiphany or an instantaneous knowledge conferred upon the birth of her first child. In the interview with Heintjes, Johnston spoke of the challenges of becoming a mother, dismissing popular stereotypes of beaming new mothers cradling beatific babies, somehow gifted with an all-knowing, all-loving comprehension of maternal discernment. Madeline Yonker, drawing on work from Patrice DiQuinzio, argues that "to admit that mothering is not emotionally fulfilling and completely rewarding—is to admit failure, or worse; to admit that mothering is not fully satisfying in and of itself is to deny the very natural duty that women are made for" (Yonker 40). In the interview with Heintjes, Johnston revealed a very personal and very potent truth, one that is rarely stated for fear of condemnation, that to act as a mother is not an innate ability. Motherhood is difficult and complicated and not always satisfying,

FIGURE 2.9. Lynn Johnston. *For Better or For Worse.* September 15, 1979.

a theme also expressed in *For Better or For Worse,* although in such a way as to be palatable to the public at large.

In *FBoFW,* Johnston enacts Burke's notion of identification to forge a bond with readers, who, when forming a connection with Elly as mother, come to forge a sense of "consubstantiality," a working together to establish a new understanding of motherhood, replete with the difficulties as well as the joys. Lindal Buchanan argues, "Maternal ethos is typically simple and straightforward, transforming a complex, multifaceted woman into a familiar, reassuring character. This flattening effect derives from motherhood's affiliation with dominant social, historical, and ideological constructs of gender, which the code presents as natural, eternal, and inevitable" (118). Johnston engages the audience with Elly, a mother the audience can relate to and sympathize with, reifying and "flattening" her into a "reassuring character," yet she also invokes the messier moments and the failures of a mother, subtly redefining maternal ethos.

Humor, as in Burke's comic frame, is an essential strategy in establishing this sense of identification with another, which, in turn, leads to consubstantiality, which Brooke and Hogg define as "Burke's fancy word for acting together where separate individuals or groups undertake common projects or form common ways of living." Yonker explains, "The use of humor as a rhetorical strategy can create a kind of performative layer that allows both writer and reader the comfort of distance from the specific topic or concern of the entry" (183). Johnston wittily renders the trials of a mother and family, forging a bond with the audience while positing another "way of living" and understanding of the role and authority of mothers.

rhetoric & the comic frame + motherhood

humor + identific. rhetoric

consubstantiality define

On September 15, 1979, the strip posed a pointed question through the character of Michael (see figure 2.9). In the three-panel strip, Elly is depicted picking up dirty clothes as son Michael follows her through the house. In the first panel, Elly is positioned at the right of the panel, stooped at the waist, bending low and picking clothing up from the floor. One arm is already full of clothing and a doll. The background depicts toys on the floor and jumbled on a low table; the wall behind them scrawled with childish doodles. Elly's young son Michael occupies the left side of the panel, taller and more dominant due to his mother's bent position. Michael wears a "Star Wars" T-shirt and checkered pants. He gazes down at his mother and asks, "You weren't a mom before I was born, were you, Mom?" "Nope," Elly replies. In the second panel, Elly has straightened to her full height and towers over her son as she holds a pair of pants in front of her, scrutinizing a hole in the knee. But Michael's speech balloon rises above hers, as he looks at his mother, wondering, "So, when I was born, I turned you into a mom, right?" Her reply comes in small, capital letters, the balloon partially hidden by her son's: "Yeah." In the final panel, Elly appears to be walking out of the frame, clutching an article of clothing. She doesn't meet her son's eyes; in fact, she hasn't actually looked at him for the entire exchange, but in this final moment her eyes are stricken with wrinkles and her lips are turned down in a worried frown, for Michael, gazing up at his mother's back, has asked, "Did I do you a favor?" In this scene, Elly has spent the entire conversation not actually seeing her son, but rather engaging with the work of motherhood, of domesticity. She is cleaning and mending and seeing to the household. Is this all that motherhood is? Has Michael done her a favor? The question is unanswered, with the reader left to draw their own conclusions.

FBoFW presented another candid, unvarnished domestic moment that serves to inspire a connection with readers on March 9, 1980 (see figure 2.10). The eight-panel Sunday strip plays out a heartbreaking scene, once again between Elly and Michael. After the initial panel announcing the strip's title, the second panel focuses on Elly in profile at a sewing machine, pins in her mouth, and a grawlix-filled speech balloon indicating frustration with the project. Dark lines limn her eyes and her mouth turns down. In the bottom right corner of the panel, Michael fiddles with some string. In the third panel, Michael queries, "Do you love me, Ma?" Receiving no response as Elly continues to sew, he renews his inquiry in the fourth panel,

For Better or For Worse
by Lynn Johnston

FIGURE 2.10. Lynn Johnston. *For Better or For Worse.* March 9, 1980.

"Mama? **Do** you love me?" Elly only grunts in response. The fifth panel shifts the perspective, facing Elly head-on, although her face is completely obscured by the sewing machine. Michael's pleas escalate as he pokes his mother, indicated both by his hands and the text. He asks, emphatically: "Ma? Ma? **Ma?** . . . Do you like me, then, Ma?" Elly's speech balloon offers only a "Mumble?" This appears to be the last straw for Elly, who loses her temper in the sixth panel, leaning out from behind the sewing machine to look down on Michael, rage etched in her posture, her eyes, and her wide mouth as she screams, "Yes! I'd **LIKE** you to get lost!" Michael stumbles backward, his eyes and mouth wide with shock, his arms spread upward. The penultimate panel depicts the immediate aftermath; Elly's expression has softened to worried disbelief, sadness etched in her downcast mouth, in the lines around her eyes, and the hunching of her shoulders. She stares as Michael turns from her, eyes squinting with tears and his mouth open in a wail, as his speech balloon cries, "Waahh," the text dripping with tears, emphasizing his despair. In the final panel Elly is finally alone, her now-abandoned sewing project positioned in front of her, a spool of thread on the table. Elly is bent with despair, hands on her knees, her face etched with lines of anguish. A thought balloon reads, "Something tells me I could have handled that better." This is not a funny moment, but rather, a profoundly sad one, but one that many mothers could immediately identify with—an instant of frustration and failure. Why include such a strip if not to establish a common connection with the reader, to share an honest error in judgment? Johnston explained that she was often led by emotion in creating the strip: "I started letting some of this guilt flow out onto my drawing board—therapy, you could call it—and to my utter amazement, I discovered that others actually identified with me" (*I've Got 6*). Burke would argue that link helps create consubstantiality, a new vision or understanding about how we can act together and "handle things better" next time. Furthermore, this authentic and flawed moment offers an alternative construction of motherhood—one that acknowledges the missteps and imperfections.

When Elly works for a few days at John's dental clinic, expanding her identity and her role, the choice to work outside the home leads to a critique of her maternal instincts, as seen in a strip from November 5, 1980, in which Elly's friend Anne suggests that Elly doesn't truly enjoy motherhood (see figure 2.11). In the first panel, Elly extends her arm, offering money to her friend Anne, who holds baby Elizabeth on her hip. There are no speech balloons to record their conversation; instead, Anne's dialogue hangs in the air unfettered. Anne argues, "I couldn't accept payment for taking care of the kids, Elly!" In the second panel, Anne leans over Elizabeth and a toddler, smiling beatifically and directing them to play with some blocks as she explains, "I'm just one of those moms who <u>loves</u> being with children. It was a pleasure!" Elly's face hovers in the upper, right-hand corner, disconnected from her body and the domestic scene, frowning with what appears to be dismay. By the third panel, the two women have moved to a table and are seated in profile across from one another, drinking out of mugs, suggesting a coffee klatsch or friendly chat between friends. Elly listens closely to her friend, her hands covering her chin and mouth, as Anne speaks, a wide smile on her mouth and her hands gesturing widely: "While you were gone, Lizzie and Mike had a warm, stable home environment here!" However, it isn't until the final panel that Anne delivers the coup de grâce, grinning widely as she lectures, "So relax!—Some of us enjoy parenting . . . some of us don't!" Elly reacts violently, her eyes shut tight as she spews liquid from her bulging lips; her mug flies, suspended in the air, and her hands are splayed with surprise. She makes no verbal retort, other than to spit out her beverage, obviously astonished. Anne, in her cheerful way, argues that because Elly chooses to leave her children and go to work, she does not "enjoy" being a mother to her children and that in Anne's supe-

FIGURE 2.11. Lynn Johnston. *For Better or For Worse.* November 5, 1980.

rior care the children enjoy a "warm, stable home environment," something she implies is not possible with the mother working outside the home. Elly remains silenced and removed throughout the strip, unable to counter Anne's images of domestic bliss while surrounded by the children. Elly is suppressed and disconnected by this vision of maternal perfection. Johnston noted, "Most people don't joke enough about things that worry them—and parenting must be one of the biggest sources of worry of all time. Or call it insecurity. And then there's the guilt." This panel shares that guilt in leaving one's children to work. However, as Elly is the hero and main character readers identify with on a daily basis, the strip also insinuates that Anne is the actual villain, shaming Elly for her choice, and, once again, creating a sympathetic bond between audience and characters, as readers balk at Anne's overbearing comments and commiserate with Elly's frustration at being painted as an uncaring mother.

Career and Children

Despite criticism from others, Elly pursues a career outside the home, putting forward the notion that mothers can work and be good parents. In her quest to find satisfaction in her working life, Elly represents one of the dearest tenets of the women's liberation movement—equal opportunities for women—but does so within the lens of a mother balancing employment and family obligations. Elly takes courses at the local college, eventually taking a position at a library and writing for the local paper. In later years Elly works at and pur-

More representative of women's lib?

FIGURE 2.12. Lynn Johnston. *For Better or For Worse.* September 17, 1982.

chases a bookstore, but in the early years the struggle to mother and to work was particularly prominent. For example, in one early strip from September 17, 1982, Elly is delighted in one of her earliest work triumphs, but her family demonstrates a distinct indifference, quickly pushing Elly back into domestic role (see figure 2.12).

In the strip Elly shares the news that she will be publishing a column on "Library News" for the local paper, telling John, "Look at this, John. My column's going right there!" as her husband smiles at her. In the second panel, John fades to a dark silhouette in the background as Elly beams, eyes wide as she continues, "I am going to report the library news as it's never been reported before!" In the third panel, Elly attempts to engage the attention of son Michael, exclaiming, "Did you hear that, Michael? Your mother is now a career woman!" but her son is too busy playing with a rolled-up paper to meet her gaze. The final panel features Michael alone, one eye shut as he peers through the rolled-up paper. Clearly unimpressed, he responds, "Neat. What's for supper?" Elly's family appears to care little for her professional triumph. John smiles but fades away quickly, while her son gives the briefest sign of acknowledgement, "neat," before quickly placing his mother back into her role as caregiver, asking what she is preparing for dinner. The strip suggests that a mother who looks for fulfillment from her career may not have her aspirations supported by her family.

Elly's career goals are similarly overlooked when her library column finally appears in print, as evidenced in a strip from October 6, 1982, in which Elly must celebrate her accomplishments alone, as her family offers her little support, encouragement, or even acknowledgement in her professional success (see figure 2.13). In the first

FIGURE 2.13. Lynn Johnston. *For Better or For Worse.* October 6, 1982.

panel of the strip, Elly holds up the newspaper, showing it to son Michael and husband John. They lean in as she smiles widely and announces, "There you are. Bottom of page 4. 'Library Corner'—by Elly Patterson." The males appear utterly disinterested in the second panel, turning away from Elly and appearing to depart the left side of the panel, offering only a desultory, "Nice, honey," and "That's good, Mom." Both offer small encouragement while reminding her of her position in the family as "honey," and "Mom," as Elly watches their backs, her expression downcast. The fourth panel features a close-up of Elly's face and partial torso, downcast and silent, but in the final panel she rebounds, with a wider shot showing Elly holding out the newspaper and declaring, "Elly—You are sensational!" Absent the affirmation she desires, Elly chooses to celebrate her accomplishment alone. There is no background evident in the last two panels, emphasizing her solitary moment. The family offers only halfhearted praise, physically turning their backs on her, and thus Elly must choose to savor her victory alone, perhaps suggesting that to choose a career is to choose a path alone and apart from the domestic scene.

Yet, despite their indifference to her professional identity, Elly's children tender her with another kind of success as a mother, underscoring her achievements at home and presenting themselves as sometimes mischievous but always good. It is these moments of familial bonding and success that render an idealized image of the children, for despite their flaws they make all of the sacrifices worthwhile, as they did in a strip from December 2, 1979, in which Elly finds redemption in a few kind words (see figure 2.14). The nine-panel Sunday strip depicts Elly struggling to cook a meal while balancing baby Elizabeth (and reading the book "The Adequate Chef").

For Better or For Worse
by Lynn Johnston

FIGURE 2.14. Lynn Johnston. *For Better or For Worse.* December 2, 1979.

The family consumes the meticulously prepared meal with a series of "burps" and "guzzles" before wandering off, leaving Elly surrounded by the mess. But Michael approaches Elly in the midst of the chaos, stating "Mom, you made a really good supper," to an exhausted and tremulous Elly, who realizes, in the final panel, that it is "strange how a few kind words can give you the strength to carry on," as she carries a stack of dirty dishes with a smile. With these few words, Elly's son has made all of the work and drudgery worthwhile, and so she continues on in the cycle of cleaning, cooking, and cleaning again.

It is in these thoughtful gestures from the children, such as Michael's words or in a gift, as is the case of the strip from August 28, 1980, in which Michael presents his mother with a birthday present (see figure 2.15), that Elly finds peace and joy. In the first panel, Michael gives Elly a badly wrapped gift with a tag marked "Mom." She beams down at him, as he declares, "Happy Birthday, Mom! I wrapped this all by myself!" Elly opens the gift in the second panel as Michael continues, "I chose it all by myself, an' I made the card all by myself!" In the third panel, mother and son embrace, Michael cuddled in her arms as she clutches what appears to be a small bottle, declaring, "It's lovely, Michael." John stands to the right side, cheerily observing the hug. Mother and son hold one another even more tightly in the final panel as Elly looks up to John, her eyes wide open

FIGURE 2.15. Lynn Johnston. *For Better or For Worse.* August 28, 1980.

as she says, "Thank you." This is a moment of pure, sweet, innocent delight. The child's inherent goodness and light exemplifying the best of family—love and acceptance. In these moments, a reader connects and joins with Elly in celebrating her birthday and her delight in the love of a child.

In these early strips Johnston showcases the triumphs and the challenges of motherhood—a mother struggling within culturally determined gender stereotypes and idealized images of the perfect mother as well as one attempting to reconcile her desire to work outside the home and forge a new identity, one she must realize for herself and without the support of her community, or, for that matter, her family. Looking back on these early years Johnston, reflected, "When I look back at the earliest efforts, I see such negativity hidden beneath the humor" (*Suddenly Silver* 3). In fact, in her mind, the strip "began with hesitant lines, disjointed ideas, and a rather dour attitude, but it was funny" (*Suddenly Silver* 4). Yet in these tentative lines, *For Better or For Worse* helped sketch a new, more complicated image of a mother, one that readers could identify with, in accomplishment and defeat, acting together through a comic frame to find another, more complicated vision of motherhood. Kenneth Burke argues that "the comic frame is the most serviceable for the handling of human relationships" (*Attitudes* 106), and furthermore, that "whatever poetry might be, criticism had best be comic" (*Attitudes* 107), and through this gentle comic strip, *For Better or For Worse* criticizes essentialized notions of motherhood with wit and empathy, moving beyond simple stereotypes of maternal perfection and binaries to present a messier, more authentic reality.

CHAPTER 3

PUNK ROCK GIRL

Constituting Community in Barry's *Girls and Boys*

> I actually had a hard time with girls for a really long time, and it was only when I started to teach that I was able to calm down around women because they just seem—and I still feel to this day that they're the most vicious creatures.
>
> —Lynda Barry, Personal Interview with the Author

I N THE SUMMER of 2016 at San Diego Comic Con, in a crowded ballroom full of the most elite, most lauded comics creators, longtime best friends Lynda Barry and Matt Groening were inducted into the Will Eisner Hall of Fame. When accepting her award, Barry bounded up to the front of the room and, full of exuberance, tearfully thanked her own influences, particularly Bill Keane, exclaiming, "This means more to me than I can explain." Groening, the creator of the animated television show *The Simpsons,* as well as the lesser-known but critically acclaimed *Life in Hell* comic strip, made the trip to the podium to accept his honor, and announced "Lynda Barry is my influence." For Barry, the honor recognizes an astounding body of work over her extensive, winding career, from her longrunning strip *Ernie Pook's Comeek,* to the vibrant novella turned play *The Good Times Are Killing Me,* in addition to the cult-classic illustrated novel *Cruddy,* her dazzling collection *One! Hundred! Demons!* and the more recent heuristic workbooks *What It Is, Picture This,* and *Syllabus,* all of which culminated in a 2019 MacArthur Genius Grant. Barry has been blazing her own path as a cartoonist since the late 1970s, charting a course of her own design, moving between styles and genres with relative ease. She is known as a truth-teller with particular skill at rendering childhood authentically, as well as a generous and quirky spirit with a commitment to preaching the power of creative expression for everyone. Recently, scholars have begun to study Barry's work in earnest, and her enormous oeuvre certainly merits extended critical attention. However, her earliest works have, to date, received little academic consideration, even with the publication of *Blabber Blabber Blabber: Volume 1 of Everything* by Drawn & Quarterly in 2011. The volume collects the entirety of her first collection, *Girls and Boys,* originally published in 1981, as well as early miscellany, including samples of the short-lived strip *Two Sisters.*

Barry's early work from the late 1970s and early 1980s as represented in *Girls and Boys* presents a curiously circumscribed vision; peripatetic and erratic, the work stands staunchly apart from mainstream culture, yet hints at themes that would come to dominate her later career. At almost the same historical moment, *Cathy* launched into mainstream consciousness in the daily paper, an "everywoman" struggling to find a balance juggling career and family, but ultimately finding "the worst of both worlds," and Lynn Johnston's Elly lamented her frustrations as a stay-at-home mom in *For Better or For Worse*. As *Cathy* and *For Better or For Worse* focused on presenting female characters finding their identities in the midst of the women's liberation movement, and Nicole Hollander's *Sylvia* even more directly challenged sexism through satire, Lynda Barry presented a very different kind of strip with a decidedly different perspective. Barry's various comic experiments of the time appear more insular and isolated, focusing not on the emergent feminist movement, but rather on a punk rock aesthetic untethered to recurring characters or the serialized narratives that would come to be the hallmark of her later work. In fact, in *Girls and Boys,* Barry employs constitutive rhetoric to construct a community of readers revolving around the punk aesthetic, simultaneously proposing a shared culture of destruction and authenticity through her weekly strips. However, in forging this group, Barry concurrently separates her work from the broader public conversation around feminism and Women's Liberation. This chapter focuses on this early collection, exploring this particularly rich moment in Barry's long career.

Personality Crisis: Origins of an Image Whisperer

biography

Lynda Barry was born on January 2, 1956 in Richland Center, Wisconsin, to Bob Barry, a meat-cutter of Irish-Norwegian descent, and, Pearl Landon, from an Irish and Filipino background. Her family, including her two younger brothers, moved to Seattle, Washington, when she was five, and she spent her formative years in the Pacific Northwest, reading and drawing not to "escape reality," but "to be able to stay" and endure a troubled childhood, as she clarified in 2008's heuristic writing workbook *What It Is*. Barry explained to Joe Garden that she drew inspiration from many sources in her youth, including, "Dr. Seuss, Don Martin, Dave Berg, R. Crumb, Tom Robbins, Grimm's fairy tales, Mrs. Piggle-Wiggle, Anderson's fairy tales, hippie music, Peter Maxx, the Broadway musical *Hair, Ripley's Believe It Or Not!, The Family Circus, Archie,* [and] *Nancy.*" Barry met two of her formative influences, Marilyn Frasca and Matt Groening, while attending Evergreen College in Olympia, Washington. Groening, the editor of the school newspaper, published some of Barry's earliest works, and the two formed a friendship that has lasted for over forty years. Barry also found inspiration working with art professor Marilyn Frasca, developing a way of looking for the "aliveness" in images that she has practiced throughout her career.

After graduating from Evergreen, Barry worked a variety of jobs until her cult-favorite weekly comic strip *Ernie Pook's Comeek* was picked up in the *Chicago Reader* in 1979, where it ran for over thirty years. In 1986 the popular strip introduced the world to the iconic characters Arna, Maybonne, Freddie, and fan favorite Marlys. Over the years *Ernie Pook* told many stories, placing the featured children in a gritty neighborhood and addressing issues such as child abuse, rape, racism, and homophobia. Barry noted in an interview with Pamela Grossman, "My strips are not always funny, and they can be pretty grim at times, and I know I lose readers because of it, but I can't do anything about it—my work is very much connected to something I need to do in order to feel stable."

style & motif

In *Ernie Pook,* Barry established the drawing style she is most known for—a raw, edgy aesthetic that underscores the tumultuous experience of childhood. Her unaffected cartooning style accentuates the emphasis on childhood, and she is also frequently noted for the loquacious, often elegant narration within panels, as well as her use of telling details that highlight poignant memories of youth. In regards to her style, critics often note that Barry's figures appear as if drawn by a child's hand, and she is widely praised for capturing the essence of children's speech. *Ernie Pook's Comeek* was reprinted in popular anthologies including *Big Ideas* (1983), *The Fun House* (1987), *The Freddie Stories* (1999), and *The! Greatest! of! Marlys!* (2000), and even after the strip ended in October 2008, the characters have made guest appearances in various other projects.

Although Barry is most known for her comic art, she has achieved success in many genres. Barry has contributed to essay collections, written for newspapers, and written two novels, *The Good Times Are Killing Me* (1988) and *Cruddy* (1999). *Good Times* was inspired by Barry's art show featuring portraits of quirky and tragic musicians that was originally exhibited at the Linda Farris gallery in Seattle, Washington, in 1986. The project first became a novel (or "novellini" as Barry has called it) and was later adapted into an award-winning play that examines two young girls in the 1960s, one Black and one White, as they experience racism firsthand. *Cruddy* garnered a devoted following for its harrowing, hyperbolic depiction of young heroine Roberta Rohbeson revisiting her father's murderous rampage in a search for lost treasure. This horrifically violent and gruesome story demonstrated Barry's skills in text-based fiction and further established her credentials as a novelist.

Furthermore, Barry continues to blur the boundaries of comic art, creating a new genre, "autobifictionalography" with her celebrated collection *One! Hundred! Demons!*, a series of loosely autobiographical comic strips that originally appeared online at Salon.com before publication as a collection by Sasquatch Books in 2002. *Demons*, inspired by Barry's experimentation with sumi brush painting and *The Art of Zen*, encouraged Barry to call up her own demons, and the resulting collection of strips won a coveted Eisner award. In the anthology Barry also experimented with a collage style, including interstitial collages that blended comic art along with assorted ephemera to create a layered, textured affect. In the conclusion of *Demons*, Barry offers a "Do-It-Yourself" tutorial in which Barry encouraged readers to draw their own demons.

In recent years, Barry has taken on an even more active role with her audience, teaching "Writing the Unthinkable" workshops across the country and sharing her creative process with eager students. In these workshops Barry urges others to create simply for the delight of engaging in the sort of imaginative play that often disappears in adulthood. Barry extends her pedagogy in the workbooks *What It Is* (2008), which focuses on writing images, and *Picture This* (2010), which encourages drawing, painting, and other artistic methods, and *Syllabus* (2014), a compendium of syllabi and teaching materials from her classes at the University of Wisconsin as well as the creative workshops she conducts across the country. *What It Is* acts as a visual Künstlerroman/writing workbook/philosophy text and extends Barry's technique, blending collage and comic art to convey Barry's development as an artist and to argue for the power of her writing process. *Picture This* functions as an art book of sorts, shifting the focus from the creator to the creative process, and revisits old favorite characters Marlys and Arna while introducing a new character, the Near-Sighted monkey, a muse and trickster figure. *Syllabus* provides an inside look at Barry's pedagogy as a "professor of interdisciplinary studies" at the University of Wisconsin. In these books, Barry develops a hybrid genre to showcase her evolving skills, and the varied techniques featured in each demonstrate Barry's willingness to adapt and extend her artistic pursuits, developing and cultivating her approach, and continually exploring different ways of seeing. Author and cartoonist Ivan Brunetti told Christopher Borrelli that Barry's "become one of the most important cartoonists we have—however quietly people are recognizing it. She was first to do fictional comics that felt autobiographical, which is the draw today with graphic novels, and she was the first strong female voice in comics." Miriam Harris argues that "Barry creates a new breed that challenges the traditional canon" (135). Clearly, Lynda Barry is a legend, but her earliest comics experiments are just that—experiments. And these nascent endeavors bear additional scrutiny, as evidence of a time and moment in history and of Barry's development.

As previously mentioned, after graduating from Evergreen, Barry worked a variety of odd jobs while creating comics. She copied and stapled together little books of her work, some of which landed at the shop, Printed Matter. Barry recalled in an interview with Thom Powers, "I got dumped by my hippie boyfriend and then started drawing. Then the stuff just started getting printed by accident" (62). At the time Barry identified as punk, as she articulated to Anne Elizabeth Moore: "I was a punk rocker too. I was very heavily into punk. I smoked a lot and I didn't eat, so I did all these comics that were about these guys that were cactuses." The cactus-focused series *Spinal Comics* was followed by the strip *Two Sisters*, focusing on young twins Rita and Evette Fisk. It was just after *Two Sisters* ended that the tenor of her work changed, and her career launched in earnest, as she related to Thom Powers, "It all just really happened by accident. I was selling popcorn, and my comic strips were being printed in the local paper for—I think it was $5 a week. Bob Roth called me from the *Chicago Reader* as the result of an article Matt [Groening] wrote about hip West Coast artists" (63). In an interview with Joe Garden, she further explained:

> When Robert Roth at the *Chicago Reader* called me in Seattle and picked up my comic strip the *Reader* paid $80 per week. My rent was $99 a month. Lordy! I was rich. This was when I was 23, so around 1979-ish. Punk time. Actually, a little post-punk time. Punk time for me was college. So it was, uh, new-wave time. I remember my comic strips being called "new-wave." It bugged me. But being called anything (except "Princess Kitty") bugs me.

Although she balks at labels aside from Princess Kitty, Barry's comics of the time bear the hallmarks of the punk/new wave movement as her work moved from a softer, sweeter manner to an edgier, uglier style in both form and content. While the early strips occasionally featured children, they frequently focused on adults. Emma Tinker argues that the nascent efforts "are primarily gag cartoons, often barely definable as narrative texts" (115). For her part, Barry considers the early work as a part of her development: "I was a real know-it-all and I was in my twenties and I didn't know anything. But that's the beauty of being in your twenties and being a teenager, where you're just like, 'Well, I have this shit figured out and I know why people don't get along'" (Rogers). Critic Douglas Wolk commented that the comics "are mostly one-off absurdist gags rendered in an arch, brittle, new-wave style (She really like drawing decorative patterns.)."

At the time, Barry adopted a rougher drawing style and chose to delve into dark topics, swearing off a comical punchline. Emma Tinker observes:

> Significantly, the protagonists of these strips are not identifiable as individuals; they are generic young men and women in typical situations, and their stories do not require continuity to make sense. These comics exhibit a distinct stylistic simplicity reminiscent of

defining punk

Punk & women

R. Crumb's line-only phase, but more importantly, they exemplify the <u>defiantly messy, handmade aesthetic</u> of punk. Where underground, for all its supposedly liberal hippy ideology, tended to exclude women, punk had more room for female musicians, writers and artists, although the subculture was still heavily male-dominated and women are seldom allocated much space in histories of punk. (116)

avoided punk label but nevertheless embodied it

And, indeed, although she eschews the label (and the vast majority of labels, for that matter) Barry seemed to find inspiration from punk, in turn, exemplifying many of its core tenets.

"Something Better Change": Picturing Punk

Lawrence Grossberg argues that by the late 1970s, "pleasure had become passé" (60) as punk as a movement began to take shape. In "Postmodernism and Punk Subculture: Cultures of Authenticity and Deconstruction," Ryan Moore notes that "the term 'punk' first appeared in the world of popular music during the 1970s, when American rock critics used it to describe relatively unknown 'garage bands' of the previous decade and a developing music scene centered in Manhattan's Lower East Side" (309). Eventually, "the epicenter of Southern California punk rock in the 1980s was neither Hollywood nor East LA, but rather the suburbs and beach towns of the South Bay and Orange County" (316). But punk was more than a musical style or movement; it infiltrated art, fashion, and politics:

> As forms of style, music, and attitude, the punk subcultures of the late 1970s and early 1980s represent divergent responses to the condition of postmodernity. Though characterized by a wide range of practices and meanings, each of the various subgenres of punk have taken as their point of departure the implosion of boundaries between media and reality and the deepening of commercial culture. (322–23)

Moore goes on to argue that <u>punk culture embraced two sometimes contradictory reactions to postmodern thought</u>: an impulse to deconstruct <u>narratives while creating authentic</u> art. According to Moore, the "'culture of deconstruction' expresses nihilism, ironic cynicism, and the purposelessness experienced by young people. On the other

Both/And of punk & how Barry's strips represented such

hand, the 'culture of authenticity' seeks to establish a network of underground media as an expression of artistic sincerity and independence from the allegedly corrupting influences of commerce" (305). And during the late 1970s and early 1980s, Lynda Barry exemplifies these dual impulses through her comic strip, effectively constituting a community of punk comics readers.

As Lynda Barry and Matt Groening began their careers, it was, according to Pat Grant,

> a bizarre moment in comics history, when the ability to make weird drawings and say honest, confronting and/or inappropriate things was a genuine asset. It was the late '70s and the tail end of the underground "comix" movement, when staying hip meant you had to be into weird comics. Small alternative newspapers were popping up in every city in America, opening up doors for cartoonists with unusual sensibilities.

Anne Elizabeth Moore noted that Barry's "early frenetic linework secured her a place in the New Wave canon of cartoonists, an avant-garde if smallish group who pushed storylines out of the 1970s navel-gazing underground and into new territories: space, youth culture, post-apocalyptic landscapes. Melinda de Jesús maintains, "Stylistically Barry's work is seen as embodying the spirit of 'New Comics' as well as 'wimmin's,' or feminist, comics. 'New Comics' describes comic art oppositional to the corporate-produced and syndicated comics strips" ("Of Monsters" 2). For her part, in a personal interview with the author Barry acknowledged the attempts at categorization, "Primitive. Faux naïve is another thing . . . And I don't agree." Barry stated, "I don't feel like I am in any group with comics, certainly in the mainstream." I think Barry's reticence to be categorized is fair, particularly for an artist and author who was created in many genres, with her style and subject matter changing and evolving over time, sometimes to the consternation of readers and editors.

Yet, at least for a time, Barry was linked fairly directly with punk. Larry Reid, the manager and curator of the Fantagraphics store, commented that Barry made a major contribution to punk in Seattle with the iconic 1982 "Poodle with A Mohawk" poster. With the illustration, Reid has remarked, Barry "made punk rock cute and cuddly and acceptable to a Seattle that was still stuck in a Birkenstock lifestyle. People considered it threatening, but Lynda made it funny" (qtd. in Appelo). Still, given the vastness and variety of her oeuvre, it is not possible to tidily label and categorize all of Barry's work with one broad stroke, although I contend that the early works as represented in *Girls and Boys* exhibit the dual and dueling punk responses to the postmodern condition, and, in doing so, help constitute a punk community, much as people rallied around her "Poodle with a Mohawk" poster.

"If the Kids are United": Constituting Community

James Boyd White insists that rhetoric is "the central art by which culture and community are established, maintained, and transformed" (28), and that, through "a wealth of constitutive social practices," including "expressions of pleasure at a shared language and culture, affirmation of a shared history, participation in shared grief, expressions of gratitude; pledges and promises," a rhetor actually calls a community into being (15). Maurice Charland expanded on this idea, as Martha Thorpe explained in "Making American: Constitutive Rhetoric in the Cold War," for Charland, constitutive rhetoric "does not just invite a member of an audience to be a part of a particular community, but actively creates that community as the rhetor engages with the audience. Constitutive rhetoric is powerful stuff in that it does not just describe the characteristics of a group, but involves the group in its own creation" (4). Lynda Barry, through her comic strip and the forum of the weekly alternative paper, helped constitute a community of punk—an audience that simultaneously sought to destroy mainstream notions of what a comic strip "should" be, while positing something more authentic, more real in its wake. To do so, Barry works within what Leff and Utley call an "interpretive frame," a "process that demands attention to: (1) the rhetor's construction of self, (2) the rhetor's construction of the audience (what Edwin Black calls the 'second persona'), and (3) the enactment within the text of the relationship between rhetor and audience" (40). A closer examination of the strips helps reveal Barry's craft in establishing her ethos as creator, building an audience, or "second persona," and instituting a connection with that audience.

In rhetorical theory, while the first persona refers to the rhetor, the second persona refers to the audience the rhetor attempts to create and address. Christopher Medjesky, drawing on the work of Edwin Black, posits that "the second persona is the person in the crowd

. . . who hears the speaker. By focusing on the implied auditor, the rhetor shifts the emphasis from instrumental to constitutive. A focus on the second persona forces the rhetoricians to consider the moral dimension of a text" (5). The genre of *Ernie Pook's Comeek* provides a frame by which to initiate the second persona. While, for many years, a daily newspaper had a presumed mainstream audience of newspaper readers, the alternative weeklies served a different readership. Published once a week or less frequently, alternative papers by name and definition targeted a readership that sought an "alternative" to the mainstream newspaper system. The implication is that the perspective of the paper is somewhat slanted, edgier, more incisive, and ultimately and unapologetically more opinionated than traditional journalism, which purports to be unbiased. Furthermore, the alternative newspapers operated on a different business model than traditional newspapers, generally given out for free and supported by advertising.

In a piece on the decline of alternative weeklies, Jack Shafer noted, "It may sound corny, but one hallmark of a great alt-weekly investigation was a variety of fearlessness that was beyond the ken of the big dailies that worried about offending advertisers and readers." And Barry capitalized on this kairotic moment—in the pages of various alternative weeklies, Barry's strip was fierce and fearless. Barry needn't fear upsetting the audience of the alternative weeklies, as strips syndicated in daily papers, like *Cathy* and *For Better or For Worse,* did. In fact, Barry links her success to the rise of the alternative weekly, recalling that her rise "happened at the same time that alternative newspapers started to really come about in every city, so for a brief time, there was a place where there were alternative newspapers where they wanted alternative comics" (personal interview with author). A space that recurred weekly, rather than daily, allowed Barry and her readers more time to breathe and process between strips. She was able to establish an audience seeking information content outside the mainstream, and her work was supported by a business model that did not demand consumers purchase the paper each day to support the company. In this space and at this pace, Barry could embrace the moment of rebellion. Of course, even as rhetors such as Barry worked to establish a second persona and develop a bond with this audience, there are those not included in the group, what Philip Wander terms the "third persona"—the "audience left out of the exchange" (qtd. in Medjesky 5). In choosing to focus on publication in alternative weeklies, and later, through small presses like Real Comet, Barry was effectively inviting one audience and ignoring another. The insular nature of the strip portended a cult status—the cool insiders knew of Barry's work, while mainstream outsiders were mired in the conventional likes of *Hi and Lois* and *The Wizard of Id*. As a result of its created audience and the audience it disregarded, *Ernie Pook's Comeek* was able to develop into a distinctive kind of strip, and consequently left a singular kind of legacy.

While Barry balks at labels, the early examples in *Girls and Boys* just look punk. Emma Tinker declares that "Barry successfully ignores many of the conventions of professional cartooning" (117) and that her "punky, DIY aesthetic also reflects a commitment to inclusiveness" (124). Özge Samanci comments on the ways in which Barry "blurs the *professional aesthetic* of mainstream comics" (185), and, "as a result of her unplanned and naïve formal approach, Barry communicates with her audience honestly and obtains credibility. Hence, she locates herself not above, but equal to her readers, and establishes a more democratic relationship in comparison to mainstream's hierarchical approach" (188). In strips like "How to Draw Cartoons," Barry does, indeed, as scholar Sandra Harding suggests, operate on the "same critical plane" (9), as the audience, establishing an ethos of camaraderie and equality as is evident in the interactive strip "How to Draw Cartoons" (see figure 3.1).

In the square-shaped strip, which is subdivided into four smaller squares, Barry immediately establishes herself as an approachable creator through the signatory attribution, which is set within an embellished circle positioned in the upper left-hand corner of the upper-left side panel. A strange, misshapen baby doll figure resides within the sphere, its eyes askew and sporting an awkward wisp of hair sprouting from the irregular head. The body is lumpy, resembling a beanbag or potato, and stubby, little limbs protrude from the trunk, with lines for fingers and toes. Small dots cover the nipple and pubic area. An arrow points to the figure, the capitalized text indicating, "By the famous artist teacher Mrs. Lynda." Özge Samanci links the rough drawings and explanatory arrows to a juvenile aesthetic: "As a result of thick contour lines, missing formal details, flat representations, and aimlessly drawn hatch lines, the identification of Barry's object requires the arrows signifying descriptive titles, as happens in children's drawings" (187). The undersized figure appears handmade and humble, suggesting the homespun aes-

FIGURE 3.1. Lynda Barry. "How to Draw Cartoons." *Girls and Boys*. Seattle: Real Comet Press, 1981, pp. 6–7.

thetic Barry is known for, a design also linked with punk culture. Ryan Moore argues that "within punk subcultures, the process of creating independent media and interpersonal networks in opposition to the corporate media is referred to as the "do-it-yourself," or DIY, ethic" (307), and the DIY punk ethic is very much in evidence in this small figurine. Beneath the character, the circle is bisected by a line underneath which cursive handwriting states, "I can teach you to draw so that anyone will want to be your partner. -L. B." This credit establishes the ethos of the creator as an "artist" and "teacher," but

ethes & first persona [handwritten margin note]

also offers a friendlier moniker of "Mrs. Lynda," rather than a more formal form of address. This instructor is the approachable one who maintains authority but encourages informality, linking the honorific with a first name. The quote underscores the author's connection with the audience, the first persona "I" reaching out and arguing that through this method "Mrs. Lynda" will teach the skill of drawing so well that "anyone" will want to be the reader's partner.

This strip further showcases Barry's verbose nature; each panel is crowded with text to the point that it pushes traditional understandings of comic strips. But Barry delights in the look and feel of text so that it, too, becomes meaningful image. Miriam Harris comments of "How to Draw Cartoons," that "a raw exhilaration drives the shaping of her words and images, so that both text and image can be considered expressive marks, as well as signs denoting meaning they share the same space with each other, without the usual demarcations of speech bubbles or boxes" (133). Furthermore, "letters swell voluminously, cast shadows, sprout spikes and tendrils, beam hallucinogenic rays. They are letters belonging to a new mutant species" (133). For Barry, the shape and feel of the letters is integral to the storytelling, guiding the reader through the interpretation of image, text, and text as image.

The text in the first panel parodies instruction manuals and the drawing classes advertised in comic books, poking fun at the serious, bombastic tone, intoning, "The first thing you'll want to think about is what you'll say in the interview with *Time* magazine after they select you as cartoonist of the year!!!" In addition to Barry's credit line, the panel features images of a cartoonist's tools: a pencil, pen, paper, and a human brain, once again carefully indicated with explanatory text and arrows. The second and third panels call upon the readers to "Learn from Others," with several examples of different shapes of heads: a masked superhero from "Spiderman," the traditional globe-like head of Charlie Brown for "Peanuts," a mass of curls atop a round head for "L'il Orphan Annie," the recognizable visage of "Nancy," and, finally, a strange, abstract doodle for "Lynda Barry." Below the expressionless faces, there are four, extremely tiny squares subdivided into twelve even smaller squares. In this exercise, Barry exploits the punk "culture of deconstruction," showing "the constructed and arbitrary nature of popular culture, reappropriated past images with a sense of irony and self-reflexivity, mimicked the fragmentation and distortion of mediated perception, and embraced

punk ethos [handwritten margin note]

Punk ethos

hybridity and simulation as a means of semiotic disruption" (Moore, *Postmodernism* 323). But even as the activity disrupts the past and reappropriates it, the text also encourages the reader, "Now you try. Be sure to use all of the space provided. You have room for 12 different shapes so let your imagination 'go-go' wild! You're probably going to have to draw pretty small!! But cartoonists must draw small so it will all fit in that comic strip! On Sundays you can draw bigger!!" In this panel Barry invites the audience to dismantle and repurpose these very common cartoon faces, made uncommon by the lack of features. As Lawrence Grossberg argues, "Punk cut up every style or surface and threw the pieces together" (59), just as Barry instructs the readers to do, particularly in the next panel.

The third panel encourages the reader to "mix 'n' match" the eyes, noses, and mouths, offering a chart displaying representative features in the styles of "Spiderman," "Peanuts," "Nancy," and "Lynda Barry," with more tiny squares for practice below, along with four samples of mixed-up faces: Nancy's head with a Spiderman face, Charlie Brown with abstract "Lynda Barry features," and so on. The narrative text of the final panel explains, "Now: all we need is a story. Here's the key: Keep it simple." Playing on a visual pun, an arrow points from the phrase "Here's the key" to an image of a key. Arrows below the key point to the word "Originality." A small profile pokes out of the right-hand corner, a speech balloon stating, "Hmm—That's sorta tough." Text framed in a box offers: "How about one just to help you get started." The text is positioned next to the image of a pencil, under which the following story is printed: "A young girl has to have extensive dental work. The young dentist finds himself falling in love with the girl. When she falls off the dental chair by accident the young dentist finds himself looking up her skirt. 'Dr. Hix!' she exclaims." The narrative text jokingly states, "OK-Good luck with this one!" Barry has chosen a strangely inappropriate story for the audience to adapt into cartoon form. The scene is framed as a love story in which a dentist falls in love with his patient, but he does so when sexually assaulting her by "looking up her skirt." The woman, or in this case "girl," responds by exclaiming the dentist's name, but it isn't clear the feelings or intentions behind her response. Is she angry? Amused? Barry as narrator points to the difficulty of the scene when she wishes the reader "good luck." To aid the audience, Barry provides yet another tiny practice space, four small frames are placed at the bottom of the panel, adjacent to a small hand holding a diploma, again indicated by an arrow and explanatory phrase, "your diploma." "All done?" the texts queries, underneath which is a dotted line and the phrase, "Sign here."

The strip deconstructs the commonplace imagery of the standard comics pages of the mainstream daily newspaper. Ryan Moore explains that "punks have recycled cultural images and fragments for purposes of parody and shocking juxtaposition, thereby deconstructing the dominant meanings and simulations which saturate social space" (307). Other than her own work—referenced as a rough and comical counterpoint—Barry here references conventional comics, cutting up the hallowed features of the vaunted superheroes and sweet children of the comics world. Furthermore, Barry works to demonstrate a more authentic, honest space, pointing out the difficulties of drawing comics ("draw really small") and encouraging her readers to make their own comics.

Moore points out that for punk communities, "doing it themselves, they made the ephemeral world of consumption into a grounds for durable identities and participatory community" ("Postmodernism" 321). The DIY aesthetic is a clear feature of Barry's aesthetic, but the strips go one step further, directly addressing the reader and inviting them to participate in dismantling common comics tropes, creating his or her own comic strip and establishing identities as creators and active contributors. In calling out to the reader, Barry helps establish a connection and a community of participants immersed in punk principles.

In addition to repurposing the quiz format to engage the reader, at times Barry provides abundant free and open space within the panels, a striking contrast to her typically wordy panels, and these absences encourage readers to project their own ideas into the strips, as in the strip "I Remember," originally published in 1980 (see figure 3.2). The strip features the profile of a woman repeated with little change over four panels. Positioned in the left-side of the panel, she stares into the distance, resting her chin in her hands. The figure is abstracted and angular—a Picasso-like deconstruction of a woman. The right side of the first three panels is filled with a looping cursive; free of a speech balloon or other tethering, the text suggests the character's stream-of-conscious reverie. She ponders:

> I remember a lot of things about my childhood. Memories of the most ordinary things come to me and I wonder "What made me

FIGURE 3.2. Lynda Barry. "I Remember." *Girls and Boys*. Seattle: Real Comet Press, 1981, pp. 30–31.

think of <u>that</u>?" Like my dog's bowl or a T.V. tray that was my favorite. And then if I think about these things I always become very sad. I think of the people I knew and what we did, I think about how I was mean sometimes and I feel sorry. Or I will remember my parents. My mom washing dishes how the water sounded in the sink. Or my dad. I often feel as if I can go to them again. I will visualize the house, the furniture. But they always seem to be in the next room. It is dim. I go into each doorway to find them. To say something to them. And then it all fades and I am here. Sitting still. (30–31)

In the final panel the woman's profile remains, but the dense text that crowded the previous panels is gone, leaving an enormous lacuna made all the more striking given the contrast from the repetition of the previous three panels. Barry made her intentions for the strip clear to Mary Hambly: "The process of remembering and then it stops and in the final square you fill in with your own memories and in that way it becomes personal, it's your own cartoon" (26). Barry begins the strip by sharing an intimate contemplation, a shared confidence, and then provides a space for the reader's own thoughts and memories.

Barry pushes the reader from a passive to active stance in individual panels and strips and, moreover, does so within the "free" space of an alternative weekly. The work positions the audience as a community held together by shared interests and actions. The building of bonds is key, for as Moore further argues, punks "must also build alternative institutions which allow ordinary people to communicate, create, and participate in opposition to a society which relegates citizens to the position of spectator and consumer, and here again the punk do-it-yourself ethic serves as an exemplary model" ("Postmodern" 325). This space is not the docile, impassive mainstream newspaper that parrots dominant narratives of the hegemony, but one that challenges the received images, encouraging the audience to cut, paste, and remix the words and images of others into something entirely new.

Barry's work as anthologized in *Girls and Boys* challenges the very notion of the comic strip as funny or humorous, taking on the darker themes, and confronting commonly held, largely sacred narratives of the innocence of childhood, as seen in a very early comic originally printed in 1979, in which two children jump on the bed and argue while their mother is away (see figure 3.3). In an interview with Hillary Chute, Barry reflected on the time immediately after she finished working on her *Two Sisters* strip, when she began tackling bleaker subject matter:

> I started doing the first strips that you see in *Girls and Boys*. That very first one, if you see it, I think it's the kids who are left at home, and a kid's jumping on the couch and saying, you know, "When mom comes home you're going to get in trouble," and the other kid says, "Mom's never coming home. She's going to marry a bum." So that was the first stuff that I did and the drawing was really kind

FIGURE 3.3. Lynda Barry. "I'm Going Out." *Girls and Boys.* Seattle: Real Comet Press, 1981, pp. 8–9.

of gnarly, too. It was really rough, compared to Rita and Evette, which is very sort of sweet. It's not *sweet* sweet drawing, but it's sweeter. . . . So I started doing these comics that had trouble in them, and people were very upset and I wasn't in many papers at that time. People were very upset, because there weren't many comic strips that had a lot of trouble, that weren't funny, you know? (Interview 52)

But it was through strips such as this one that Barry discovered that "a comic strip could contain something sad, like a song. And I realized I could discuss anything in comics" (54). While the comics are clearly historically associated with humor—the word itself linked to comical content—the visual/verbal form of comics most certainly does not have to be funny.

Through strips such as this one, Barry disassembles the commonplace notion that comic strips require a tidy punch line or must inspire hilarity. Barry also confronts romanticized understandings of the sanctity of home and the goodness of children, concepts that permeated much of popular culture of the time, particularly as repre-

Challenges mainstream ideologies often espoused in comics

sented on the mainstream comics page. If one were to find Barry's strips tucked into an alternative weekly such as the *Chicago Reader* or the *Village Voice,* a quick glance at the strip would reveal the flattened, grotesque drawing style, quite a contrast to the sweet, innocent style of comics stalwarts like Charles Schulz or Bil Keane. Barry's comics also represent one of the rare depictions of people struggling financially at the time.

As Barry pointed out, these are by no means "sweet" illustrations. The art flattens the characters, abstracting and exaggerating their flawed features. The mother, daughter, and son are all unattractive, their mouths stretched into angry grimaces and, in the case of the daughter, a tight rictus of grief. The panels themselves are overwhelmed with kitsch and chaos, cluttered with repeating, hand-drawn decorative patterns, clashing on every surface—walls, shirts, pants, dresses, and tablecloths. Even tears take on a rhythmic pattern, spilling across the girl's cheeks. It is the darkness of the primary figures that causes them to stand out from the overwhelming patterns, for their hair and clothing (though also patterned) is darker and holds more weight in each panel. In the first panel a middle-aged woman faces the reader, but her eyes shift to the right as she addresses her absent children through a speech balloon, stating, "I'm going out to pick Grandma up from bingo. I want you to stay home till I get back. No roughhousing and **no** fighting—Do you two understand?" (*Girls and Boys* 8). Speech balloons drift in from the right of the panel, indicating the children's response, "Yes Mama!" and "OK Mama!"

In fact, speech balloons dominate much of the space, with rough, wavering balloons enclosing the characters' fevered arguments. In the first panel, a woman stands facing the reader in the left side of the panel, a table cluttered with cups and an ashtray to her right. She is wholly unattractive, her eyes tilted and angry and her mouth turned down in a snarl. She wears a short, polka-dotted tank top that reveals her midriff and tight, patterned pants. In the second panel, it is evident that that the mother has departed, for a young girl points up to a boy, who is jumping up and down on a bed, his arms held up high behind him and small lines shooting down from his feet, indicating his ascent. Once again, the panel contains a multitude of intricate, clashing patterns, drawn onto the wallpaper, the bedspread, and the children's clothing. The young girl is positioned in the bottom left of the panel, pointing up at her brother (in mid-flight), lecturing, "I wouldn't jump on Moms bed if I were you Ernie. You hear me Ernie? Im gonna tell Ernie. That's rough housing Ernie. Thats just what you're doing right now and Im tellin." The daughter, placed in the lower-left panel, occupies the submissive position, attempting to act in her mother's stead and discipline her brother, but he inhabits the upper right-hand quadrant of the panel and shuts down her dogmatic monologue, replying, "Shut-up creep."

The brother becomes even more dominant in the third panel, a tighter shot that features a closer look at him bouncing in mid-air, much of his body outside the right side of the panel. He peers down at the face of his sister, which is trapped in the lower-left of the panel, weighted under the speech balloon, in which he explains, "Besides Im not too worried about you telling for two big reasons. One is that Im Superman and the other is Mama isn't ever comin hom. She's gonna get drunk and marry a bum and never come home." The sister, completely dominated and silenced by this diatribe, weeps, tears spilling down her cheeks as she looks up to her brother's vicious, but confident face. At this moment, the brother is in the position of ultimate authority, perched high above his sister. In addition, he has he taken on the name and mantle of the Man of Steel, Superman, and he spins what appears to be a somewhat convincing and utterly devastating possibility that crushes his sister's fragile emotional state.

The final panel reverses the situation from the first. The mother now stands outside the panel, but her words enter in through a speech balloon positioned at the very top of the panel, "What on earth is wrong with you Lisa?" The two children are now pictured on equal standing. The daughter faces the reader, tears still flowing freely, her hands clasped in front of her as she exclaims, "Ernie said you were never coming home Mama. He jumped on your bed and said you were gonna marry a bum." Her brother looks to the side, his face in profile, as he exclaims, "What a liar! Lisa stubbed her toe and now shes makin up a lie to get me in trouble! And I bet you're gonna believe her. You always take her side!" The sister, who was acting as her mother's surrogate, now occupies her parent's original place, foreshadowing her eventual role, while her brother suggests that the mother will take the daughter's side, as she apparently always does. Of course, his lament is prefaced by a lie about Lisa stubbing her toe and lying, indicating an error in judgment compounded by yet another lapse in discernment. And then, the strip simply ends without humor or even a sense of finality or closure. Will Ernie be punished? Will Lisa be comforted? Will the mother run off? The strip implies no resolution, leaving the reader to create their own conclusion, or accept the ambiguity, for, as Lawrence Grossberg argues, "locating punk in this broader context . . . makes it a set of strategies for living in the face of the collapse of meaning and increasing paranoia" (59). In the absence of conclusions, of finality, and without the ability to determine meaning and value from narratives, punk culture works to establish a way of existing in the absence of the dominant narratives of church, state, and family, which previously guided behavior. The punk culture survives without the benefit of received wisdom, life lessons, and easily consumed, consumer-driven stories. This comic requires the reader to process and make sense of the strip, or discount it, without the comfort of previous forms to guide the way. And those reading who suffer from inattentive parents and difficult childhoods find a point of connection with this comic, its creator, and the wider audience. Representing this subjugated narrative graphically illustrates that those without stable families are not alone.

However, in spite of the darkness, there is reason to hope, for the content is open to interpretation, something that a reader immersed in the punk culture of the alternative weekly would be able to fashion from context, understanding the definite pathos of the piece. Barry realized she was defying convention by bucking any sort of humorous intent. She explains, "The setup for a comic strip is four panels and that last thing should be a punch line, so when people didn't get that punch line they became very upset and they would write furious letters to the editor about how there's nothing funny about child abuse, and it's like the strip wasn't funny, it was sad" (Chute, Interview 52–53). The strip is sad and unresolved and thus provokes a connection with the audience based on emotion, a piquant sadness. For as Barry actively recruits a punk community of deconstruction as her readership, she simultaneously posits this second persona as an active one who participates in the act of making meaning and forging connections inflected with empathy.

Lynda Barry, Love Doctor: The Relationships Between *Girls and Boys*

A few of the earliest strips in *Girls and Boys* focused on childhood scenes and younger characters, foreshadowing the post-1986 focus of the strip on recurring, cult-favorite characters Arna and Freddie Arkins and Maybonne and Marlys Mullens, but in the beginning there was no focus on recurring characters or serialized storytelling, nor were children the norm. In fact, the majority of the strips centered around men, women, and relationships, perhaps because, as Barry told Michael Dean, "it was a period in my life when I thought I had love and relationships . . . figured out—this was when I was all of 23 or 24, and I wrote from that perspective" (42). In another revealing interview, this time with Thom Powers, Barry reflected on the early days, and what inspired her at the time:

childhood & relationships Barry inspiration

> So I always drift toward what gives me the most kind of terrified yet thrilling feeling. It's almost like the work has this kind of stream-of-consciousness hippie attitude. It's the hippie attitude that led me to it. When I did *Girls and Boys,* there was a lot of childhood stuff that moved into relationships, and then moved out of relationships back into childhood stuff. I think that the two things are really tied to each other. I think the reasons we choose the people we choose have a lot to do with our childhood. (66)

Thus, Barry found herself studying relationships, as she did in the strip, "Finding Your Perfect Love Mate," originally published in 1981 (see figure 3.4). The strip is addressed to women and girls, with the profile of the narrator perched in the lower-left corner of the first panel, calling out, "Calling all girls! Calling all girls! Yoo-hoo ladies!!" This strip, at least superficially, appears to address women, and, in fact, much of Barry's work, both early in her working life and throughout it, centers around female characters and experiences. However, although feminist theorists and literary critics have attempted to claim Lynda Barry as a "feminist cartoonist" for years, for her part, in the early 1980s, Barry didn't identify as a feminist or with the "Women's Liberation" movement, pleading ignorance in a 1982 interview with Mary Hambly. Barry hedged, "I don't know what the goal is or the definition of feminism, so it's hard to say. But in terms of being a woman I'd say my work is almost exclusively about being female in a real average way" (30). Studying these early works the concentration on female experience, in all its messiness, is readily apparent. However, this emphasis occurs apart from any sort of explicit political argument and the author herself suggests a lack of information on the purpose of feminism. While *Sylvia* directly

center on women's experiences though not tied to feminism

FIGURE 3.4a. Lynda Barry. "Finding Your Perfect Love Mate." *Girls and Boys*. Seattle: Real Comet Press, 1981, p. 40–41.

challenges misogynist media figures and *Cathy* champions the Family Medical Leave Act, and even Elly examines her own mixed feelings about "Women's Lip," in *Girls and Boys* the characters flounder about in the dating world without acknowledging the politics of feminism raging in the real world.

In a personal interview, Barry explained that she was a tomboy growing up, and, as indicated in the epigraph, she didn't necessarily feel comfortable with women. She elaborated, "Girls are into hierarchy. Guys have power stuff, but you can at least see it. It's where you

connection to Cathy & other comics

FIGURE 3.4b. Lynda Barry. "Finding Your Perfect Love Mate." *Girls and Boys.* Seattle: Real Comet Press, 1981, pp. 42–43.

can see it. With girls, it's a whole other thing. So, yeah. It took me a really long time to relax . . . unless I was around other tomboys. Then it was all right. It is interesting that, given her self-identification as a tomboy, Barry places herself as separate from other women and even from the feminist movement. And this division is evident in the comics themselves, which, though they show women and girls who read as authentic and true and honest, the strip does not directly address feminism or Women's Liberation as a movement. Barry confided to Mary Hambly, "I want to say, 'Yes, I am a feminist,' but I think the

Barry's disconnect or issues w/ other women are (unintentionally) reflected in her comics

why Barry unidentified w/ feminism (handwritten annotation)

Feminists would say I was out of my mind, that my work is about men and women and that none of my women are strong, good role models" (30). Barry's statement to Hambly suggests that she believes she would be unwelcome as a feminist, and, furthermore, that in order to claim the title of feminist, one must present "strong, good role models," not the awkward, complicated characters depicted in her work. *Girls and Boys* presents numerous strips depicting bad relationships in which women wait by the phone for feckless partners to call, or cling to dirty socks as reminders of lovers long gone. As Barry suggested, neither the men nor the women are "role models." Özge Samanci observes of the strips:

> Torturer males appear as the result of the unconscious choice of females, since females repeat their separation-attachment-disapproval trauma between them and their mothers with their selection of mean boyfriends. As a result, Barry does not make a cliché generalization of saint females and bastard males. She brings a wider view based on psychoanalytic theory to explain the repetitive pattern: while looking for attachment, approval, and love, females fall in love with inattentive partners. (194)

These strips divest notions of romance and love in awkward, ugly encounters, made even more grotesque through the jarring, abstracted aesthetic.

Based on these relationship comics, Barry was hired to create monthly comics for *Esquire* magazine, a series that began in 1984. These comics, edited by Jay Kennedy, were full-color cartoons originally entitled *Modern Romance* and later renamed *On the Home Front.* While the *Modern Romance* series is beyond the scope of this analysis, it certainly bears additional scholarly attention, even though Barry lamented in a private interview that "I hate that stuff with all my heart. . . . The drawing part was miserable, the writing part was miserable. . . . I don't feel like they're mine at all." Although she reveled in dissecting the foibles of love and relationships, Barry clearly preferred the freedom of the alternative weekly over the constraints of a men's magazine.

Despite Barry's qualms about a feminist label, scholars have been quick to claim Barry as a feminist cartoonist, with Özge Samanci claiming, "Barry's themes and various narration devices locate her work at the intersection of feminist humor, women's humor, and

is it important that she identifies as a feminist?

male humor" (181) and Emma Tinker positing that "Barry does identify herself as feminist" (109). Regardless of scholars desire to classify Barry, or the creator's demure evasion of the past, the comic strip "Finding Your Perfect Love Mate," spoofs the utter absurdity of quizzes found in popular women's magazines such as *Glamour* and *Cosmopolitan* that call on women to debase and belittle themselves in an effort to "catch a man."

her comics spoofs normative romance

"Finding Your Perfect Love Mate" is a longer-than-ordinary, eight-panel strip comprised of two separate, subdivided squares and represents an example of Barry at her most loquacious. All but the eighth and final panel are crowded with dense lines of text, sometimes scrawled in tight cursive and sometimes lettered in lowercase print. Barry's handwriting certainly helps tell her story, from the frantic pinched cursive to the looping lower-case printing, the writing takes on the qualities of speech—sometimes frenzied and desperate. As Barry explained to Michael Dean, "Handwriting is drawing. And it contains an image too—the image is the thing we recognize when we recognize someone's handwriting" (44), and Barry's handwriting adds intensity to the breathless narrative commentary. In addition to the layers of text, tiny images mark the corners, with a helpful narrator popping up in profile to guide the reader through each of the panels, distinguished by headings such as "Success Begins at Home!" (Panel Two), "Just Who is Mr. Right?" (Panel Three), "What do I do once I Spot Him?" (Panel Four), "What Shall We Talk About?" (Panel Five), "What Shall We Do on Our 1st Date?" (Panel Six), "Is it Love? How Can I Tell?" (Panel Seven), and "Planning Your Future" (Panel Eight).

handwriting

The first panel opens with "Wonderful News for Every Woman Who Worries About Finding Your Perfect Love Mate" and offers "a few hints to help you in your fabulous search for Mr. Right" from the narrator, a smiling woman featured in profile, wearing bold earrings and a beaded, multi-colored necklace, along with a striped shirt. The right side of the panel is dominated by the head of a man, his face blank, apart from a large question mark surrounded by smaller question marks. The face is surrounded by a gilded frame with a banner below, indicating that this anonymous visage is "Mr. Right." The blank face is notable for the large, bouffant, fifties-style hairdo, with an enormous curl hanging down the forehead. The button-up shirt, sweater, and bow-tie suggest an old-fashioned notion of a "nice young man." The face is surrounded by hearts and dollar signs and words such as "tall," "intelligent," "handsome," "roman-tic," "funny," and "kind." The narrator addresses the reader with her words but also seems to be clasping her hands and offering a sort of prayer to this blank visage, a simulacrum of the perfect mate.

The second panel offers the "keys to happiness," two actual keys in which are inscribed, "Attitude" and "Appearance," above several questions which inquire, "Am I cheerful and clean?" and "Do I want a boyfriend for the right reasons?" The third panel asks the reader to study various categories, including "Looks," "Brains," "Sense of Humor," "Penis Size," "Money," and "Job" to determine "Who is Mr. Right." The fourth panel takes a more active approach, offering "tips 'n tricks" for meeting Mr. Right, including "shoot a spitwad at him," Stare at him and smile," "Let him do the work," and "Go over to him and ask politely, 'Is this seat taken?' and then point to his lap." The fifth panel offers tips regarding what to talk about on a date, such as "Let him pick the conversational topic. Try to figure out just what you think he'll say then timidly say it first—as if you 'aren't sure.'" At the bottom of the panel the narrator demonstrates the technique with small speech balloons, stating "Yes. Uh Huh. Oh, really," among other flattering and obsequious comments.

Interestingly enough the sixth panel focuses on eating together, but rather than extolling the hazards of eating messy food or having a large appetite, the text urges the reader to watch the date, for "you can tell what sort of lover a man is by how he eats." The seventh panel addresses the question of whether it is truly love with a picture of the narrator lying prone, apparently knocked out and clutching a heart at the top of the panel. The quiz asks, "Which of these things can you no longer do? Anything? Everything?" Finally, the last panel breaks up the text-heavy monotony with a cluster of images, designed to help the reader with "Planning your Future Together." A couple kisses in the upper left, the man marked with an arrow denoting "Romeo' and a tail of sorts trails from his back into a path-way to a sweet home replete with chimney and apple tree, marked "Love nest." Below the couple and home, the joy seems to diminish somewhat with an illustration of two hideous "matching hula shirts" and a "cat named Damien," most likely an evil portent. The lower left features the couple's further devolution, picturing a myriad of "birth control pills," and, finally, "fights," showing the previously kissing couple from the upper-left hand corner now buried in the lower-right, their faces contorted with rage, the woman swinging a rolling pin as they each point angry fingers at one another. As the reader's eyes move through the images, his or her gaze follows a trajectory from fairy tales, as indicated by the passionate embrace, the "Romeo" moniker, and the quaint, homey cottage, to the more mundane realities of awkward domesticity, suggested by the embarrassing bourgeois Hawaiian shirts and a domestic pet with a villainous name. By the bottom of the panel the myth of the perfect romantic has completely dissolved, as evidenced by the detritus of copulation—condoms and pills and diaphragms. And, in the end, the perfect mate has been replaced with a domestic squabble. The quiz posits the question—how does a woman find a perfect mate?— as a jest, but the answer is that, despite the ludicrous posturing and perambulations a woman endures to find this partner, no such mate truly exists.

[margin note: the "perfect mate" doesn't exist]

The interactive and wholly unsettling quiz presented in "Finding Your Perfect Love Mate" satirizes the ridiculousness of female subservience as attractive to potential romantic partners, a theme frequently represented in glossy magazines. It is brutal and honest, invoking the culture of authenticity espoused by punk culture and inviting readers to participate in what is represented as a shared and genuine experience. Ryan Moore reasoned that, for punks, this "culture of authenticity"

[margin note: punk "culture of authenticity"]

developed as young people attempted to insulate themselves from the culture industry and consumer lifestyles in their search for expressive sincerity and anticommercial purity. Those who embraced the do-it-yourself approach transformed media and consumer identities into independent networks of cultural production, which enabled a sense of local community, allowed spectators to become participants, and created a space for public debate and dissent. (323)

In "Finding Your Perfect Love Mate," Barry dismantles the popular narrative of "one true love," as well as the ethos of women's magazines targeted at bolstering the romantic fiction, concurrently inviting the reader to move beyond a spectator role, check the boxes, and become a part of the deconstruction. The strip operates within the sphere of alternative weeklies, outside the mainstream newspapers that must be bought, and encourages the reader to contribute to the rebellion. Julia Round believes that the comics form provides a

[handwritten note at bottom: Barry deconstructs & dismantles & invites the reader to do so, too.]

unique opportunity to establish a bond between creator and reader: "The reader works alongside the creators as a kind of contributory author, both by interpreting the panel content, and by filling in the gaps" (317), and Özge Samanci contends that Barry, in particular, calls out to the audience, for "Barry invites the readers to enter her world, to remember and to develop an insight in several ways" (191). This participatory bent is key to Barry's work and ethic: she compels the reader to join in, to play a part in the community, an *agora* marked by rebellion against the establishment.

Barry's ethic based on reader participation

gathering place

The strips of *Girls and Boys* display a particular kairotic moment, in which Barry constitutes a punk community marked by the deconstruction of dominant narratives as well as a commitment to DIY authenticity. The strip's placement in the alternative weeklies solidifies her positionality, as does the raw aesthetic and the dark and disruptive subject matter. Furthermore, Barry truly invites the reader into the comic, asking each individual to participate, sometimes by checking a box or taking a quiz, other times by filling in the gaps of understanding. She creates an open narrative into which a reader might project him or herself. Maurice Charland argues, "While classical narratives have an ending, constitutive rhetorics leave the task of narrative closure to the constituted subjects" (143). Thus, while older, modernist dominant narratives present a closed loop with subjects only able to observe the conclusion, a narrative designed as constitutive rhetoric enables the subject to complete the narrative. In fashioning this community of insiders participating in the punk readership, Barry establishes a second persona that exemplifies the tenets of punk culture. Ryan Moore contends of punk that "the emphasis on creative access has opened spaces for artists representing a wide range of perspectives, and occasionally these bring the cultures of authenticity and deconstruction together in fresh and powerful ways" (324). However, as evidenced in the strips themselves, at the time *Girls and Boys* represented an insular community, removed from wider, mainstream culture. The strips do not address politics, feminist or otherwise, as *Cathy, Sylvia,* or even *For Better or For Worse* did. For Emma Tinker, "it is surprising that one so rarely encounters treatments of race" (113) in these early works, not to mention government policies or affairs of state. Despite Barry's own difficulties with reconciling her Irish-Norwegian-Filipina heritage, as explored in *One! Hundred! Demons!,* she does not explicitly depict characters of color nor does she address racism in these early examples. Barry

Punk ethos

rhetoric reader

overall analysis

lack of diversity in comic

kairotic: perfect time & place

revealed to Mary Hambly that she simply "would not be good at studying politics. I would fall asleep. I am good at eavesdropping and remembering funny things that happen as I move through the world. You have to keep up with politics to do political cartoons" (28), and so Barry chose to concentrate on developing a community made up of a shared commitment to creating small and authentic moments that disrupted received wisdoms.

Over time Barry's community has widened enormously, and when she strode onto the stage in 2016 to accept her inauguration into the Will Eisner Hall of Fame, her work had progressed and changed greatly from these early endeavors. While hints of her interest in representing childhood, and in particular the experiences of girls, were evident in these nascent projects, her world expanded as she continued to produce works in other genres. In *One! Hundred! Demons!*, Barry examines race, class, gender, and passing, as well as sexual assault, even occasionally making a foray into politics. In *The Good Times Are Killing Me,* she tackles racism at length, and in *Cruddy,* she presents an explicit and painful meditation on abuse. Yet across the years and throughout many genres, Barry's creations have retained an emphasis on participatory connections with readers, and later evolved to embrace a wider culture. However, in establishing the second persona and constituting the punk comic community through the youthful strips of *Girls and Boys,* a third persona is also instituted, a group excluded by virtue of not reading or not participating. Philip Wander suggests, "What is negated through the Second Persona forms the silhouette of a Third Persona—the 'it' that is not present, that is objectified in a way that 'you' and 'I' are not" (49). While these early strips create a powerful community of creativity and rebellion, what Julia Round might call a "postmodern artefact" (317) of a certain place and time, they also operate in relative isolation—a place apart from the world at large.

[handwritten annotation:] participatory audience (second persona) that contributes to a punk ethos, but by extension there is a third persona, or a group excluded/not present

CHAPTER 4

NICOLE HOLLANDER'S *SYLVIA*

Menippean Satire in the Mainstream

Thus, satirists write in winters of discontent. And they write not merely out of personal indignation, but with a sense of moral vocation and with a concern for public interest.

—Ruben Quintero

Mercy, it's the revolution and I'm in my bathrobe.

—Nicole Hollander, 1982

IT'S SOMETHING of a mystery that Nicole Hollander's caustic, biting *Sylvia* ran from 1981 to 2012 in many mainstream newspapers, positioned next to the placid charm of *Hi and Lois* and *Family Circus*, while providing caustic social commentary through the use of deliberately raw, static images coupled with highly literate and literary text. In the strip, the roughly drawn character of Sylvia often rested in her bathtub, pontificating on the news and skewering various injustices; however, she also addressed concerns about weight, dieting, and finding a romantic partner. Over the many years of the strip, *Sylvia* effectively employed a type of Menippean satire, and did so in a particularly appealing way, enacting a playful (and occasionally punishing) rhetoric of display and resisting dominant narratives through what Northrop Frye might call a "display of erudition" (11), an erudition pronounced with unabashed vigor from Sylvia's bathroom. *showing great knowledge/learning*

This chapter draws from rhetorical theory to consider *Sylvia*'s scathing opposition to social ills and, in particular, her argument for a more radical form of feminism through the use of Menippean satire, a technique that challenges and persuades her readers through

136 *menippean: attacking mental attitudes vs individuals & entities*

argument

a daily comic strip, positing a particular strand of feminism as the only truly logical position, while lampooning sexism and stereotypes, loudly sounding an alarm and alerting the audience to community crises and inequities. However, before engaging in a close analysis of the strip itself, this chapter introduces Hollander and the history of the strip, and presents key concepts of satire that help illuminate *Sylvia*'s contributions to the historical dialogue surrounding feminism as understood in popular culture.

"Everything Here Is Mine": The Genesis of *Sylvia* *biography*

Nicole Garrison Hollander was born in Chicago in 1939 as Nicole Garrison. Growing up, Hollander's humor was informed, in particular, by her mother and her mother's friends. In an online article for the Jewish Women's archive, Hollander recalls, "I noticed that around our house, my father was to be amused and danced around. And he was amused by my mother and me. He had very little humor himself. I always thought of women as the funny ones." However, her father, whom she describes as a "difficult man," stimulated her interest in politics. She explained of her father that "his legacy to me was politics; a vision of the world in which there are 'haves' and 'have-nots' and your duty is to be on the side of the 'have-nots'" (Jewish Archive). Her father also influenced her perspective on religion. In *The Sylvia Chronicles,* Hollander reflects, "My father was an atheist. On days when other Jews were fasting he encouraged me not to. . . . He was a member of the carpenters union and when I balked at joining the union at the Cook Country Department of Public Aid, he asked if I felt comfortable having others fight for my rights while I did nothing. That's what I remember of his political and religious philosophy" (4). Thus, Hollander inherited her mother's wit and her father's moral code, qualities very much in evidence in *Sylvia.*

As a child, Hollander enjoyed comics, but her enthusiasm waned as she grew up. In *The Whole Enchilada,* Hollander recalled, "I know that I loved the comics. . . . I know I stopped reading comics, but I can't remember why. . . . Maybe the comics stopped being relevant to my life because they were all written by men, filled with male characters" (7). Instead, Hollander pursued studies in the fine arts, receiving her B. F. A. from the University of Illinois and her M. F. A. in painting from Boston University, and, she recollects, "as a student I

trained in art

FIGURE 4.1. Hollander's First Comic for the *Spokeswoman.* 1978. Republished in *The Whole Enchilada*, p. 8. New York: St. Martin's Griffin, 1986.

was torn between choosing a career in which I could help others and one where I would stand in front of a canvas painting images from my darker self" (Hollander, *Tales* 243), and, indeed, it would take her several more years before she found her true calling as a cartoonist. In 1962 Hollander married sociology graduate student Paul Hollander while studying painting at Boston University; they divorced four years later. Post-graduation she held a number of jobs, including working in a bakery, at a day care, and selling cold custard. She also held positions as an art instructor, a hat maker, a telemarketer for a bank, a sandwich maker, and a graphic designer (Hollander, *Tales* 244–45). She especially enjoyed working for nonprofits and artistic groups, and it was while doing graphic design at a feminist newsletter that Hollander finally found the passion that would lead to her long-term career. Hollander reveals, "Only when I started working for the *Spokeswoman,* a national feminist newsletter, as a designer and illustrator did I see that I could combine drawing, humor, and politics and I was hooked. . . . I had found my career at forty" (*Tales* 246). Hollander brought her politics and life experience to her art while publishing small cartoons and doodles for the *Spokeswoman* in the late 1970s. Her first strip for the paper featured a woman cleverly distracting her male dining companion while swiping his much larger piece of pie in a three-panel, wordless cartoon (see figure 4.1). Her style at the time was sturdy and straightforward, with the figures solidly outlined and facing directly toward the reader. This early endeavor is a simple cartoon, and far less complicated than her later work. Of this neophyte effort Hollander suggests, "I thought I could go on forever doing cartoons without words" (*Whole Enchilada* 8), a far cry from her later, extremely text-heavy work.

These early *Spokeswoman* cartoons were collected in her first book, *I'm Training to Be Tall and Blonde,* published in 1979 by St. Martin's Press. In the article "Hokinson and Hollander: Female Cartoonists and American Culture," Patricia Alley argues that this book "satirizes female stereotypes on television, from ethnic groups, and as housewives. Sylvia infrequently appears in this volume. The focus is on male-female relationships and women in and out of history. Hollander keeps apprised of current issues in her frames" (12). However, later in the chronology of the strip, Alley argues, "In the 1980s, the feminist issues are not quite so prominent as in the late 1970s, but the 1980s preoccupation with economics appears often" (12). Thus, as the strip evolved and moved from the smaller, focused audience of the *Spokeswoman* to the larger, broader, syndicated audience, the strip also widened its perspective, incorporating feminist concerns along with more comprehensive topics such as the economy and the environment.

[handwritten margin note: independent to syndicated changed scope/focus]

The character of Sylvia first appeared in the late 1970s, and, according to Hollander, in these initial sketches she was "not yet named, her politics were a little shaky, her profile undeveloped, but with backless mules and cigarette firmly in place" (Hollander, *Whole Enchilada* 9). As Alley notes, the eventual main character appears from time to time in these early endeavors, but the figure became more central over time, particularly after the strip entered syndication in 1981, first through Field Enterprises and later by Hollander herself. The focus and structure of the strips collected in *I'm Training To Be Tall and Blonde* and her second book, *Ma, Can I Be a Feminist and Still Like Men?: Lyrics from Life,* published in 1980 and featuring more *Spokeswoman* cartoons, differ from her later work, as evidenced in a comparison of these two initial books with the next anthology that brought together her syndicated work from the daily newspaper, *That Woman Must Be on Drugs: A Sylvia Collection,* published in 1981. The initial strips focused primarily on sexism and gender stereotypes, as befitting the context of publication, and lack the organizing principal character, to whom the reader can relate to or revile, as the case may be. In the first few years, the art was rougher (in a strip already known for a rough style) and less consistent. For the most part, the images from the first two collections do not have the strict and easily recognizable comic strip structure of panels found in a syndicated newspaper, but are more flowing, free-form doodles—

loose in composition but circling firmly around gender stereotypes and sexism.

However, over the long course of the strip, from the early beginnings as collected in *I'm Training To Be Tall and Blonde* through over sixteen anthologies, including *The Whole Enchilada: A Spicy Collection of Sylvia's Best* (1986), and *The Sylvia Chronicles: 30 Years of Graphic Misbehavior from Reagan to Obama* (2010), *Sylvia* evolved and changed, but her commitment to skewering politicians and championing the underdog never wavered. Given the focus on the Women's Liberation movement as reflected in popular culture, the bulk of analysis for this particular chapter rests on the years from 1978 to the early 1980s, as the strip developed from the loose, unformed sketches created for the already-feminist audience of the *Spokeswoman* to the more structured strip that aimed to convert a wider audience to her way of thinking.

After nationwide syndication, *Sylvia* regularly featured the eponymous character along with her daughter, Rita, and a cast of rotating characters, including Harry, a bar owner and Sylvia's ex, her best friend Beth-Ann, Gerniff the alien, and others, including, "The Woman Who Lies in Her Journal," the Devil, and the fortune teller Grunella. Yet even as other characters would come and go, they seem to orbit around the solid, steadying presence of Sylvia—who stolidly resisted change, never aging or adapting to the world around her. Hollander explains, "I created Sylvia to say what I couldn't. . . . She comments on everything. She says the things I can't or, in fact, don't even want to say" (*Sylvia Chronicles* 6). The strip is unapologetically feminist and political, her style raw, and the panels cluttered. The strip varies from day to day, sometimes featuring one long, narrow panel, while on other days the strip is divided into two or three smaller panels. But the artistic aesthetic remains constant; the art features dark lines scratched in a raw, rough style, the backgrounds encumbered with debris. In contrast, the lettering is, for the most part, straightforward and legible, with a quirky combination of bold capital and lowercase letters, as if to emphasize the import of the text, while allowing the reader to draw his or her own inferences aside from any overly ornate or expressive script. Hollander rarely uses speech balloons to indicate dialogue from her characters, preferring free-floating text with a quick line drawn to indicate the speaker, creating unfettered and unenclosed speech, implying that the char-

FIGURE 4.2. Nicole Hollander. "A Political Questionnaire." Comic Strip originally published September 7, 1988. Republished in *Sylvia Chronicles*, p. 15. *The Sylvia Chronicles: 30 Years of Graphic Misbehavior from Reagan to Obama.* New York: New Press, 2010.

acter's words, and their power, cannot be contained or corralled, but rather soar over the scene, suspended in mid-air. However, balloons usually encase the frequent speech emanating from televisions, radios, as well as Sylvia's typewriter, indicating that these mediated speech acts are shaped and contained within the balloon, and thus are interpreted and enclosed within the diegesis, insinuating that this speech is tightly regulated and constrained (see figure 4.2).

Not only does Hollander use her words to persuade, but her characters also work to combat dominant narratives. The figures in *Sylvia* do not conform to stereotypical beauty standards and have something of a punk, DIY feel. Sylvia is not predictably cute, nor is she conventionally attractive. Hollander explains:

> I should confess that I only drew Sylvia once, saw that it was good, and knew I'd never be able to get that nose exactly right again. Thanks to the invention of photocopiers and full-sheet removable Avery labels, I never had to draw her again. The nose was born. And with that nose came attitude and permission for my character to give her opinion on everything. (*Sylvia Chronicles* 8)

Patricia Alley reflects that Sylvia is not "glamorous," but rather "she has perfect logic, the guts to say anything, and, as a result, evokes one laugh after another" (129). While pontificating on numerous subjects, Sylvia, in all her glory (and often in her bathtub), offered pointed satire on the politics of the day from the early 1980s until 2012. And the strip, surprisingly, did so while embedded among other, blander syndicated comic strips. A closer look at the biting and prescient wit of the strip reveals an especially thoughtful use of rhetoric, and in

argument

particular Menippean satire, to make a case for a variety of liberal positions.

Menippean Satire and the Mainstream Comics Page

Sylvia falls into a long tradition of political satire, from the gentle ribbing of the Roman poet Horace (c. 30 BCE), to the more pointed barbs of the Roman poet Juvenal (second century AD), to the satires of the Roman cynic Mennipus. This analysis looks to these predecessors to better understand Hollander's methods, with the understanding that, as Ruben Quintero argues, "we are better able to circumscribe than define satire, though we continue to try" (6). It is intriguing to note at the onset of this exploration of rhetoric, and more specifically the satirical tradition, that comics scholarship has rarely examined the connection between satire and comics. In fact, despite the satirical bent of many comic strips, and the long tradition of editorial cartoons, there are very few critical works examining how satire plays out in comic strips, with notable exceptions being Kerry Soper's work on *Doonesbury* (2008) and *Pogo* (2012), as well as works by Berger (1994), Hendley (1983), and Goldstein (1992). It thus behooves the comics scholar interested in satire to turn to rhetorical theory for guidance.

rhetoric
satire
comics

inserts self; gaps

Satire has, according to Patricia Meyer Spacks, "a public function, and its public orientation remains" (363) The satirist observes the failings of society, and brings them into focus for an audience, and does so with the intent to persuade. However, for all of their civic mindedness, satirists maintain a rather sullied reputation. Jackie Stallcup posits that "from the perspective of many adults, satire is a rough-and-tumble, ill-bred form that strips away illusions, attacks hapless targets, and flays the world open to reveal humanity in all of its ugly glory" (172). In *The Art of Satire,* David Worcester contends, "Many persons instinctively shrink from satire as they might from a scorpion" (38), thus summarizing the feelings of numerous readers. Despite this "rough-and-tumble" status, a status, I might add, shared by cartoonists who are also generally disdained by various members of the public, scholars regularly posit that satirists speak out for what the creator believes to be the public good. Ruben Quintero claims:

rhetoric of satire

A true satirist must be a true believer, a practicing humanitarian, responsible even in his or her subjective indulgence or personal indignation. . . . Satire also moves heart and mind through building tension and provoking conflict, but, unlike tragedy and comedy, stops short of any reconciliation with its subject. And as the prism does to light, it leaves its subject refracted and disharmonized. Satire remains militantly rhetorical and hortatory. (3)

The windows provided by the panels of a comic strip thus act like the facets of the prism, splitting a subject into smaller pieces, illuminating each frame and shining light in new directions. Not only do political cartoons and comic strips break apart the subject, they also invite the reader to participate in the process of making meaning. Satire is dialogic by nature, engaging in a conversation between creator and audience, encouraging a connection and an eventual action, and this special reciprocal relationship is an enduring one, for, from Horace to Hollander, the satirist pokes fun at "the haves" and fights for the "have nots." Laura Egendorf clarifies, "Yet even as the context shifts and the specific targets change, the purpose of satire—to expose flaws, cruelty, and hypocrisy—has remained the same throughout history" (8). In order to enter into this exchange, Matthew Hodgart indicates that "the political satirist in particular must try to reach a wide public if he is to achieve his ends, and any popular medium will serve his purpose" (163). Thus, the medium of the comic strip as housed in the newspaper has been uniquely positioned to reach a wide, and public audience, and the newspaper has long been the site for significant satire.

In fact, satire has a special link with comic strips and the particular form of Menippean satire has enjoyed an extensive and varied tradition, having recently come into vogue among academics. Ruben Quintero, for his part, comments, "Even though a universal definition of Menippean satire may be a will-o-the-wisp . . . scholars continue to enlighten us about this especially complex art form" (7). In his comprehensive book on Menippean Satire, *Grotesque Anatomies: Menippean Satire Since the Renaissance,* David Musgrave maintains, "Since the proselytizing work of both Northrop Frye and Mikhail Bakhtin in the second half of this century, . . . there has been a revival of interest in the genre, although the quality of work produced on the subject has varied widely" (33). Indeed, much of the work of the scholars writing about Menippean satire supports a particular theoretical agenda, with Frye conflating Menippean satire with "anatomy" and Bakhtin focusing on the "carnivalesque" aspects of the form. Musgrave argues, "There is no Menippean satire which is quintessentially Menippean: there is no paradigmatic Menippean satire and there is no such thing as a 'pure' Menippean satire. A form which is based on disjunction and impurity can have no final, refined form" (67–68). Menippean satire, then, has a slippery history and seems to shift meaning depending on the philosopher or critic and his or her intentions and argument.

Menippean satire's elusive nature is perhaps no surprise, considering the ambiguity of its presumed creator, Menippus, a Cynic philosopher working around 250 BCE.[1] The writings of Menippus are lost, further complicating attribution, with Bakhtin arguing that "Mennipean satires were written by Aristotle's contemporary Heraclides Ponticus, Antisthenes, a pupil of Socrates, and Bion Borysthenes" (qtd. in Musgrave 1–2). While it is easy, according to Musgrave, to get "bogged down" trying to verify the author and originator of Menippean satire, Bakhtin seems to believe that "a genre of sorts existed from multiple points of origin whose most influential avatar was Mennipus" (Musgrave 2). The now-lost works of Mennipus did seem to inspire followers, particularly the Roman poet and philosopher Marcus Terentius Varro, who wrote prolifically in the style of Mennipus, to the point that some conflate Mennipean and Varronian satire. Mennipus also features as a character in Lucian's "Dialogues with the Dead," and through Varro's work, Mennipus became a curious sort of philosophical celebrity, even though his actual writings remain lost.

The man and the tradition he inspired have a mysterious, somewhat comical bent, for the creator can be remade and refashioned to suit the follower. Thus, as has been indicated by others, there is no single, pure, unassailable definition, but rather a malleable construct which, with a nod to history and an understanding of ambi-

---

1. For an in-depth consideration of the history of Mennipus and Mennipean satire, see Northrop Frye, *Anatomy of Criticism* (Princeton: Princeton UP, 1957), Howard Weinbrot's *Menippean Satire Reconsidered: From Antiquity to the Eighteenth Century* (Baltimore: John Hopkins UP, 2005), David Musgrave's *Grotesque Anatomies: Menippean Satire Since the Renaissance* (Newcastle on Tyne: Cambridge Scholars Press, 2014), and Bakhtin's *Problems of Dostoevski's Poetics* (Minneapolis: U of Minneapolis P, 1984).

positionality

guity, can be defined by the critic. Therefore, while I acknowledge the long tradition and varied definitions of Menippean satire, I find myself persuaded by David Musgrave's careful historical research and thorough reading of the literature, and my interpretation relies primarily on his work to explicate the form for contemporary texts. In Musgrave's informed and thoughtful exploration, which traces the history and genealogy of Menippean satire, he indicates that a few key features of the genre stand out throughout time and in reference to various examples attributed to Menippean satire. Musgrave argues for the following qualities "structural heterogeneity," "stylistic heterogeneity," "thematic heterogeneity," "grotesque iconography," "extreme eccentricity," "encyclopedism," "catachresis," and "digression" (Musgrave 57). While these qualities have been primarily linked to the Menippean satire found in narrative political commentary, and later, novels, they are also very much in evidence in politically focused cartoons, such as *Sylvia*. Furthermore, examining *Sylvia* through the lens of Menippean satire brings her shrewd use of rhetorical strategy into sharper focus, illuminating the methods by which the strip makes an argument for a different world view, and against dominant narratives that serve to stereotype and oppress.

Connection to Sylvia

Satire and *Sylvia*

As a comic strip, *Sylvia* is clearly a hybrid form and represents a mixing of genres—the characteristic of structural heterogeneity as realized in Menippean satire. While in text-based literature this pastiche of structural elements might include snippets of poetry or verse alongside prose, in comics this fusion is inherent in the juxtaposition of text and image, for the commingling of word and picture is one of the hallmarks of comics.[2] Furthermore, the context of the syndicated comic strip, as it appears within the daily newspaper, surrounded by a curious mélange of fact-based journalism and hyperbolic advertisements as well as other comic strips of wildly varying styles and subjects, only emphasizes the curious amalgamation of forms. And while satire in general and Menippean satire in particular is primarily attached to the novel, the serial nature of the comic strip, entering

structural heterogeneity

---

2. Obviously silent or wordless comics do exist, but I refer to the majority of comics art, which features both text and image.

into the lives and homes of readers on a daily basis, is arguably a superior representation of the form, for it is peripatetic and disjointed by the interruption of each daily installment, each strip realized in short, sharp bursts of connection. Yet a comic strip is also recursive and quotidian, greeting the audience on a daily basis with a comforting reunion with familiar characters. The regular newspaper reader can recognize the style of individual strips and distinct characters quickly; with time and habitual study, the reader will instinctively know where to look on the page each day to find his or her favorite strips. And even on the micro level, the shape that *Sylvia* the strip demonstrates is a variety of panel formats on a daily basis, sometimes with one, two, or three or more panels, eschewing a standardized four-panel layout.

Sylvia further exhibits stylistic heterogeneity in the language of the narrative text, with a peculiar mix of dialects, including the alien tongue of Gerniff, as well as the stilted jargon frequently emanating from televisions and radios, juxtaposed with the casual vernacular of Sylvia and friends. The audience must negotiate a sophisticated multi-dialectalism to make meaning from the various linguistic registers in order to comprehend each strip. Artistically, although the very first strips differ slightly in style, after 1980 Hollander's aesthetic does not vary much over many years or between days; as Hollander reported, Sylvia's profile changes very little, as if copied from panel to panel and from day to day, with only minor embellishments marking the passing of the time. Her characters remain static, both in style and, for that matter, within the panels; they rarely move, but rather remain suspended in bathtubs or in armchairs. Sylvia exhibits very little character movement; this is not a strip of pratfalls and slapstick physical humor. Yet this rough, repetitive, and constant artistic style contrasts with an extremely literate and literary text-based narrative as her characters discuss philosophy, history, and current events with evident erudition, further emphasizing the curious amalgamation of high and low cultures in style and structure.

While the art remains static, thematically *Sylvia* roams widely, and in doing so tackles a wide range of subjects, veering from intellectual to unrefined in the space of a panel. While gender stereotypes are a frequent subject (particularly in the *Spokeswoman* entries), she doesn't hesitate to discuss douches and macro-economics and the danger of chipped cups along with healthcare reform and LGBTQ+ rights. These drastic contrasts stress the absurdity of the political situations, bringing the news to another level and, in fact, into bathrooms and bars, just as Sylvia's television becomes the voice of the media piped into the domestic, enclosed spaces of the strip. *Sylvia*, by and large, takes places in these intimate domestic spaces—the kitchens, bathrooms, and living rooms of women. And though the characters occasionally meet at the neighborhood bar (which acts as an *agora* in which Sylvia can interact with outsiders and antagonists), the strip's most frequent setting depicts Sylvia in a domestic space, such as soaking in a tub in the bathroom or resting in a lounge chair in the living room, surrounded by the clutter of familial life—potted plants, mugs, and food—while a television or radio blares out snippets from the news. Inevitably, Sylvia makes a biting, witty comeback in response to the outside influence, rendering the world outside and the news of the day absurd and illogical, while she appears all-wise and all-knowing. And once again, although this setup is a recurring one, the topics addressed fluctuate widely, and *Sylvia* covers a great deal of territory.

In addressing these various themes, *Sylvia* presents additional traits of Menippean satire, such as numerous digressions as well as displays of encyclopedism. Certainly, a long-running syndicated comic strip would have to vary its content over many days and years, but *Sylvia* is particularly itinerant. While providing a mirror of the news cycle, mocking key political figures and movements, the strip wanders frequently, spending a day lamenting an onslaught of killer bees or showcasing the superiority of cats before lambasting a political figure. There is no continuing plotline or growth nor is there any character development to speak of. A reader does not need to be familiar with the history or the strip in order to appreciate it. Rather, the reader would be best served by a knowledge of current events and political theory. Although the strip displays a meandering focus at best, highlighting its nomadic perspective, it does remain rooted within the home. This is not a strip about work or careers or adventures in foreign lands. That is not to say that the strip is not highly intelligent, for the daily strips repeatedly invoke encyclopedism, showcasing a didactic knowledge in the form of informational snippets as well as comical checklists and quizzes that draw attention to the absurdity of the news and to the idea that complex social ills can be captured in bulleted lists and taglines (see figure 4.3).

Hollander uses lists and fill-in-the blanks to display information and to emphasize the dialogic nature of the strip, which encourages

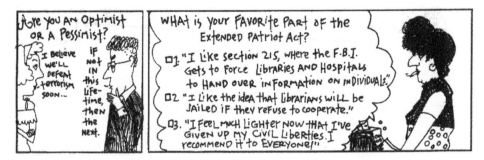

FIGURE 4.3. Nicole Hollander. "Are You an Optimist?" Originally published May 27, 2004. Reprinted in *The Sylvia Chronicles*, p. 94.

FIGURE 4.4. Nicole Hollander. "The Sylvia School." Comic Strip originally published February 18, 1983. Republished in *The Sylvia Chronicles*, p. 24.

the audience to participate in the making of meaning. Hollander also playfully employs catachresis, intentionally misusing words and phrases for comedic effect, as in figure 4.4.

This circuitous style features a rotating cast of characters with Sylvia positioned steadfastly in the center, and the alternating narrators, who directly address the reader, share an eccentric and sometimes extreme point of view, another mark of Menippean satire. As Musgrave contends, "eccentricity, foolishness, extreme behavior, or abnormal mental states are frequent in the narrator and/or characters" (23), or, as Miranda Gill explicates, a Menippean figure "hovers between genius and madness, wisdom and foolishness" (32). Sylvia, flouting convention and spouting hyperbole, can certainly be said to exemplify an eccentric character, yet when her statements are juxtaposed with the absurdity of the news of the day, her position is less clear—is she melodramatic or reasonable? This uncertainty

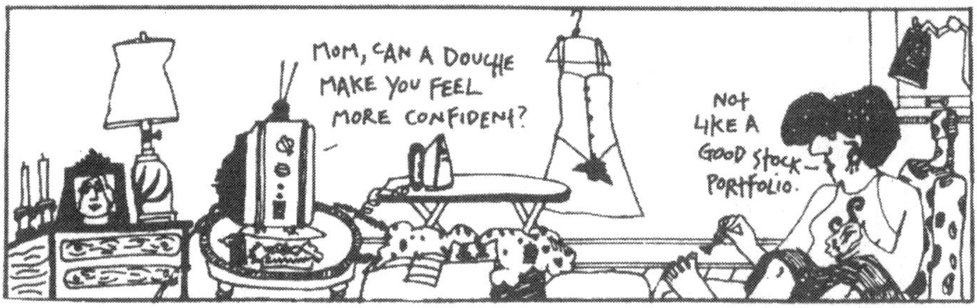

FIGURE 4.5. Nicole Hollander. "Sylvia Gets Offensive." Comic Strip originally published September 11, 1984. Republished in *The Sylvia Chronicles*, p. 37.

carries over into the recurring characters, including "The Woman Who Lies in Her Journal," "The Woman Who Does Everything Better Than You," "The Fashion Cop," and the "Super Cop," who all sound ridiculous via introduction, but frequently dispense sound advice, thus embodying the common trope of the "wise fool" frequently found in satire.

Not only does *Sylvia* revel in the unusual point of view, it also proudly displays a grotesqueness of iconography in theme and art, sometimes overtly, such as when the Devil takes center stage, and sometimes more subtly, as represented by the large nose and rumpled figure of Sylvia, or, at times, in the concentration on bodily functions as points of discussion. The strip did not hesitate to mention hemorrhoids, douches, and sigmoidoscopies, a fact which bemused the creator and dismayed some audiences. In *The Sylvia Chronicles*, Hollander reprinted a cartoon that suggested that a "good stock portfolio" would make a woman "feel more confident" than a douche (as advocated by a commercial blaring from the television), and which some readers found offensive, in addition to a letter to the editor that originally appeared in the newspaper, *Prince George's Journal* (see figure 4.5). The letter decried the strip as "offensive and quite unnecessary," wondering "what has happened to honest modesty?" (*The Sylvia Chronicles* 37).

For her part, Hollander felt the ugliness of the exchange resided in the idea "that there might be something offensive about women's bodies, something that can be made right with a scented over-the-counter product" (*Sylvia Chronicles* 36). While one might argue what, exactly, was grotesque in that particular strip—the mention of a product designed to clean a female's genital area or the idea that such an invention was actually necessary, Hollander was certainly intentional in her position, and as Harry Thurston Peck has argued, "if the Menippean satire was anything at all, it was scrappy, eccentric, and purposely grotesque" (90). Of course, the aforementioned Devil represents the most obvious example of the grotesque, operating as the epitome of divinity debased, yet in *Sylvia* the Devil pops in from time to time with the nonchalance of an annoying neighbor, making questionable bargains for souls but once again seeming to be more of a wise fool trope than a dangerous threat—the more dangerous characters appearing to be the politicians and/or the government. *Sylvia*'s Devil points out the monstrousness of human behavior, acting as a foil for the truly evil—the humans themselves.

While these attributes attest that *Sylvia* bears many qualities of Menippean satire, it is important to remember that it is not a "precise form" (Musgrave 23), and scholars still debate its definition. Still, most critics agree on the primary feature being a "disjunctional nature" along with, according to David Musgrave, "a medley . . . concerned with the absurd, irrational and the contradictory" (23). Through the embrace of the absurd, a lampooning of the contradictory, the delightful pastiche of themes, and the incorporation of the grotesque, *Sylvia* surprises and persuades readers through highly sophisticated rhetorical techniques, urging the audience to view the news of the day through another, more focused lens. Yet, to what end does *Sylvia* employ the practices of Menippean satire? The next section takes an in-depth look at several representative strips to examine *Sylvia*'s powerful, feminist argument and her skillful use of rhetoric.

At Work: *Sylvia*'s Argument

As a stalwart feminist, Hollander used her strip to influence public opinion, lambasting gender stereotypes and sexism in the public forum of the newspapers across the country, and, even more intimately, in reader's homes. Through techniques of Menippean satire

FIGURE 4.6. Nicole Hollander. "Good Old Days." Reprinted from *That Woman Must Be On Drugs*. New York: St. Martin's Press, 1981.

radical feminism

she argues for a more radical strain of feminism, one which seeks to upend the system. While the incipient version of the Women's Liberation movement of the 1960s sought to fight for equality within the system, Christine Stansell argues that in later years the movement fractured into many pieces, with radical feminism pushing for another system altogether: "Radical feminism was searing, melodramatic, and rambunctious. Its proposals to liberate women captured and transformed a national audience, a public alternately appalled and enthralled, scandalized and persuaded" (222). And *Sylvia* playfully advocates for overturning the patriarchy, as she does in this strip from the 1980s (see figure 4.6), which reminds readers that, for women, there were no "good old days."

In the three-panel strip, a serious man in a suit sits in profile at a table clutching a cup. His face is dour and his mouth is closed, although stiff, thick capital letters emanate, stating, "Days would go by when the only words from my father were: 'Pass the gravy.' When he wasn't at work or bowling, he was taking a nap. Did anyone expect him to be sensitive?" In the next, smaller panel the man has raised his arm, middle figure pointing out aggressively in a gesture that bisects the panel and his speech. His mouth is slightly parted now, as if shouting, "No! He brought home his paycheck on Friday, and we respected him. He was like a king in that house." "I hate it." His final words linger, alone and unfettered in the final panel, the largest one, which depicts the rest of the table, including an ash tray, some popcorn, a birdcage housing two birds, a class of wine, and, at the far end, Sylvia, smoking a cigarette and holding a pen to paper. She wears an outrageous, feathered hat, and a patterned dress with beaded necklace. Sylvia responds, "Sid, women are lucky. We don't have any 'good old days' to long for." In this example, the man thus appears ridiculous and disgusting. He is alone, antagonistic, and hopelessly old-fashioned, while Sylvia, the more intelligent figure, enjoys the food and luxuries, all positioned in her panel. She can smoke and drink and enjoy the company of the birds. She has no need for Sid, and humorously points out that women have nothing of the past to hold on to or to cherish. The structure of the panels further underscores the contrast between the figures, with the man trying, unsuccessfully, to dominate. As Patricia Alley notes, "Sylvia deviates decidedly from the cartoons showing male dominance. Sylvia is always dominant, as are the other women in Hollander's cartoons" (131). In this encounter Sylvia, though undeniably and happily eccentric, is the expert with the witty comeback, the wise encyclopedist, while the man is grotesque and foolish.

Feminist M. Satire

Hollander deftly deploys comical wordplay characteristic of much Menippean satire in another example, which continues this acerbic belittling of men who denounce equal rights for women (see figure 4.7), yet again featuring an overbearing man expounding while sitting at a table. This time the man, also drawn in profile, sits at what appears to be a bar, holding a drink in a dainty glass. His drink looks to have a cherry, a lemon, and a striped straw—a frivolous cocktail, to be sure, contrasted with his heavy, masculine appearance. He has square glasses and thick features—dark hair and muttonchop sideburns, a full moustache, and bushy eyebrows. His sweater and patterned collar suggest a man concerned with appearance, and in the first panel he sits on a stool, alone at the bar with unenclosed dialogue, arguing, "Equal rights for women is unnatural." The second

FIGURE 4.7. Nicole Hollander. "Equal Rights for Women is Unnatural." Reprinted from *That Woman Must be On Drugs*. New York: St. Martin's Press, 1981.

panel is slightly larger, and as in figure 4.5, this man also raises his arm to point at Sylvia as he declares, "What is natural"—the final panel, as with the other example, is the largest one, and depicts Sylvia across a long countertop while the man's speech concludes—"is men wanting to protect women." To which Sylvia responds, "From earning too much money." Sylvia wears a patterned dress and fabulous hat and continues to smoke. This time her purse and ashtray, as well as the newspaper she has been reading, separates them, providing a bulwark against his stupidity. Sylvia is anchored by the news, her luxuries, and her possessions, coolly denouncing this common trope of male protectors, with Sylvia indicating that this condescend-

rhetoric
&
feminism

ing attitude of the male protector as natural and equality as unnatural is a joke. In finishing the man's sentence, Sylvia uses the rhetorical device of *anacoluthon,* which interrupts a sequence and serves to emphasize the logic of the second half of the statement. Feminism is seen as the logical conclusion, and thus this radical notion appears as common sense, whereas the old trope is worthy of ridicule.

However, while *Sylvia* is, at times, representative of radical feminism, it also turns mother/daughter relationships upside down, suggesting a disruptive, heterogenous perspective that doesn't confirm to any one, singular viewpoint. As previously mentioned, in the 1970s the older form of feminism associated with the National Organization for Women came to be seen as stodgy, and the more radical wing embraced a more extreme point of view, a point of view often reflected in *Sylvia*. However, this more radical form also took a dim view of procreation in general and mothers more specifically. Christine Stansell maintains that, for radical feminists, "mothers, too, came in for disdain, for their capitulation to a soul-crushing system, their timidity before male power, their compulsion to conscript their daughters into the same circumstances that crippled them. This was a politics with the habit of lashing out at intimates rather than august authority" (221), and that "women's liberation perpetuated daughters in revolt, not mothers in thrall" (262). Yet Sylvia dismantles this conceit, for in this representative example from the early 1980s, the mother Sylvia articulates the more radical perspective, counseling her somewhat clueless daughter Rita (see figure 4.8).

In the three-panel strip Rita sits across the table, chatting with her mother. Rita wears a striped tank-top and has an elaborate hairstyle while Sylvia sports a housedress and kerchief. A cake sits between them, diminishing in each panel (as if by magic, the eating takes place out of the frame) until only one slice remains. In the first panel Rita expressed her intent, "Ma, I'm thinking of marrying Dennis soon." To which Sylvia responds, "I'm sorry to hear that." The second panel is almost a duplicate of the first, apart from the diminishing cake and Rita's raised hand. "Why?" wonders Rita, to which Sylvia responds, "Because I always dreamed of you getting married in white." The final panel Sylvia is depicted alone as she delivers her parting words, "White hair." Sylvia, the safe, wise woman, employs humorous wordplay and disrupts the expected convention of a woman wearing white at a wedding, arguing that her daughter

Sylvia disrupts (feminist) stereotypes of the mother

FIGURE 4.8. Nicole Hollander. "Getting Married." Reprinted from *That Woman Must be On Drugs.* New York: St. Martin's Press, 1981.

FIGURE 4.9. Nicole Hollander. "Culture Alone." Originally published July 13, 1983. Reprinted in *The Sylvia Chronicles,* p. 26.

shouldn't get married as a young woman, but wait until she is much, much older. Sylvia, pictured alone in the final panel, is smiling, content to have the cake all to herself. Once again Sylvia is the eccentric but wise sage, offering wit and wisdom, and disordering not only the dominant narrative of the pure, young virgin wedding in white but also the notion that mothers uphold the conventions of marriage and long-held notions of female roles.

With that said, stereotypes of male and female behavior remain in Sylvia, as does what critics have called, "male-bashing." Patricia Alley observes that in the strip females "worry about their weight. They are over forty. They diet and hate it, or they fight the notion that they should diet. Their clothes are not stylish, and they are never pretentious. They struggle with children and with men who are the straight characters" (124). In *Sylvia* women obsess over shoes and appearances, while men are shown as universally loving sports, stereotypes that essentialize gendered behavior. And, Hollander herself admits to a reverse sexism at times, as in some strips that make a case that women are superior to men (see figure 4.9). *stereotypes*

& -reverse sexism"

→limits of comic

In this single panel example Sylvia sits in her extremely cluttered living room in a chair facing toward the reader (something she rarely does) while reading *Crime and Punishment.* She is surrounded by domestic detritus, including a clock, numerous jam jars, telephone, mirror, chandelier, and a number of cactus plants. The television, on the far-left side of the panel, sits on top of the oven, indicating that this domestic tool is never used. The face of a man is barely visible on the television screen, and a small dash indicates his speech: "Culture alone doesn't make us who we are, the brain is differently wired in men and women." To which Sylvia responds, "In men the wires are loose," clearly indicating men as faulty, while she stands as the voice of reason and erudition, as evidenced by her lofty reading material. This cartoon makes it clear that women are superior, something Hollander refuses to apologize for, as she indicates in the marginal comments of the anthology: "I got a letter from a reader who was outraged about this cartoon. He chided me: two wrongs don't make a right. Actually, I think they do. I think men have to suck it up for a couple of years until sexism is really dead, not just nodding off" (*Sylvia Chronicles* 26). For her part, Sylvia not only dismantles the status quo, she reverses it entirely, placing women at the top of the hierarchy.

Sylvia overturns convention and hints at the future in the form of intersectional feminism, expanding the focus to include the LGBTQ+ community as well as people of color. Hollander frequently depicts two friends discussing the news of the day, one Black and one White (see figure 4.10.) In this example from 2001, the friends discuss Colin Powell, the newly instated Secretary of State, as a token political gesture that "looks good," but does little to actually improve conditions for Black Americans. In the side notes, Hollander reflects, "Two women chat over dessert at a café; you can tell they are old friends. One is black, one is white. Of course, these relationships exist, but I don't see much of them in real life, so I make it happen in the strip" (*The Sylvia Chronicles* 91). Thus, Hollander creates an aspirational panel in which friendships across ethnic groups are common. And in doing so she makes an argument for another vision of society in which women work together for empowerment. This is a powerful statement at a time when most comic strips did not represent people of color, nor did they show close friendships across races. Hollander also frequently championed gay and lesbian rights, skewering conservative viewpoints, and bringing LGBTQ+ rights to the forefront

FIGURE 4.10. Nicole Hollander. "Bad Girl Political Chats." Originally published February 7, 2001. Reprinted in *The Sylvia Chronicles,* p. 91.

of the strip, once again when these issues were rarely taken up in the mainstream.

Sylvia was fueled by hope and by rage, and worked to initiate change through a witty and powerful satire, and, rather shockingly, did so successfully within one of the most staid, conventional public forums: the daily newspaper. But Hollander had a powerful motivation. In a journal from January 1983, Hollander reflected that she

> talked to Paula (therapist) about anger. She says anger affects your work, your body. I say but my work isn't affected: of course not! My work is my anger. Sylvia expresses my anger, why would I shut off that wonderful, invigorating flow. That's why my work is always my salvation. I can truly lose my anger, lose my tight self. Not that I approach it easily, it's difficult to start it to charge into that mode, but then like my Vega, rusty and protesting I charge into high gear and soar! (*Hollander Archives,* NH 3 Folder 28)

For Hollander, her work reflected her anger about societal ills, but it also represented a world she wished to see. Jackie Stallcup argues, "Satire may be presented as a mode with reform at its heart—a didactic form that seeks to reveal folly and/or to make readers recognize and reject vice" (174). While Sylvia smokes like a chimney and doesn't necessarily seem inclined to urge readers to reject personal vices, she does invite the audience to recognize inequity and social ills. Through her fantastic, exaggerated figures she says what those in polite society feel they mustn't, sounding the alarm and inspiring a rueful chuckle. Yet the daily strip also roams and rambles into different arenas, relieving the pressure and allowing an opportunity to laugh at shared mundanities—the wisdom of cats and the fear of bees. According to Ruben Quintero, a "true satirist

ending argument

must be a true believer, a practicing humanitarian, responsible even in his or her subjective indulgence or personal indignation," and as a "true believer," Nicole Hollander, through the social contract of *Sylvia,* challenges the audience to act as responsible citizens, witnessing injustice and countering it with wit and wisdom, while soaring through the pages.

CHAPTER 5

"THE LESBIAN RULE" IN ALISON BECHDEL'S *DYKES TO WATCH OUT FOR*

> Finitude cannot measure what cannot be confined, and limitations of consistency are to be construed not as a rigid regulus but as a Lesbian rule.
>
> —J. R. Lucas, "The Lesbian Rule"

N THE "Cartoonist's Introduction" to *The Essential Dykes to Watch Out For,* a harried avatar of Alison Bechdel reflects on the origins of her long-running, cult favorite comic strip as she navigates the "archives" of the strip, a cavernous room filled with enormous stacks of file cabinets. As Bechdel's avatar rifles through the papers, rummaging through VHS tapes and boxes of slides marked "Precambrian DTWOF," "Mesozoic DTWOF," "Cenozoic DTWOF," and "Big Bang DTWOF," she ruminates on her original goals for the strip: "I saw my cartoons as an antidote to the prevailing image of lesbians as warped, sick, humorless, and undesirable. Or supermodel-like Olympic pentathletes, objective fodder for the male gaze. By drawing everyday lives of women like me, I hoped to make lesbians more visible not just to ourselves but to everyone" (xv). While Bechdel initially felt that lesbians were "essentially . . . well . . . more highly evolved" (xv), her plan to present their "essential" superiority was ultimately doomed, for, "inducing the general from the particular doesn't really hold water. Let alone millions of lesbians. My tidy schema went all to hell in the nineties. Lesbians could be reactionary provocateurs. And colonels. Arch conservatives and Neocons could be gay. Oh, and apparently no one was essentially anything" (*Essential* xvi). Thus, as the strip evolved over time, Bechdel came to a new understanding of the diversity of the "dykes" she portrayed and the culture of friends they developed. As Bechdel's character ruminates on the collapse of her plan during her prefatory monologue she becomes increasingly rattled, her eyebrows raised with concern.

In the final panels of the "Cartoonist's Introduction," Bechdel looks out at the reader from the depths of her archives; she is surrounded by files, books, photos, boxes, a record player, and a slide projector, as well as various insects pinned to the wall and a tabby cat clawing at her leg. From the clutter, the figure breaks the fourth wall and appears to toss a copy of *The Essential Dykes to Watch Out For* directly to the reader, asking, "Have I churned out episodes of this comic strip every two weeks for **decades** merely to prove that we're the same as everyone else? Here, you decide. Essentially the same? Or essentially different?" (xviii). The questions seem to haunt Bechdel's figure, who invites the reader to "make yourselves comfortable. Clearly, I need to rethink this thing" (xviii). She then turns away from the spectators, departing the archive in the final two panels, stating that she must go "back to the drawing board. Most disconcerting" (xviii). Ultimately, she is seen in silhouette at the darkened threshold of a doorway, ostensibly a passageway back to the world apart from her collection—from this collection—swearing comically, "&$@#." Bechdel thus invites the reader to draw his or her own conclusions on the experiment by reading the book, for she, playfully and begrudgingly, must "go back to the drawing board," continuing, explicitly, to draw this world she's created, even though she has come to no final determinations on the legacy of her long-running comic strip. In this meditation, Bechdel contemplates her goals and her (supposed) failings for the strip—to reveal the veracity of lesbian nature, a goal that eventually changed and evolved into something else—a study of a wider culture, a bringing together of many individual storylines into a larger, more telling narrative of human nature.

This process of bringing together disparate parts that don't quite fit into other contexts, and shaping them into a more cohesive, more powerful whole finds a somewhat surprising corollary in the architecture of Ancient Greece and in particular the isle of Lesbos, where the builders there mastered the art of bringing together irregular stones to form a consistent structure, developing a style that came to be known as "Lesbian masonry." In fact, the builders of Lesbos were so well known for working with these nonconforming building materials that they developed a special tool, a flexible ruler known as "the Lesbian rule," which, according to the *Oxford English Dictionary,* was made of lead and could be "bent to fit what was being measured." The Lesbian rule was so well known in Ancient Greece that Aristotle found the tool a useful analogy in his discussion of *epieikeia,* or equity, in his treatise *Nichomachean Ethics*:

Aristotle; epieikeia/ equity; justice; Lesbian rule

> When the law speaks universally, then, and a case arises on it which is not covered by the universal statement, then it is right, where the legislator fails us and has erred by oversimplicity, to correct the omission—to say what the legislator himself would have said had he been present, and would have put into his law if he had known. Hence the equitable is just, and better than one kind of justice—not better than absolute justice but better than the error that arises from the absoluteness of the statement. And this is the nature of the equitable, a correction of law where it is defective owing to its universality. In fact, this is the reason why all things are not determined by law, that about some things it is impossible to lay down a law, so that a decree is needed. For when the thing is indefinite the rule is also indefinite, like the leaden rule used in making the Lesbian moulding; the rule adapts itself to the shape of the stone and is not rigid, and so too the decree is adapted to the facts. It is plain, then, what the equitable is, and that it is just and better than one kind of justice. (Book V)

Aristotle thus urges his listeners to understand the importance of *epieikeia,* or equity, apart from universality, from a singular law or dominant narrative. True justice is not marked by absolutes, but by flexibility and by understanding individual experiences and lives. Equity must "adapt" to circumstances, as the Lesbian rule measures the reality of what exists, in all of its roughness and variability. In her article, "Universal Justice and *Epieikeia* in Aristotle," Annie Hewitt notes that for Aristotle, *epieikeia* was an important concept, a corrective for overarching laws that failed to account for individuals:

> As laws are written in 'universal terms' they offer inadequate guidance for those difficult cases that do not fall neatly under one general rule or another. While Aristotle is clear that written laws are essential to secure justice in a political community, he is quick to

recognize that alone they are insufficient to achieve this aim. Bridg-
ing the gap between legal principle and concrete situation is Aristotle's concept of *epieikeia*: that virtue which "corrects" the law where
it falls short. (115)

connection
to
Aristotle
& Lesbian
rule

argument

While Aristotle's words are far removed from Alison Bechdel's
archives, could her comic strip "bridge a gap" between an abstract,
dominant narrative of gender identities and the practicality of actual
lives? I would argue that, as the Women's Liberation movement
of the 1970s waned, Alison Bechdel's *Dykes to Watch Out For* represented a form of *epieikeia* as exemplified by the Lesbian rule, a flexible concept of equity that countered the essential, universal rule,
and a binary, heteronormative standard, molding to fit the context
of the actual world in all of its diversity. *DTWOF* offered an embodied performance that gently shaped readers' perceptions, disidenti-
fying with stereotypical heteronormative narratives of community
and rendering a perspective of intersectional feminism that embraced
individuals and their lived experiences. This chapter examines the
history of *DTWOF* before exploring the ways in which it enacts and
rebels against earlier conceptions of feminism, proposing tenets of a
more diverse and more representative intersectional feminism. The
focus then turns to queer theory, studying the ways in which *DTWOF*
presents figures that disidentify with stereotypes, before finally turning to the evolution of the strip over time, and the ways in which it
came to celebrate equity through a wider, more varied perspective.

In the Beginning: Origins of *Dykes to Watch Out For*

Given the success of her autobiographical comics as well as the popular play based on these works, Alison Bechdel's early years have
been chronicled and studied in great detail by a wide audience in
the popular press as well as in academic circles. However, given
the many intersections of her life and her work, it is worth briefly
recounting Bechdel's personal history. Alison Bechdel was born
on September 10, 1960, to Bruce and Helen Bechdel and spent her
childhood with two younger brothers in Beech Creek, Pennsylvania. Her father was an English teacher and also managed the family
mortuary. Bechdel focuses on her father's closeted sexuality and his
eventual suicide in the graphic memoir *Fun Home* (2006). Bechdel's

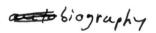 *biography*

mother worked as an English teacher, but was also a frustrated art- *trained*
ist and performer. Bechdel tells of her tense relationship with her *artist*
mother in the follow-up graphic memoir, *Are You My Mother?* (2012).
While attending Oberlin college, where she doubled majored in art
and art history, Bechdel came out to her parents in a letter. In 1980,
a few weeks after, Helen requested a divorce, and four months after
Alison's letter, her father committed suicide by stepping in front of
a truck. After graduation, Bechdel moved to New York, where she
struggled to find a suitable career; she applied to various art schools
but was rejected. According to the introduction to *The Indelible Alison
Bechdel,* she began *Dykes to Watch Out For* in 1982 as a single drawing labeled "Marianne, dissatisfied with the morning brew: *Dykes
to Watch Out For,* plate no. 27." An acquaintance recommended she
send her work to *WomanNews* newspaper, which began to publish
the strip regularly beginning with the July–August 1983 issue. After
a year, other outlets began running the strip. According to Robin
Bernstein, "Over the 1980s, *Dykes* grew into a multipanel, biweekly
strip," and "throughout the 1990s, *Dykes* developed a strong fan base:
Bechdel self-serialized *Dykes* in roughly seventy publications, and by
2008 the strip had been collected in thirteen volumes" (127). Bechdel
has named numerous influences whose inspiration can been seen in
Dykes, including R. Crumb, Harvey Kurtzman and *Mad* magazine,
and, in particular, Howard Cruse.

The first anthology, *Dykes to Watch Out For,* appeared in 1986, and
was quickly followed by several more collections, including *More
Dykes to Watch Out For* (1988), *New, Improved! Dykes to Watch Out For*
(1990), *Dykes to Watch Out For: The Sequel* (1992), and the most comprehensive collection, *The Essential Dykes to Watch Out For* (2008),
which collects most (but not all) of the strips. In addition to the physical anthologies, a smaller archive of the strips is available online at
Bechdel's online site: dykestowatchoutfor.com. However, despite
the reach and scope of *DTWOF*, it is her two graphic memoirs that
Bechdel is most known for, and the vast majority of scholarship on
Bechdel's work focuses on *Fun Home*.[1] Only a few academic pieces
have analyzed *Dykes to Watch Out For,* and those that do, focus almost
exclusively on the gay and lesbian themes as presented in the strip.

Kirtley inserts self; the "gap"

---

1. Numerous critical pieces have focused on the importance of *Fun Home,*
including its contributions to autobiography (Chute, Cvetkovich, El Refaie, Rohy),
its structure (Lemberg, Watson), and its literary influences (Freedman).

Judith Kegan Gardiner provides an exception to the trend, studying *DTWOF* in concert with *Fun Home* in her article, "Queering Genre: Alison Bechdel's *Fun Home: A Family Tragicomic* and *The Essential Dykes to Watch Out For.*" While the piece does study LGBTQ+ themes as presented in Bechdel's work, it makes the argument that *Dykes to Watch Out For* "is a coherent and accomplished work in its own right" (Gardiner 188) and, consequently, merits additional scholarly investigation. Adrienne Shaw delves into a number of lesbian-themed comics, including *Dykes to Watch Out For,* in the article "Women on Women: Lesbian Identity, Lesbian Community, and Lesbian Comics." Shaw observes that Bechdel confronts identity politics within the LGBTQ+ community in her work:

> In her strip Bechdel repeatedly addresses the difficulty of defining queer communities and identities. Race, disability, religion, transgendered characters, bisexuality, and so on are not presented as unproblematic, easily navigated issues. Although Bechdel generally presents an inclusive community, the strip acknowledges that identities and community boundaries may clash. (93)

Bechdel explained to Louise Gray that "one of my goals is to document the experience of my generation" (8). Judith Levine describes the creator "as something between a journalist, a historian, and a soap-opera writer" (55). The serialized soap opera found numerous fans, including noted comics creator and herstorian Trina Robbins, who argued, "Too bad about homophobia. Had there never been a Christian right wing, *Dykes to Watch Out For,* far funnier than *For Better or For Worse,* might have run as a nationally syndicated newspaper strip; or, more engaging than *Desperate Housewives,* it might even have been adapted as a TV soap opera" ("Desperate Housemates" 11). Louise Gray argued that *DTWOF* was "one of the most subtle comedies of modern manners to come along in the last two decades" (8). And, indeed, the strip earned a following of devoted readers who tracked the characters' follies and exploits devotedly over the many years of its publication.

DTWOF was published primarily in LGBTQ+ focused newspapers, with the business side being managed by Bechdel herself. While the audience was initially comprised primarily of readers of these alternative papers, with the anthologies, as well as the attention Bechdel garnered from the success of her graphic memoirs and the stage play based on *Fun Home,* the collections undoubtedly found a wider audience as fans from her other·celebrated works decided to track down her other creative endeavors. The strip was published every two weeks from 1983 (although it was not, at that time, in its later form, nor did it feature its recurring characters) until 2008. The strip is serial in nature, with the characters aging and growing, though not strictly in real time.

Over time the strip developed from short doodles and gags into a regularized ten- to twelve-panel layout. The first panel featured the title of the strip (often a literary joke or gag) in varying display lettering, which helped emphasize the feel and tone of the strip to follow. The panels were extremely regular and although not necessarily uniform in size, with some square-shaped, and others larger and more rectangular, the panels are very much little boxes at right angles, with floating space between each panel, rather than shared borders. The effect is something like photos pasted into an album—steady, consistent, and even. Bechdel does not experiment with bleeding images or unconventional panel shapes or an unusual layout. While some might consider the content progressive, the layout and panels are, quite literally, rather "square." The layout smoothly guides the reader through the decoding process.

Although the very first strips appear somewhat shaky and unfinished, as time goes on Bechdel comes into her own as an artist, developing a style that is both accessible and appealing.[2] In fact, flipping through the *Essential* anthology "flip-book style," it is as if a slightly blurry, unfocused picture gradually comes into very sharp focus. Bechdel's mature art features finely detailed backgrounds and careful, precise linework; the aesthetics are elegantly simple, clear, and unfettered, allowing for the audience to identify easily with the characters and the community. Bechdel is also known for her detailed renderings of characters, scenes, and set dressing, the numerous objects embedded within each panel producing a rich "underlife," a complimentary narrative thread. Bechdel explained to Lynn Emmert:

> I don't, strictly speaking, do thumbnails. I write the strip in Illus
> trator, on my computer, so I can map it all out in terms of the pan
> els and the speech balloons, and I have an idea of how the action

2. This evolution in style is especially apparent when reading *The Essential Dykes to Watch Out For* compilation, which presents most of the strips from the beginning until Bechdel retired the strip in 2008.

is going to break down. I might do a little bit of rough sketching if I'm having trouble visualizing something. But I don't really do any sketching until I've got it pretty much written. Then I begin my complicated, anal, many-layered process of sketching and revising and revising and revising. You know, maybe I *should* do more drawing earlier in the process. Because I keep writing myself into these incredibly complex panels where I have to draw six characters all interacting in a particular way against a complicated backdrop, doing activities that entail a huge amount of visual research. (44)

Adding to her workload, Bechdel doesn't use assistants to draw her strip. When asked about receiving help with her work, she replied, "No. I don't know how people do that. I'm strictly an *auteur*" (Emmert 45). *Dykes* is drawn in black-and-white pen, with cross-hatching that provides shading and depth. Bechdel explained to Lynn Emmert that black and white is her preference, and that *Fun Home*'s color wash technique was a decided departure for her:

Noooo, I hate color. Actually, I sort of balked at the notion of tinting that wash layer at first, because like my dad was a huge color freak, and he really inhibited and intimidated me about color. That was his turf. I always hated painting for that reason. There are too many variables. I think in a way that's why I became a cartoonist, because I didn't have to worry about all that shit, just soothing, simple black and white. (48)

The language of the strip and characters is highly elevated and erudite, foreshadowing her later work in the graphic memoirs. The discourse is sophisticated; characters pontificate on current events, politics, and literature with a wide vocabulary and cerebral understanding of the world at large. This is an intellectual community, well read and knowledgeable. The characters present an ethos marked by intelligence, and understanding the high-minded humor establishes a relationship with the reader who shares a similar awareness. The text is hand lettered in an extremely readable style—a straightforward, capitalized script with occasional bold type. The lettering is more creative on sound effects and, in particular, on embedded objects within scenes. For her graphic memoirs, Bechdel used computerized lettering based on her handwriting, but after a brief experiment using it on the strip, she reverted to hand lettering, as she made

*levels
of
text*

clear to Lynn Emmert: "For a while I was using the digital font in my comic strip too, just to save time. But I really don't like how it looks there. It's way too regular and uniform" (45).

There are several layers of text, beginning with the display lettering introducing the title of each strip; this is generally the most playful use of creative lettering to set the mood for each episode. *narrator* Occasionally the title is followed by narrative text from an extradiegetic narrator explicating the scene and/or catching the audience up on relevant happenings. This narrative voice is usually positioned distinct from the panels, and sometimes ends strips, teasing and building tension for the next installment. This extradiegetic narrator acts as an omniscient force operating outside the narrative, sounding much like the bombastic voice-over on a soap opera or a wise and (wise-cracking) Dickensian narrator. This narrative text establishes a sense of importance for the strip, an ethos of import evident in the grandiloquent manner.

While the narrative text of this narrator is minimal, the characters converse frequently and at length, and significant space is devoted *characters* to speech balloons in each panel. The narrative text and speech balloons are lettered in a similar font, which doesn't vary from the narrative text or from character to character. The personality derives not from the lettering but from the content and context. The speech balloons are similarly forthright. As previously mentioned, the text *objects* depicted on objects within panels, however, exhibits a great more variety, showcasing a wide variety of styles and fonts. This intradiegetic text is particularly significant in the realm of *DTWOF*, acting * as another narrative strand that works in concert with the images and speech balloons. Ann Miller notes, "The only text which can be fully integrated into the diegesis is that which occurs on decors or objects within the fiction" (98), and these integrated textual objects add another level to the fiction.

As previously indicated, during the first few years, *Dykes to Watch Out For* consisted of unconnected strips without a regular cast or serialized storyline, as can be seen in the very first collection. Bechdel introduced two of her regular characters in 1987 while living in St. Paul, Minnesota, in a strip titled, "One Enchanted Evening." More characters followed, forming a small, tightly knit community. Monica Testa, or Mo, the main character, acts as an avatar for creator Bechdel, and she is easily identifiable by her ubiquitous striped shirt, glasses, and curled forelock, as well as her unceasing complaints about the state of the world. Mo works a variety of jobs before settling in at MadWimmin bookstore, owned by Jezanna. Later, Mo becomes a librarian. While at the bookstore, Mo is frequently joined by Lois MacGiver, a free-spirited drag performer. The strip also features Clarice Clifford, Mo's former lover who becomes a successful lawyer; Toni Ortiz, an accountant and Clarice's wife; and Stuart Goodman, a straight man married to Sparrow Pidgeon, an activist and self-identified "bisexual lesbian." After years of romantic turmoil, Mo eventually settles down with Sydney Krukowski, a Women's Studies professor. The two endure despite infidelity, financial woes, and Sydney's breast cancer. And, over time, the cast of recurring characters expands a great deal beyond the central core to include even more children, friends, and relatives. Gabrielle Dean maintains that in her "careful inclusion of all 'kinds' of dykes" Bechdel produces "a cast of stereotypes: none of them is complete in her own right, but together they produce a puzzle-picture of the community of choice" (212). However, it is clear that in the many years of the strip each of these key players develops a distinct point-of-view and personality.

Furthermore, while the strip originally focused on a small circle of lesbian friends, all of whom shared a similar worldview, as the years progress, the strip began to include a wider range of characters with different backgrounds, ethnicities, philosophies, and orientations. Bechdel explained, "I may be writing from a very minor perspective, but these characters are as human as anyone else, and I really am insistent about letting them be universal. . . . The strip is about all kinds of things, not just gay and lesbian issues, although the world is seen through that lens. These events-births, deaths and everything-in-between happen to everyone" (Gray 8). Thus, the perspective of the strip came to embrace a wider community, while remaining solidly centered on the intimate, domestic lives of its characters.

Each of the main characters has visual cues that act as a short-hand and allow the reader to quickly identify each individual, such as Mo's striped shirt. The characters range in age, size, and ethnicity. While main character Mo is White, the cast is ethnically diverse. The characters themselves are generally rendered more abstractly, while the backgrounds are richly detailed, with careful attention paid to ordinary household objects, such as a remote control, a magazine, or a photograph. This approach allows the reader to connect with the slightly more generalized characters while feeling the importance of commonplace objects and scenes. Bechdel is a master of layering narrative strands of text, image, and imagination to create a larger, more resonant story.

Mo and the Women's Movement

Dykes to Watch Out For began in the early 1980s, in the waning days of what many call the second wave of feminism, and thus bears the imprint of the various and overlapping women's movements. According to Christine Stansell, "The fireworks of women's liberation spluttered out in the 1970s with the fall of the New Left and the depletion of millennial expectations. But the way of seeing the world bequeathed by radical feminism, the great refusal to proceed with business as usual, endured in the psyche of a generation of daughters" (228). Unfortunately, this waning form of feminism also maintained a complicated relationship with gay rights. While many early and influential activists in the Women's Liberation movement, such as Audre Lorde, Adrienne Rich, and Kate Millett, identified as lesbians, according to Nina Renata Aron, many feminists associated with the Women's Liberation movement felt that "that a lesbian aesthetic or 'agenda' would compromise feminists' political power or mar their image in the broader culture." However, "few went so far as to overtly exclude lesbians." Unfortunately, in 1969 Betty Friedan, author of *The Feminine Mystique* and leader of the National Organization for Women (NOW), posited that associating with lesbians and lesbian groups would damage the Women's Liberation movement, labeling the threat, "the lavender menace." In the First Congress to Unite Women, Friedan excluded lesbian groups from the roster, causing Rita Mae Brown to resign her position with NOW. Later, Susan Brownmiller made light of Friedan's concerns, arguing lesbianism was not a menace, but rather a "lavender herring." The tension came to a head at the 1970 Second Congress to Unite Women. Yamissette Westerband explains:

feminism vs lesbianism

> Lesbian activists such as The Radicalesbians chose this conference to educate feminists regarding the political obstacles faced by lesbians. At this event, the "Lavender Menace" attempted to rush the stage to present lesbian issues and distributed copies of "The

Woman Identified Woman." Although the lights were doused before the stage was rushed, this action led to pro-lesbian resolutions being passed at the conference's final assembly.

Although Aron points out that within a year of the Second Congress, "NOW had adopted a resolution recognizing lesbian rights as 'a legitimate concern of feminism,'" many felt that the public face of feminism, particularly as institutionalized through NOW, failed to include and recognize the LGBTQ+ community.

Over time, as the term "feminist" had fallen out of favor in the general public, what has come to be called the third wave of feminism rose up in response to what many perceived as the failures of the earlier approach, including the exclusion of LGBTQ+ concerns. Third-wave feminism, a term coined by Rebecca Walker in her 1992 article for *Ms.* magazine titled "Becoming the Third Wave," promoted a global feminism and endorsed a more inclusive movement that actively embraced people of color as well as the LGBTQ+ community, responding to criticism that the second wave was heterosexist and largely ignorant of the needs and desires of people of color. R. C. Snyder remarks:

> Third-wave feminism makes three important tactical moves that respond to a series of theoretical problems within the second wave. First, in response to the collapse of the category of "women," the third wave foregrounds personal narratives that illustrate an intersectional and multiperspectival version of feminism. Second, as a consequence of the rise of postmodernism, third-wavers embrace multivocality over synthesis and action over theoretical justification. Finally, in response to the divisiveness of the sex wars, third-wave feminism emphasizes an inclusive and nonjudgmental approach that refuses to police the boundaries of the feminist political. In other words, third-wave feminism rejects grand narratives for a feminism that operates as a hermeneutics of critique within a wide array of discursive locations, and replaces attempts at unity with a dynamic and welcoming politics of coalition. (175–76)

In the questions that frame the "Cartoonist's Introduction" to *The Essential Dykes,* Bechdel clearly puzzles over the debate between the essential nature of identity as opposed to its socially constructed nature, and the strip traverses back and forth across the

FIGURE 5.1. Alison Bechdel. "Pride and Prejudice." *The Essential Dykes to Watch Out For.* New York: Houghton Mifflin, 2008, p. 10.

boundaries of the second and third waves of feminism as they, too, struggle with notions of nature and nurture.

It is clear, however, that *DTWOF* depicts an intersectional feminism that embraces difference and argues for action over theory. In the 1987 strip "Pride & Prejudice," Mo attends a Pride March with friends Clarice, Toni, and Harriet, and Mo is startled by the many voices and many individuals in attendance, and the groups they represent (see figure 5.1). The first panel features the symbolic triangle with large, chubby letters announcing the title, as if the letters are simply bursting with pride. The second panel establishes the scene, as Toni and Clarice walk amidst a large crowd of people, and call out to Mo. Toni and Clarice hold hands, and they are surrounded by men walking with their arms around one another, while others hold signs for "Pride '87" and "We're Not Going Back!" Balloons drift into the crowded scene, adding a celebratory feeling. In the third panel, in a tight shot of the four women, Mo (clearly recognizable in a striped tank top) is introduced to Harriet (who will later become her lover), and, in the fourth panel, Harriet announces, "Nice to meet you, Mo! We were just agreeing that **gay pride** day is our favorite holiday of the year," as the scene widens slightly to include a very hairy, bare-chested man in the background. Mo, clutching the straps of her back-pack, responds, "Yeah? Me too! But don't you think the whole thing is getting kind of **conservative?**"

By the fifth panel the scene has widened a bit more, as Mo continues her rant, "Don't you see the influence of **Reagan** and **AIDS?** This country is in **political retrograde** and **Gay Pride** is going along!" Toni, positioned next to Clarice behind Mo, whispers, as evidenced by her shaky, intermittent speech balloon, "Uh-Oh . . . Here she goes," indicating that the couple is well used to Mo's diatribes. A variety of people appear in the background, wearing dark leather jackets and holding, "Fight Aids Not Gays" signs. In the next several panels, Mo stands to the side of each panel, gesturing toward the various groups she finds offensive, including the "Gay & Lesbian Catholic Martyrs," the "Gay Men's Chorus," and the "Lesbian Investment Bankers." Mo gestures at the happy, smiling marchers as they pass, complaining:

> "Look at this **March!** We've stopped saying, 'We're queer and happy that way, so you'd better get used to it.' **Now** it's more like, 'See we're just as patriotic, god-fearing, and red-blooded as the rest of you wholesome Americans. **Religion!! Patriotism! Financial Security!** Doesn't anyone realize? We're **conspiring** in our **own oppression**! Where has our old **spirit** and **consciousness** gone?"

In each successive panel as Mo monologues, the scene widens, displaying more and more people, smiling and enjoying the scene. The groups hold banners before them as they march, full of glee and goodwill. In her ire, Mo represents a feminism that opposed dom-inant forces by reversing traditional binaries, but at times failed to understand the faultiness of the binaries. Clark A. Pomerleau explains:

Oppositional rhetoric meant to create collective feminist identity often used binaries that symbolically reversed normative values, but women disagreed on whether these dichotomies had essential or social constructionist origins. Women transgressed feminine passive acceptance of norms by willingly hearing or reading feminist critiques. Feminist consumers of rhetoric, however, might resist one interpretation by privileging their own experience and values over another's. Women's actions also signaled the effectiveness of rhetoric meant to change behavior. For all the effort to reevaluate dominant views, feminist views on sexuality sometimes blended with societal biases, and radical propositions created in the late 1960s through mid-1970s have remained at odds with neoliberal values. (188)

Mo not "the lesbian rule" ✱

For her part, Mo privileges a certain kind of activism, and a certain kind of "queerness," but succumbs to her own biases in interpretation; she is like the rigid, wooden ruler rather than the "lesbian rule," unbending and unwilling to shape her vision to accommodate the diversity of the crowd.

Mo essentializes the LGBTQ+ community, arguing that one cannot simultaneously be gay and be "conservative," a refrain that resounded many years later with Pete Buttigieg's run for US President in 2020, when he was criticized widely by groups such as "Queers Against Pete" for being too "straight," too "conservative," and "not gay enough." Mo complains that the Gay Pride march has evolved from celebrating a distinct LGBTQ+ identity apart from the heteronormative mainstream American culture to rejoicing instead that "we're just as patriotic, god-fearing, and red-blooded as the rest of you wholesome Americans," a critique widely lobbed at Buttigieg, a White, upper-class man who identifies as Christian and served in the Army before becoming mayor of South Bend, Indiana, in addition to identifying as gay.

connection to present day

Mo's friends, however, argue for a more inclusive LGBTQ+ community; one that welcomes everyone. The ninth panel focuses on the four friends to the left of the panel, and two new figures to the right. Mo is pressed against the left side of the panel as Clarice, to her side, argues, "Mo, there's **plenty** of spirit and outrageousness here! Will you **lighten up** and take a look around? You get so worked up, you only see the things that support your depressing theories!" Mo is chastened, her face downcast. To their right, a grinning woman leans on a sign reading, "Fuck Gender." She is bare-chested, wearing a tutu, suspenders, biker boots, a hat, a watch, and sunglasses. A man is just to her side, his face and legs visible beneath a large, full-body condom costume. He, too, smiles, his mustache turned up and his eyes crinkled with laughter. Mo's friends encourage her to look beyond her own prejudices and really see all of the people honoring Pride Day, in all of their diversity—from the Lesbian Investment Bankers to the grinning man in the condom costume.

Thus, Mo confronts her own prejudices and preconceived notions of what it is to be gay, prejudices still very much in evidence in 2020. Feeling chagrined, Mo laments, "Jeez! Maybe you're **right!** Maybe I otta just wander off into the **crowd** and stop **ruining the** march **for you guys.**" Harriet leans toward Toni, her jagged speech balloon indicating that she is whispering, "Is she **always** like this?" to which Toni responds, "You get used to it." This scene indicates a shift in the LGBTQ+ movement and in third-wave feminism, which both worked to celebrate a diversity of voices within a community, even those voices that might once have seemed contrary to the movements. R. C. Snyder notes, "By rejecting a unified category of women and embracing the anarchic imperative of direct action, third-wave feminism necessarily embraces a philosophy of nonjudgment" (188). Mo still struggles with nonjudgment, arguing that the pride parade is in "retrograde," but her friends pull her out of her spiral, encouraging to see all that is there, rather than only viewing through her own lens.

Dwelling on judgment and exclusion within her community is a frequent issue for Mo, who often speaks from the perspective of an older, more monolithic strand of feminism, as she did in the 1990 strip "Feelings" (see figure 5.2). In the strip Mo is discussing the coming out of Marvin Liebman, the cofounder of the *National Review,* although he is not mentioned by name. In the fourth panel of the strip, Mo barges through a doorway, met by Lois and a barking dog. Lois, smiling in the left half of the frame, states, "Mo! Nice ta see ya! Come on in and **vent** your **spleen!**" Lois's smile suggests she is amused by Mo, who has disrupted a gossip session about old loves and new girlfriends. But Mo doesn't pause to find out what the group is discussing, but rather intones, "I don't know what this country is coming to! Did you see the paper? The co-founder of the **National Review** just came out!" In her anger Mo seems to push the happy dog's paws from her waist, and by the second panel, she is shak-

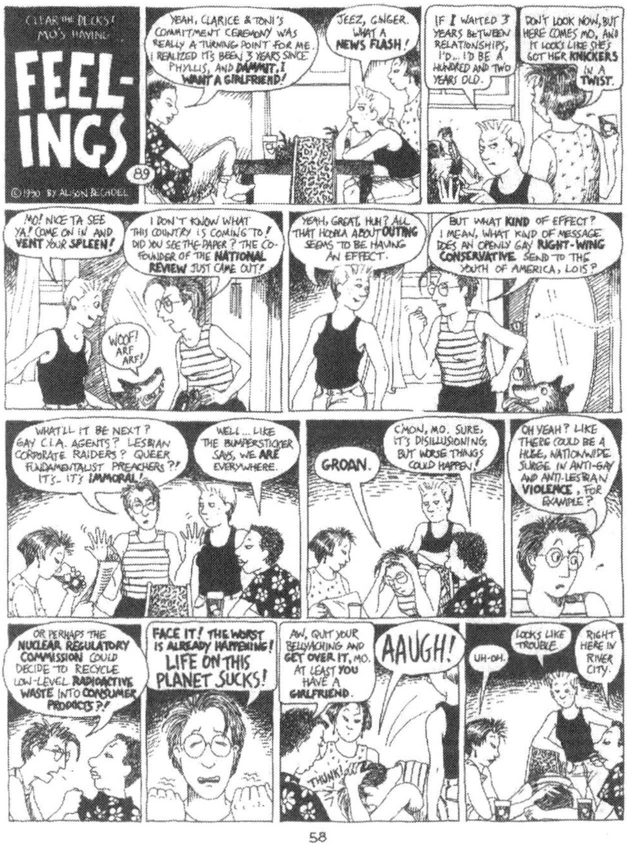

FIGURE 5.2. Alison Bechdel. "Feelings." *The Essential Dykes to Watch Out For.* New York: Houghton Mifflin, 2008, p. 58.

ing her fist with rage, despite Lois's genial comment, "Yeah, great, huh? All this hoopla about **outing** seems to be having an effect." For Lois, this moment of truth from a conservative public figure is good news, evidence that the world is becoming more accepting if a staunch Republican feels comfortable self-identifying as gay. But Mo is having none of it; she does not accept Marvin Liebman's admission, suggesting that he is the wrong kind of gay, a dangerous example for others to follow. With the door open behind her and the dog, tongue hanging out, smiling, Mo continues her rant: "But what kind of effect? I mean, what **kind** of message does an openly gay **right-wing conservative** send to the youth of America, Lois?" Mo represents an essentialized notion of what it is to be LBGTQ+, suggesting that an "openly gay right-wing conservative" sends the wrong kind of message to young people. Are LGBTQ+ people only allowed to be Democrats? This challenge to her essentialized notions of sexuality startles and angers Mo.

Mo continues to rant on the subject of acceptable notions of LGBTQ+ behavior in the seventh panel, surrounded by her disinterested friends, who are seated at a table, drinking and reading. Mo stands in the center, facing the reader, her expression angry, and lines indicating her hands are gesturing aggressively. She states, "What'll it be next? Gay C.I.A agents? Lesbian fundamentalist preachers? It's . . . It's immoral!" Mo once again struggles to accept the diversity of LGBTQ+ individuals, suggesting that a gay person couldn't possibly want to work for the government as a C.I.A. agent, nor could any lesbian choose to be a fundamentalist preacher. Comically, she even mimics the arguments hurled at the LGBTQ+ community—"It's immoral."

Ginger, however, smiles serenely while sitting at the table, simply stating, "Well . . . like the bumper sticker says, we **are** everywhere." Citing the popular slogan, Ginger points out that, in fact, gay, lesbian, and transgendered people are everywhere and in every occupation, not simply the ones endorsed by "the old guard," or those that fit within a certain worldview, as held by Mo. Feminism was changing and expanding, as were LGBTQ+ communities, and, as Mo makes clear, growing pains were inevitable. Yet the strip also suggests that it is equitable and just to adapt to the varied people and perspectives, creating a community comprised of delightfully irregular building materials.

Disidentification in *Dykes*

One of *DTWOF*'s notoriously difficult characters, Sydney Krukowski, a professor of Women's Studies, frequently mocks academic inquiry in general, and Queer Theory in particular, but the discipline, which came to prominence in the 1990s and resides at the intersection of Queer Studies and Women's Studies, encourages new ways of reading and theorizing texts. The subdiscipline of queer rhetoric developed through the connections of queer theory and rhetoric and composition, and, as described by Alexander and Rhodes, "Queer rhetoric is certainly concerned with lesbian, gay, bisexual, and transgender (LGBT) issues, identities, and politics, but it is not exclusively linked to them and may in fact resist certain kinds of gay and lesbian normalization." Furthermore, "embedded in much queer theorizing is the rhetorical practice of disidentification, or the ways in which one situates oneself both within and against the various discourses through which we are called to identify" (Alexander and Rhodes). José Esteban Muñoz clarifies:

> Disidentification is about recycling and rethinking encoded mean-
> ing. The process of disidentification scrambles and reconstructs the
> encoded message of a cultural text in a fashion that both exposes the
> encoded message's universalizing and exclusionary machinations
> and recircuits its workings to account for, include, and empower
> minority identities and identifications. Thus, disidentification is a
> step further than cracking open the code of the majority; it proceeds
> to use this code as raw material for representing a disempowered
> politics or positionality that has been rendered unthinkable by the
> dominant culture. (31)

Whereas some in marginalized groups attempt to identify with a cul-turally sanctioned identity group, others prefer to counteridentify, defining oneself in opposition to the dominant identity. While there is power in rejecting stereotypical narratives, it can also be limiting, in that it asks the person to define him or herself by perpetuating limit-ing binaries. However, to disidentify is to pursue another option, one that encourages individuals to accept all of the parts of their identity.

While Mo frequently remains mired in the binaries of the com-mon stories of an older form of feminism, contemporary feminists and queer theorists argue for a disidentification from dominant narratives, rereading texts and creating new ones, moving beyond dualistic thinking. Lois, Mo's friend, stands at the forefront of dis-identification, lobbying for more inclusive understandings of gen-der fluidity in the 1994 strip "Au Courant" (see figure 5.3). The first panel introduces the title and theme with a black background and a contemporary font announcing the title, "Au Courant," or "well-informed," and establishes the scene, depicting Mo standing behind the checkout counter bagging books at her job at Madwimmin's Books, and complimenting Lois's boots. Mo's position is important, for she is stationed in a position of authority, the bulwark of the coun-ter and cash register isolating her from the others and indicating her

FIGURE 5.3. Alison Bechdel. "Au Courant." *The Essential Dykes to Watch Out For.* New York: Houghton Mifflin, 2008, p. 125.

power. Lois, however, stands away from the counter, holding a duster and admiring her boots, while a woman peruses the stock in the background. Lois explains that she got the boots "from an Australian shot-putter at the games," and that she "swapped her my Doc Martens. I was glad to get rid of 'em now that every suburban mallcrawler has a pair." Lois thus establishes her disdain for the suburban culture that has co-opted rebel culture as well as her laissez-faire attitude toward her possessions. Lois is quite willing to swap footwear with a stranger on a whim, while Mo clings to her clothing (wearing the same striped shirt every day), just as she holds tightly to her ideals.

In the third panel, Mo laments a submission to her Local Lesbian Writers Series from "Someone named Jillian who identifies as a transsexual lesbian." Lois, also working at the bookstore, with a small smile, responds, "Cool." As Mo becomes increasingly incensed by the evidence of a wider spectrum of gender identity, Lois simply smiles and laughs. Mo isn't satisfied, stating in the fifth panel, "The cover letter says, 'I hope you'll consider changing the name of your reading series for local lesbian writers to be inclusive of transgender and bisexual women writers too.' Oh, man!" Mo's exhortation of "Oh, man" takes on special resonance in her frustration, for a "man" can be so many things, and Mo simply cannot seem to accept this fluidity. But Lois leans on the checkout counter, and, with a smirk on her face, encourages Mo, "Guess it's time to get with the program, huh?" The two characters represent two perspectives, an older, essentialized notion of LGBTQ+ identity, and a more contemporary, fluid notion of intersectional identity. By the sixth panel, Mo has had it, exclaiming, "What am I supposed to do? Have bi women and drag queens come in here and read about schtupping their boyfriends?" During this exchange, Mo maintains an angry, erect posture, her eyebrows raised, first in exasperation then anger. Lois, however, remains relaxed in face and posture.

gender fluidity & fixidity

In the third row of panels, the perspective shifts, with Lois positioned on the left of each panel with the ninth panel a close-up of her face, a reflection of Mo's face from panel six. This change in perspective also represents a shift in the conversation, with Lois taking the lead. She leans back, holding her duster, and retorts, "Why not? I'm sure they'd have a unique perspective on the topic." Mo counters, "Lois, I'm still trying to adjust to lesbians using dildos! What am I supposed to make of a man who became a woman who's attracted to women?" In light of Mo's retort, Lois becomes even more dominant, albeit very playfully, in the eighth panel in which she dusts Mo, who tries to block her with her arm, and claims, "Love is a many-gendered thing, pal. Get used to it." But Mo again responds defensively, with her arm and words, bickering, "Well fine. Let people do what they want. But I'm not gonna add this unwieldy 'bisexual and transgender' business to the name of my reading series. I don't even know what transgender means!" Thus, Mo indicates a grudging acceptance of others identifying as they choose apart from her community, but also reveals her unwillingness to accept "bisexual and transgender"

Mo unaccepting of bi & trans folks

people into her carefully guarded reading group. Her lack of understanding equals a refusal to accept them.

The ninth panel focuses on Lois's face, her eyebrows raised in concern, a reflection to the angry close-up of Mo's face positioned immediately above it. Lois asserts,

> It's sort of an evolving concept. I mean, we haven't had any language for people you can't neatly peg as either boy or girl. Like cross-dressers, transsexuals, people who live as the opposite sex but don't have surgery, drag queens and kings, and all kinds of other transgressive folks. "Transgender" is a way to unite everyone into a group, even though all these people might not self-identify as transgender. In fact, the point is that we're all just ourselves, and not categories. Instead of two rigid genders, there's an infinite sexual continuum! Cool, huh?

gender & disidentification

Lois thus argues for a flexibility in gender identification, a disidentification from categories of either gay or straight, and an understanding of gender marked by recognition of the diversity of individuals' experience.

Mo, ever the skeptic asks, "How do you know all this stuff?" And in the final panel Lois, still positioned to the left of and occupying the first speaking position, reveals the twist, responding, "From hanging out with Jillian at Lesbian Avengers meetings. She told me she was gonna send this to you."[3] Mo leans back from Lois, who shakes the letter at her, and responds, "You love to watch me squirm, don't you?" Alexander and Rhodes argue that in queer rhetoric, "*ethos* and *pathos* often assume dominance, while *logos,* traditionally vaunted as the superior form of argumentation and persuasion, is less queerly compelling," but in this exchange Lois is able to marshal all three forms of appeal. She invokes emotion, playing on Mo's anger with her cool demeanor, in addition to employing the disarming comic frame to impishly weaken Mo's stature. She summons authority by stressing her association with Jillian and the Lesbian Avengers, and expertly employs rationality in her calm state and her sensible dismantling of Mo's emotional diatribe. Through this exchange Lois has successfully and resoundingly squelched Mo's protests, using logic

rhetoric

---

3. For more on the activist rhetoric of the Lesbian Avengers, see Ann Rand's article, "An Appetite for Activism: The Lesbian Avengers and the Queer Politics of Visibility." *Women's Studies in Communication* vol. 36 no. 2, 2013, pp. 121–41.

argument & rhetoric

and reason along with *ethos* and *pathos,* and her accomplishment is reflected in her switched positions and her postures throughout the strip. Mo's position, locked in the bifurcated thinking of an earlier time, is defeated with a comic twist when Lois reveals that she knew the identity of the author all along, but enjoyed watch her friend "squirm" as the faultiness of her ill-informed prejudice was revealed.

Over time Mo softens her stance a little, as her world expands beyond the small original cast. In an interview with Judith Levine, Bechdel clarified that the introduction of straight male character Stuart "shows a shift in my personal allegiance to people who share my world view, away from people who are queer like me" (58). Levine concluded, "Bechdel strives in each strip to produce a 'small moment' in which 'hardly anything happens. Just like real life' . . . Viewing herself as something between a journalist, a historian, and a soap-opera writer, Bechdel describes her challenge this way: 'To have [my characters] segue into more contemporary life, but without losing their personalities and their relationships'" (54–55). Over twenty-five years, the characters grew and evolved, mirroring the world at large. Bechdel observes, "The comic strip observes culture, but it also is culture. I see my role really as a kind of cultural anthropologist" (London 10). *Dykes* thus mirrors culture and creates it.

space

DTWOF operates primarily in the home, exploring the ways in which politics manifested in the personal. Lisa London notices that for Bechdel, "The spaces her characters inhabit are for the most part interiors: living rooms, beds, kitchens" (10). At the communal kitchen table, the group of friends, absent Mo, discuss the many changes in their family units, their community, and their understanding of gender in the 1999 strip "I. D. Fixe?" (see figure 5.4).

The title, introduced in quirky, D'Nealian style script, plays upon the phrase *ideé fixe,* a fixed idea that is resistant to change, and here refers to the challenges the group confronts with changing notions of sexual identity and, perhaps, shifting notions of family as well. The strip opens, as so many do, with a character, in this case Ginger, returning home to the family unit. Ginger enters the cluttered dining room and slaps a bridal magazine on the communal table in front of Sparrow, who is wearing a bathrobe and drinking from a mug. The leopard print chairs hint at eccentricity in the family abode, but Ginger is most shocked by the post, stating, "Your mail," and dropping it with a resounding "SLAP!" In the second panel, Ginger leans on the table, challenging Sparrow, who sits with the magazine spread

FIGURE 5.4. Alison Bechdel. "I. D. Fixe?" *The Essential Dykes to Watch Out For.* New York: Houghton Mifflin, 2008, p. 230.

before her. Ginger queries, "Is there something you'd like to tell me, Sparrow? Aside from the fact that organza is back?" Ginger radiates anger that Sparrow has presumably bought into bridal mania. Sparrow exclaims, "Oh my god! I bet my mom did this! Ever since I came out to her about Stuart, she thinks it means I'm straight. She can't understand that I'm a bisexual lesbian!" In this sequence, Sparrow struggles both with familial expectations of her mother, assuming that now she is dating a man she is straight, and her new, chosen family, Ginger, who rejects any association with the trappings of matrimony as envisioned in "Bride's" magazine.

Stuart, Sparrow's male partner, enters the dining area in the fourth panel, further complicating the group's dynamics. Stuart lumbers in happily, carrying a mug and wearing a "HMO Phobic" t-shirt, its clever slogan poking fun at homophobic discourse. Stuart approaches the table, where Sparrow and Ginger sit, a bag of "Nguyen's bagels" poised between them. Ginger studies various envelopes and argues that Sparrow's self-identification is a "nuance that can elude the best of us," while Sparrow retorts, "Look, in a perfect world, I wouldn't have to call myself anything. But for now, bi-dyke works for me, ok?" The perspective shifts in the fifth panel to encompass all three at the table, a dog snoozing in a comfy chair in the background. As he sits, Stuart voices his belief that he's "a butch lesbian in a straight man's body," but Ginger counters, "Soft butch. Maybe." This gentle teasing allows room for playful banter about gender identity, although for White male Stuart the stakes aren't so high, but for the others, including Sparrow, a bisexual lesbian of Asian descent, and Ginger, a Black lesbian, the implications aren't quite so light-hearted. Sparrow holds her hands in front of her, palms down as she contends, "It's not as simple for everyone as it is for you, Ginger! Sometimes people change. Identity is so much more complex and fluid than these rigid little categories of straight, gay, and bi can possibly reflect." While this is a difficult conversation, the characters clearly respect one another, and the home operates as a safe space for the family members to challenge one another and their own prejudices and preconceived notions.

[handwritten margin note: home as safe to challenge ideas]

Sparrow is clearly frustrated, defending herself from the expectations of others, but the conversation is interrupted by another intriguing expression of gendered identity in the sixth panel, which shifts perspective to peer over the shoulders of the group at the table to focus on the front doorway, where a bearded man in a black t-shirt chats with Lois, casual in a white t shirt and spotted boxer shorts. The man states, "You're a sweetheart, Lois. See ya later," to which Lois responds, "'Kay, Jerry. Have fun." Ginger calls out, "Who was that? Don't tell me you're seeing a man too." Ginger plainly feels uncomfortable with another housemate defying gendered expectations, but Lois is unfazed, "No, just lending him a tie. Though he is kind of hot." In her response Lois challenges Ginger by indicating that she sees Jerry as "hot," noting his attractiveness although they aren't dating.

The family unit continues their conversation on identity, and in particular Jerry's gender identity, in the eighth panel, which shows a close-up of Sparrow and Lois, with the back of Ginger's head par-

transmiss]
home a
to be to
space e
challenge
gender

tially visible. Sparrow holds her finger to her lips, deep in thought, pondering, "He reminds me of someone . . . whatserhame . . . You know, that buff babe, your mechanic?" Lois is pictured with her arm in the bagel bag; she responds, "Geraldine, exactly. Only now he's a buff trans guy, and his name's Jerry." This revelation seems to rock the group. Apparently, Jerry's transition is incomprehensible. Sparrow's eyebrows are lifted in shock, as she queries, "Are you serious? Like, with surgery? And testosterone? God, I just can't understand that." Ginger faces Sparrow, her expression serious; she retorts, "Uh . . . 'Sometimes people change'? 'Identity is complex and fluid'? Any of that ring a bell?" These characters are complicated—both generous and judgmental—and they are working through their understanding of gender identity together.

The final panels don't reveal any definitive conclusions, although Stuart does offer some comic relief to the drama. In the penultimate panel, Sparrow angrily states, "Changing your body to conform to rigid, conventional gender identity is just more binary thinking! What was wrong with being a butch dyke!" In doing so, Sparrow, who moments before lamented others forcing preconceived notions of gender onto her, now confuses counteridentification and disidentification. Sparrow feels that by changing from a "butch dyke" to a man, Jerry is buying into narrow categories of male/female gender identity, counteridentifying by rejecting one category gender and choosing the opposing category. However, once more, "disidentification is a step further than cracking open the code of the majority; it proceeds to use this code as raw material for representing a disempowered politics or positionality that has been rendered unthinkable by the dominant culture" (Muñoz 31). Jerry represents an alternate positionality outside of the binary. Lois cogently makes the argument: with her bagel almost to her lips, she casually points out that Jerry is simply living his truth: "He doesn't feel like a butch dyke. He feels like a gay man." Ginger, as evidenced by her exhausted posture, is further depressed, stating, "Skip fluid. Press 'liquefy,'" indicating that gender fluidity is not a strong enough term, opting instead for the utter destruction of "liquefy," suggesting the category, and her brain, has been completely scrambled.

dis-
identifi-
cation

It is perhaps appropriate that this family unit doesn't come to any sort of resolution in the last panel, but they do part with humor, largely courtesy of Stuart, who smacks his head, his eyes wide in an epiphany. Ginger faces the audience, her head in her hands, her expression unruffled, while Lois, shown in profile, chews, her cheek bulging with food. Stuart, in shock, shouts, "Oh my god! Geraldine from Rainbow Automotive? I used to have such a thing for her! I mean him . . . I mean . . . Wow!" Lois counters, "Don't get too excited, Stu. He goes more for the studhorse type." Stuart is also clearly struggling with Jerry's transition, and in particular his own attraction to him, but Lois teases Stuart, suggesting he isn't enough of a "studhorse" to attract Jerry.

This entire sequence is entertaining and engaging for a number of reasons. The strip features the members of a found family, all dwelling in the house, as they challenge one another on gender identity, sometimes angrily and sometimes playfully. Mo, featured in so many other strips, is absent, while the action revolves around this household of friends. The characters are diverse in terms of ethnicity and gender identification. And there is something undeniably intimate about the entire exchange. Sparrow, Stuart, and Lois are in casual morning clothes—a bathrobe, t-shirts, boxer shorts, and they are gathered around the table sharing a relaxed, shared meal, the comical "Nguyen's bagels," another sly wink at challenging cultural expectations with a common Vietnamese surname attached to bagels, a food associated with Jewish culture—yet another "blending" of traditions. The family in this house feels flawed and real. Adrienne Shaw believes, "In these comics, what it means to be part of an imagined lesbian community is celebrated, questioned, and debated; in this process the artists help define a community and identity framed by flux" (93). The lesbian community has expanded and exploded, and even as the characters debate questions of gender identity, the strip celebrates the family within. These characters, for all of their weaknesses, find love and companionship together, building something larger and stronger through their bonds to one another. In the many strips over many years in *Dykes to Watch Out For,* the hundreds of individual strips act as stones, varying in size but forming a sturdy foundation, coming together to form a larger page structure—a construct of micronarratives that offers a vision of intersectional feminism and disidentification. Contained therein are messy characters and messy situations. There isn't one "ideal" lesbian but many people, and these irregular, uneven characters assemble in a larger community, another kind of edifice. Aristotle argued that *epieikeia,* that equity, must be understood not as an impenetrable or unyielding measure, but an ideal tempered by flexibility, as exemplified by the lesbian rule, accounting for the individuality of the many building blocks. *Dykes to Watch Out For* builds an argument for this justice, this *epieikeia,* through these characters, narratives, panels, pages, and strips—proffering not a grand monolithic ideal, but a diverse one marked by a respect for singularity, polyglossia, and fluidity.

CHAPTER 6

ESTABLISHING COMMUNITY THROUGH DIS/ASSOCIATION IN BARBARA BRANDON-CROFT'S *WHERE I'M COMING FROM*

> We are all bound up together in one great bundle of humanity, and society cannot trample on the weakest and feeblest of its members without receiving the curst in its own soul.
>
> —Frances Ellen Watkins Harper, May 1866, Eleventh National Women's Rights Convention

IN MAY 1866 Frances Ellen Watkins Harper addressed the Eleventh National Women's Rights Convention, appearing alongside suffragist stars such as Elizabeth Cady Stanton and Susan B. Anthony. However, in her remarks, Harper challenged the audience to recognize her identity as a Black woman, demanding that listeners acknowledge the diversity of women as well as shared goals. Harper explained, "Born of a race whose inheritance has been outrage and wrong, most of my life had been spent in battling against those wrongs. But I did not feel as keenly as others, that I had these rights, in common with other women, which are now demanded." Harper thus foregrounds the "inheritance" of her race in fighting injustice, but further indicates her distance from the Women's Rights movement, before detailing her despair as a widow from whom everything was taken after her husband passed. She noted, "Had I died instead of my husband, how different would have been the result! By this time he would have had another wife, it is likely; and no administra-

Harper
Blackness & women's rights

187

tor would have gone into his house, broken up his home, and sold his bed, and taken away his means of support." Thus, Harper argues that "justice is not fulfilled so long as woman is unequal before the law." Yet Harper also recognized that she does not believe that "white women are dew-drops just exhaled from the skies," nor does she think that "giving the woman the ballot is immediately going to cure all the ills of life," for the "grand and glorious revolution" of the suffragist movement "will fail to reach its climax of success, until throughout the length and brea[d]th of the American Republic, the nation shall be so color-blind, as to know no man by the color of his skin or the curl of his hair." Harper critiques the White women lobbying for suffrage for their "airy nothings and selfishness," arguing, "You white women speak here of rights. I speak of wrongs." In her speech, Harper strongly argues that society cannot divide women's suffrage from civil rights, for we are "all bound up together" and can only succeed when recognizing difference *and* acting for the betterment of all.

In the 1980s, over one hundred years after Harper's impassioned speech, it would seem that feminists were still struggling with divisiveness, as evidenced in *Where I'm Coming From*, the syndicated comic strip created by Barbara Brandon-Croft. One weekly strip speaks to this division directly (see figure 6.1). In the strip, Lekesia, a young Black woman, chats on the phone with an unseen friend who, after seeing her friend's NOW "literature on the coffee table," demands, "So what's up, Lekesia, You're some kind of feminist now?" When Lekesia retorts that she's "always been for women's rights," her friend argues, "What about the rights of African Americans?! . . . Sounds like you need to decide who you stand for, White women or Black people!" Lekesia responds with conviction that "There is no division! It's a single fight against oppression." But her friend remains unconvinced, calling Lekesia out as a "traitor." This example illustrates the continuation of Harper's call to remember our boundedness and our diversity. In *Where I'm Coming From*, Brandon-Croft exploits the exceptional rhetorical situation of her syndicated strip, using association and dissociation to point out commonalities between people while simultaneously representing multiplicity and difference. This chapter draws on Lloyd Bitzer's understanding of the rhetorical situation, including the concepts of exigence, audience, constraints, and response, in addition to Carolyn Miller's revi-

FIGURE 6.1. Barbara Brandon-Croft. "NOW Literature." *Where I'm Still Coming From.* Kansas City: Andrews McMeel Publishers, 1994, p. 79.

sion of the idea of exigence, along with Chaïm Perelman and Lucie Olbrechts-Tyteca's understanding of association and dissociation to explore Brandon-Croft's argument for building a stronger bond and community to establish harmony while recognizing the many voices and strands that add to the composition.[1] This chapter begins with a discussion of the rhetorical situation as articulated by theorists and expressed in *Where I'm Coming From,* then provides context for the strip and its historical moment, and finally moves into a close reading of the strips themselves.

---

1. This analysis draws inspiration from Shirley Wilson Logan's exceptional book *We Are Coming: The Persuasive Discourse of Nineteenth-Century Black Women,* which expertly employs rhetorical theory to examine outstanding Black female speakers during the nineteenth century. In the chapter, "We Are All Bound Up Together: Frances Harper's Converging Communities of Interest," Logan uses Karlyn Campbell's "descriptive analysis" and Perelman and Olbrechts-Tyteca's *New Rhetoric* to examine the ways in which Harper creates community in her speeches. Logan's analysis of Harper was particularly relevant to my investigation of Brandon-Croft's work, and even though the texts under consideration are very different, many of the themes and techniques carry through both creators' works.

Origins, Exigence, and Argument

rhetoric as dialogue that alters reality In Lloyd Bitzer's article, "The Rhetorical Situation," Bitzer argues that "rhetoric is a mode of altering reality, not by the direct application of energy to objects, but by the creation of discourse which changes reality through the mediation of thought and action" (4). Thus, a cartoonist such as Barbara Brandon-Croft has the capacity to "alter reality" and create a new way of thinking, not by physical altercation, but rather by inviting dialogue that can transform actuality by way of intellect and engagement. For Bitzer, the "rhetorical situation" is a "natural context of persons, events, objects, relations, and an exigence which strongly invites utterance" (5). Thus, *Where I'm Coming From* operates as an individual's response in the form of a comic strip to a particular set of events. Of course, Brandon-Croft created the comic in response to a particular rhetorical situation. As Bitzer explains, "Prior to the creation of discourse, there are three constituents of any rhetorical situation: the first is the *exigence*; the second and third are elements of the complex, namely the *audience* to be constrained in decision and action, and the *constraints* which influence the rhetor to bear upon the audience" (6). The exigence according to Bitzer, is a defect, an obstacle, something waiting to be done, a thing which is other than it should be" (6). The exigence, then is the problem or issue to be addressed or rectified. However, in the article, "Genre as Social Action," Carolyn Miller revisits Bitzer's notion of exigence:

define rhetorical situation

> If rhetorical situation is not material and objective, but a social construct, or semiotic structure, how are we to understand exigence, which is at the core of situation? Exigence must be located in the social world, neither in a private perception nor in material circumstance. It cannot be broken into two components without destroying it as a rhetorical and social phenomenon. Exigence is a form of social knowledge—a mutual construing of objects, events, interests, and purposes that not only links them but also makes them what they are: an objective social need. This is quite different from Bitzer's characterization of exigence as a "defect" or danger . . . the exigence provides the rhetor with a socially recognizable way to make his or her intentions known. It provides an occasion, and thus a form, for making public our private version of things. (157–58)

Bitzer's exigence vs Miller's exigence

[handwritten margin notes: exigence as occasion / social need, intention, collective vs default / × connection to Croft / biography]

Miller carefully explicates that exigence is, in fact, socially constructed through discourse, rather than a physical condition or internal revelation. Exigence is shared by the community, a collective "occasion" inviting communal conversation. Furthermore, "Exigence is a set of particular social patterns and expectations that provides a socially objective motive for addressing danger, ignorance, and separateness. It is an understanding of social need in which I know how to take an interest, in which one can intend to participate" (Miller 158). Miller stresses the collectively fashioned nature of exigence, as well as the opportunity for the rhetor to enter into the conversation and challenge "danger, ignorance, and separateness." When she began publishing her weekly comic strip *Where I'm Coming From* in 1989 in the *Detroit Free Press,* Barbara Brandon-Croft entered into a particularly fraught time for the many factions of feminism and for people of color, and the strip confronted a moment of exigence in which to be Black and to be feminist were often seen as contradictory stances, and Black women were rarely depicted in popular culture, let alone the newspaper comics pages.

Barbara Brandon (later Brandon-Croft) came from a tradition of comics artists; her father Brumsic Brandon Jr. created the comic strip *Luther,* which ran from 1968 to 1986 (and was nationally syndicated in 1970). According to the *Trove,* "Set in the fictitious, inner-city Alabaster Avenue Elementary school, the comic wryly chronicled the experiences of black third-grader Luther, his schoolmates, and teacher Miss Backlash, underscoring themes of social justice." Barbara Brandon, born in 1958, used to assist her father with his strip and was encouraged by him to start her own. "My father made me a dare," Brandon-Croft told Constance M. Green: "Are you going to talk about being a cartoonist or are you going to do it?" Brandon-Croft pitched a comic strip as early as 1982, but the magazine *Elan* folded before the strip could take off. After working for several years as a fashion and beauty editor at *Essence* magazine, Brandon-Croft's strip was picked up by the *Detroit Free Press* and was syndicated nationally by the Universal Press Syndicate in 1991, making Barbara Brandon-Croft and Brumsic Brandon Jr. the only nationally syndicated father/daughter comics artists, an accomplishment Brandon-Croft noted was particularly important to her: "My dad, and I make the only nationally syndicated father/daughter cartoonists black or white. What I love is that it wasn't as if I took over his comic strip (like some father/son father/daughter

cartoonists have done). We made our distinction as black cartoonists in the mainstream press independently—via different syndicates and creating separate comic strips. That's pretty cool when you think about it" (*Trove*). In 2013, Karen Evans began coauthoring *Luann* with her father Gary Evans, but Brandon-Croft and her father remain the only parent/child pair to have individual syndicated strips.

Brandon-Croft maintained a sense of pride in her strip, even when she decided to end it in 2005, explaining to Dave Astor, "It's incredible that for the past 14 years—or more, including my time at the *Detroit Free Press,* where I started in 1989—I've been able to provide a running social commentary on what it's like to be a black woman in America. Years from now, I hope it offers some historical value." During its run, the book was anthologized in two collections *Where I'm Coming From* (1993) and *Where I'm Still Coming From* (1994), both published by Andrews McMeel. During the life of *Where I'm Coming From,* Brandon-Croft also experienced great changes in her personal life, officially becoming Brandon-Croft when she married musician Monte Croft in 1997 and giving birth to a son, Chase, several years later. After ending the strip in 2005, Brandon-Croft returned to magazine work, eventually becoming the research director for *Parents* magazine. Barbara's beloved father Brumsic supported her throughout her varied career choices until he succumbed to Parkinson's in 2014.

As creators of color, the father/daughter duo represented another kind of rarity in the world of newspaper comics. An article in the January 1993 edition of *Ebony* points to pioneering creators of color, including:

> Ollie Harrington . . . E. Simms Campbell, Wilbert L. Holloway, Leslie Rogers and Zelda (Jackie) Ormes . . . Robb Armstrong, creator of "Jump Start;" Stephen Bentley, who pens "Herb and Jamal;" Ray Billingsley of "Curtis" fame; Barbara Brandon, creator of "Where I'm Coming From" and the only syndicated Black woman cartoonist; and pioneer Morrie Turner, "father" of "Wee Pals." Finally, there is Buck Brown, whose panels of naughty "Granny" and other characters have made *Playboy* readers laugh for years. ("Crusaders," 36)

Not only are creators of color a rarity, *Ebony* magazine contends that representations of people of color in all newspaper comics have been overwhelmingly negative: "There was a time, not very long ago, when cartoons in the White press were everything but a laughing matter to Blacks. Too often, their sole purpose was to demean Black people by portraying them either as pathetically primitive jungle creatures or grotesque-looking, dialect muttering buffoons" ("Crusaders" 36). In the article, "Contemporary Representations of Black Females in Newspaper Comic Strips," Tia C. M. Tyree cited several recent studies, concluding that as of 2004 "96 percent of characters were White and only 2.5 percent were Black" and "representations of women were stereotypical, including women always nagging and being more emotional than their male counterparts" (48). Tyree continues on to analyze, in particular, the ways in which Black women are represented in comic strips, studying a sampling of comics from 2011. Ultimately, she found that "Black females represent 7 percent of the total sample of 464 characters. This percentage is close to the US Black female population of 6.4 percent" (55). However, according to Tyree, *representation of Black people & women in comics*

> The Black female representations in comics is both troubling and encouraging. While Black women are portrayed in a variety of social settings and appear in a majority of racially-independent plotlines, the common message is Black female adults belong in the home, do not have jobs, berate their children and are angry. They are also more likely to be present in majority Black casts as well as comics produced by Black males. Yet, within these settings, the Black female has a higher chance of being stereotyped than within comics created by White females and males. This is largely because White cartoonists keep the Black female image in the background or in minor roles. (59–60)

Unfortunately, "the noticeable absence of authorship by Black females is troubling to the future of the comics industry, as well as Blacks and women. There is no other person better suited to tell the story on the comics pages of Black females than themselves" (Tyree 62). Brandon-Croft was an important voice, and one that is clearly missed today. In *The Blacker the Ink*, Rebecca Wanzo maintains that "critical race humor is often tied to melancholia" (316), and for her part, Brandon-Croft suggests, "I'm more concerned with being thought-provoking than funny. . . . I'm concerned with recording the experiences black women are having in this country and how some of us are feeling about them" (Rule). Scholar Marcyliena Morgan con-

'vibe"
of strip

tends that "the black woman laugh . . . locates the fool—but mostly it locates the truth, even if for one quick second. When you hear 'the black woman laugh,' it's never about anything funny" (85) *Where I'm Coming From* wasn't full of physical comedy; it wasn't about the gags or goofing off. But it did inspire reflection and, occasionally, a wry smile or chuckle.

* exigence
E rhetorical
situation
of strip

The exigence of the rhetorical situation which stimulated *Where I'm Coming From,* was also marked by a turbulent rift in the history of feminism, as demonstrated by Lekesia's traitorous status as a Black feminist and earlier by Frances Harper's clarion call that "white women speak here of rights. I speak of wrongs." For many Black women in the United States, there was a feeling that the feminism of the time had no place for people of color, and Brandon-Croft used her skills as a comics creator to define herself as a Black feminist within the wider culture. Patricia Collins emphasizes the important of "self-definition" for Black feminists, claiming:

> The insistence on Black women's self-definition reframes the entire dialogue from one of protesting the technical accuracy of an image . . . to one stressing the power dynamics underlying the very process of definition itself. By insisting on self-definition, Black women question not only what has been said about African-American women but the credibility and the intentions of those possessing the power to define. (125)

Black
Feminism

Brandon-Croft set out to define and depict, disputing monolithic stereotypes of Black women espoused in the dominant culture and within the feminist movement. As Chávez and Griffin note in the "Introduction" to *Standing in the Intersection: Feminist Voices, Feminist Practices in Communication Studies,* "As the now familiar story goes, during the second wave of the US feminist movement, many white, heterosexual, middle-class feminists talked only of oppression against a seemingly unified category of women—white, heterosexual, middle-class women" (5). However, in *Separate Roads to Feminism: Black, Chicana, and White Feminist Movements in America's Second Wave,* Benita Roth argues that it is a mistake to assume that, as many scholars have done, "feminism among women of color emerged solely as a result of (demonstrably present) racism in the white movement; this is an inaccurate conception that negates the agency of feminists of color" (6). Rather, Roth claims,

white women's liberation was not a natural home for Black feminists, as white feminists were insufficiently sensitive to the importance of race and class oppression in Black women's lives. As a
result, Black feminists, beginning in the mid-1960s, and continuing
throughout the 1970s, organized as feminists *and* as Black women.
Some of these efforts were more collectivist, others more intentionally bureaucratic; some more local in scope and some ambitiously,
if only briefly, national. . . . Thus, Black feminism, with an intersectional, vanguard center vision of liberating politics, emerged into
a space created by the inability of both Black Liberation and white
women's liberation to incorporate Black feminists as activists. (127)

The powerful voices of feminists of color forced White feminists
to examine their assumptions, biases, and essentialized notions of
shared female identity.

In *The Trouble Between Us: An Uneasy History of Black and White
Women in the Feminist Movement*, Winifred Breines explains, "White
feminists were forced to deal with racism and differences. But all
feminists had no choice but to confront differences, primarily sexual preference, ethnic, and class differences within their own movements" (153). Breines continues, clarifying, "In the years since the
flowering of second wave feminism, young feminists, sometimes
called the third wave, embraced the fluidity of racial, sexual, and
geographical identities. They define themselves less rigidly than
did early second wavers" (195). Ultimately, this introspection has
resulted in an intersectional feminism which, according to Cherríe
Moraga, has "has shifted as we turned our gaze *away* from a feminism prescribed by white women of privilege (even in opposition to
them) and turned *toward* the process of discerning the multilayered
and intersecting sites of identity and struggle—distinct and shared—
among women of color across the globe" (xvi). The compelling and
transformative notion of an intersectional feminism was named by
Black feminist scholar Kimberlé Crenshaw in the essay, "Demarginalizing the Intersection of Race and Sex: A Black Feminist Critique of
Antidiscrimination Doctrine, Feminist Theory and Antiracist Politics," published in 1989, the same year *Where I'm Coming From* was
picked up in the *Detroit Free Press*, and the evidence of this intersectional focus, and, for that matter, tension, appears clearly in the strip.
Thus, from this exigence of feminism in transition and an absence of
Black characters, particularly Black women in comics, arose Brandon-

exigence ε
B.-croft

self-definition [handwritten]

Croft's creation. Patricia Collins argues that "the overarching theme of finding a voice to express a collective, self-defined Black women's standpoint remains a core theme in Black feminist thought" (110), and *Where I'm Coming From* represents a significant point-of-view, long neglected in the comics pages. In an interview with Ellie Tesher, Brandon-Croft explained, "I hope I would appeal to a general audience. These are black women talking . . . we're all here together. If by reading my strip it helps people to understand black women a little better, then I'm accomplishing" (A2) Through her strip, Brandon-Croft worked to build community while exploring difference, adding her voice and images to expose a lack in the comics pages and in feminist discourse, revealing an exigence marked by absence and ignorance. *good summary of argument* [handwritten]

Brandon-Croft's Comic Response

B. Croft as a rhetor [handwritten]

As a rhetor, Brandon-Croft crafted a response to the exigence of the rhetorical situation that spoke directly to an audience in a singular way, inviting the reader into a conversation. Lloyd Bitzer posits that "an exigence is rhetorical when it is capable of positive modification and when positive modification requires discourse or can be assisted by discourse" (7). *Particular exigence* [handwritten] The exigent situation of a lack of Black female voices in popular culture at large and newspaper comics strips in particular, as well as the rift in feminism could, indeed, be improved through dialogue, and Brandon-Croft cleverly entered the arena with style and wit, becoming the eighth Black nationally syndicated comic strip artist (her father was the third) and the only nationally syndicated Black female creator (Jackie Ormes's *Torchy Brown from Dixie* *B. Croft lack of recognition* [handwritten] to Harlem ran only in minority newspapers and not in national syndication). The Comic Book Legal Defense Fund argues that Brandon-Croft rarely receives her due as a pioneering creator, suggesting, "Although she was the first African American woman to publish a nationally syndicated comic strip, Barbara Brandon-Croft's incredible impact with her all-Black-women strip unfortunately does not get nearly the recognition she deserves." The Comic Book Legal Defense Fund observes that Brandon-Croft's comic strip had two intentions:

> *Where I'm Coming From*'s mission as a comic meant to affect change rather than just entertain was twofold. First, Brandon-Croft wanted

white readers to fully grasp the struggles of Black Americans as
people in their own right, not just characters that happened to be
brown-skinned. . . . "If mainstream folk understand the black perspective better, they wouldn't be surprised at the rage we're holding. We know white people because we're exposed to them, but they
don't know us. If we're going to have a peaceful existence, they have
to understand our perspective." . . . Arguably more important was
the second part of Brandon-Croft's mission, which was to speak on
politically charged issues through a Black woman's perspectives
and create characters that Black women readers could readily identify with.

B. Croft as a rhetor

Brandon-Croft chose to fashion what Lloyd Bitzer calls a "fitting
response" to the exigence of the rhetorical situation, one that utilized
her skills as an artist and creator and one that began to address a
very prominent absence. The choice to use a comic strip is significant,
for, as Carolyn Miller argues, its "form shapes the response of the
reader or listener to substance by providing instruction, so to speak, *challenged*
about how to perceive and interpret; this guidance disposes the audi- *comics*
ence to anticipate, to be gratified, to respond in a certain way" (159). *conventions*
Indeed, Brandon-Croft drew on the familiar form of the comic strip,
but defied its conventions in very specific, very pointed ways.

Most papers placed the weekly comic in the editorial or opinion *politics*
pages, rather than with the daily strips. This position emphasized the *vs*
political nature of the strip, in opposition to a humor or adventure *humor*
strip. Elisabeth Hickey noted that "*Where I'm Coming From* is a series
of talking heads that often speak directly to the audience. Like the
Feifer strips, *Where I'm Coming From* is designed to run on editorial or
lifestyle pages, in a bigger format than that of the comics pages" (E1).
Furthermore, Brandon-Croft explained to Hickey that she preferred
to be placed apart from the other comics, exclaiming, "I don't want
to be on the funny pages. . . . I want to be separate" (qtd. in Hickey
E1). In placing the strip apart from the "funny pages," the reader is *separate*
immediately alerted that this is a more political strip—a strip that *from*
challenges and informs in addition to entertaining. And while Bran- *funny*
don-Croft celebrated the separateness, this positionality also further *pages*
isolated her voice as being more pointed and more partisan—not a
part of the fabric of the everyday comics but something removed
and different. While a strategy that visually announced the stance of
the comic as having a unique political perspective frames the work's

Black women disconnected from the quotsdian

power, it also serves, once again, to disconnect Black women's voices from the other comic strips, marking the pages of the daily comics, dominated by White, cis men, as the norm (and, for that matter, normative) and Brandon-Croft's work as the outlier.

Still, critics of the time were looking for connections between *Where I'm Coming From* and others, noting Brandon-Croft's relationship to other artists and creators, such as one of her idols, Jules Feiffer, as well as popular celebrities of the time, particularly noting similarities with Black figures like Oprah Winfrey and Arsenio Hall. Sometimes these comparisons were relatively straightforward; sometimes they were couched in language that read like an awkward imitation of Black English. For example, Christopher John Farley observed, "Brandon's strip is an Afrocentric mix of Jules Feiffer and the Oprah Winfrey show. Its humor is a hybrid too, from the Arsenio Hall/*New Yorker* magazine 'things that make you say hmmmm' school'" (4D). Keith Thomas remarked, "Sorry, homegirl . . . Move aside, Cathy, and make way for some 'girls' from the 'hood.' . . . Call it legendary satirist Jules Feiffer (impressionable characters, humorous monologues, sparse art) meets Arsenio Hall (hip, topical, down and dope). Woo! Woo! Woo! Woo!" (B1). This last review in particular feels problematic in its language and tone, especially as the women depicted in the strip sound nothing like the review, with nary a "Woo!" in sight. Furthermore, Thomas immediately links *Where I'm Coming From* with *Cathy*, simply because they are both created by women, and with Arsenio Hall, most likely given his popularity as a Black comedian.

Audience, Association, and Dissociation

Format different

As previously mentioned, *Where I'm Coming From* appeared weekly in newspapers across the country, normally on "Opinion" or "Editorial" pages. The strip was distinct from other strips not only in placement but in format, featuring one larger rectangle with no panels or divisions, but rather a sequence of talking heads presenting Brandon-Croft's "girls," a rotating cast of regular characters including Lekesia, Nicole, Cheryl, and Alisha. According to Brandon-Croft, "girls" is simply short for "girlfriends," although "they're definitely women" (qtd. in Thomas B1). The women themselves all appear to be Black, and each, depicted only with heads and arms, has a distinctly different look, with varying hair, eyes, skin tone, and accessories, visibly and undeniably demonstrating the diversity of Black women. In an interview with Sheila Rule, Brandon-Croft argued, "Part of the point is how varied we are. . . . We are not a monolithic people as black women. I can't say I'm a spokesman for all black women." Moreover, men only appear in text through telephone conversations; they are never pictured physically.

With so much of the physical body left undepicted, the lettering, in addition to the artist's style, carries a great deal of the weight of storytelling, substituting for gesture and visual cues as to how to interpret the text. The lettering, all in capital letters, is clear and direct. Occasionally, Brandon-Croft will highlight words and phrases by writing the text in bold or an outline, drawing the reader's attention to key moments. The women communicate without speech balloons and no background details, their heads floating in empty space. Rather than speech balloons, the text simply emanates from the speaker, thus creating an "open" sequence of talking heads, usually speaking directly to the reader, and often to one another, either directly or on the telephone.

The comic is a static one, with very little movement, as necessitated by the focus on faces. Characters will gesture from moment to moment, moving a hand or raising an eyebrow, but the comic is largely cerebral, marked by ideas over action. Brandon-Croft related that this emphasis on thoughts was a very conscious one, as women have for so long been associated with the body, rather than the mind. In an interview with Harriette Cole, Brandon-Croft explained, "I wasn't interested in using full bodies. I was so sick of women being thought of in terms of their bodies." In another discussion with Keith Thomas, Brandon-Croft jokes, "Actually, I'm not good at drawing bodies. . . . Seriously, for too long in our society, women have been summed up by their body parts and not their brains. I want to change that" (B1). Rather, Brandon-Croft wanted to stress the dialogic nature of the exchange, with the characters speaking directly to readers: "I'm going to have the women talk to the reader face to face. Eye to eye. This is what I'm talking about. This is what I want you to see. You don't see anything else but what I'm saying to you" (Cole). In *The Blacker the Ink,* Rebecca Wanzo poses the question, "How can representations of black bodies or black humor move beyond stereotype to progressive political commentary, when the history of black representation is one that is always already comical, hyperphysical, and outside of narratives about 'universal' concerns in the United States?" (327). For Brandon-Croft, the answer was in the removal or absence of female Black bodies. She would rewrite them in their absence, forcing the reader away from the physical and into the intellectual plane.

The candor of the comic is also conveyed through the strong, simple artistic rendering. The lines are distinct and bold, with shading from Zip-a-Tone offering texture. The art reinforces the simple, direct appeal of the comic to readers—this is not a gag-a-day strip, but rather a conversation between character and reader. There is no narrative text, no extra-diegetic narrator distancing the audience from the events. And the focalizer becomes a part of the conversation, seeing not from above or outside the frame, but facing it.

audience

Brandon-Croft's carefully considers her subject position in invoking her audience and inviting that readership into a dialogue. Sara L. McKinnon posits, "Historical mindfulness means paying attention to significant and formative events of the past, and more importantly, paying attention to the historicity between audience and subject" (195). Thus, scholars would do well to consider the historical importance of the first nationally syndicated Black woman speaking directly to a mainstream audience through a comic on the editorial pages. And although it isn't just or fair, *Where I'm Coming From* took on consequence as readers looked to the strip for *the* Black female perspective of the time. McKinnon continues, "When marginalized rhetors stand and speak before deciding audiences, they are read not just as themselves (and who they represent) but are recognized within a reflection of the audience" (193). Brandon-Croft and her "girls" therefore came to speak for Black women, but also to reflect the hopes and fears of the larger readership.

Brandon-Croft rightly scoffed at the frequent comparisons to *Cathy* made in the press, as she explained to Elisabeth Hickey, the creator "cringes when people call her strip the 'Black Cathy'" (E1). Clearly, it is insulting to be reduced to a racialized version of the "normalized" White *Cathy,* simply because these were two of the extremely rare comic strips created by women about women. However, despite Brandon-Croft's critique of Cathy as a "self-involved character who is 'upset that she doesn't have a waistline'" (qtd. in Montresor 339), the two strips both frequently addressed themes of beauty, fashion, and relationships, as in a strip in which Judy comments on Cheryl's unsightly chin hairs, left unattended after a recent breakup (see figure 6.2).

connection/comparison to Cathy

FIGURE 6.2. Barbara Brandon-Croft. "Sorry I'm Late, Cheryl." *Where I'm Coming From,* p. 27.

By focusing on these commonplace, personal, and embarrassing moments, Brandon-Croft invokes a sense of association between author and audience. Perelman and Olbrechts-Tyteca explain: "By processes of association we understand schemes which bring separate elements together and allow us to establish unity among them, which aims either at organizing them or at evaluating them, positively or negatively, by means of one another" (190). Brandon-Croft creates a sense of "unity" between the two joking, friendly characters, but more importantly, with the wider readership, in this small, awkward moment in which one character cringes in humiliation at being called out for unsightly facial hair, a mark of failure in personal grooming habits after the demise of a relationship. The humor of the strip comes from the sense of camaraderie and connection between the two women who know one another so well, in addition to the visual of the two small hairs sprouting from Judy's chin, visible at first, then almost-but-not-quite covered by a teacup in the second scene, and once again revealed in the third panel, before Judy covers her face with her hands, her eyes wide with shock as her teacup slips from her hands and almost out of the panel. The reader watches the seamless progression of this small drama, associating with the very human moment between friends.

audience, association, unity

FIGURE 6.3. Barbara Brandon-Croft. "Ain't Life a Trip?!" *Where I'm Coming From,* p. 26.

Yet even as *Where I'm Coming From* built connections through the foibles of women struggling with unattainable beauty standards, it also confronted racist myths about female appearance, as in the strip featuring Monica (see figure 6.3), described by Sheila Rule as "a light-skinned black woman with green eyes and long, wavy hair," wondering:

> "Ain't Life a trip?! There are White folks who don't like me 'cause I'm Black. And some Black folks who don't like me 'cause I **look** White. Ok . . . So my skin **is** "high yellow." And my eyes **are** green— No, I'm not wearing contacts. I didn't ask for any of this. It was the white slavemasters who raped my ancestors that mixed my heritage. Now, who can tell me why we call this "good hair"?

The strip pictures eight faces of Monica, with four in a row above and four below, with her monologue lettered in sturdy black capitals just to the right of her face. If anything, the text functions something like the panel border, dividing each moment in the soliloquy. Monica is depicted with large, bountiful hair rising high from her forehead and flowing down her face and unseen shoulders in sweeping waves. It is the stereotypical "princess hair" of numerous animated maidens. But Monica's face, framed by the hair, is marked by wrinkles and lines indicating frustration at her intersectional position, disliked by Whites and Blacks because of her hair, her "high yellow" skin, and her green eyes. But Monica bluntly indicates her innocence in her appearance, calling out the "white slavemasters who raped by ancestors" and contributed to her appearance, wondering how this marker of White culture could ever be termed "good hair"? This direct confrontation of beauty norms that exalt Whiteness forces the reader to consider the history of slavery as well as the origins of standards of attractiveness in American culture.

Where I'm Coming From developed an association between characters and the newspaper readership in embracing commonalities and shared lived experiences, but also worked toward dismantling stereotypes through dissociation, a rhetorical practice whereby the "techniques of separation which have the purpose of dissociating, separating, disuniting elements which are regarded as forming a whole or at least a unified group within some system of thought" (Perelman and Olbrechts-Tyteca 190). Brandon-Croft breaks down stereotypes through representation, clearly illustrating the ways in which the lived experiences of Black women are different from White women and from one another, exploring the standpoint of her characters, as she does in this strip from November 8, 1993, which challenges Lekesia's racist, sexist boss (see figure 6.4).

In the strip, Lekesia, a middle-aged Black woman, is pictured in a sequence of six heads with her arms and hands gesturing and writing on a piece of paper. Lekesia has curly black hair framing her expressive face, and her eyes, eyebrows, and mouth move dramatically throughout her monologue, indicating her irritation with wide eyes and raised eyebrows, and her amusement with a softening of her brow and a slightly turned up smile. Her speech, without balloons or marks of attribution, is lettered in large, clear capitals positioned to the right of each face. Over the course of the six panels Lekesia states:

> Can you believe my boss came to me complaining about how White men are always getting dumped on? He said he's sick and tired of it. He said Black people blame him for slavery and its residual effects. Women fault him for "their inequality." He said he doesn't appreciate taking responsibility for everything from the failed economy to the threat of nuclear war. I said, "Mr. Ivory, if you can't stand your reflection . . . Stay away from the mirror."

FIGURE 6.4. Barbara Brandon-Croft. "Can You Believe My Boss . . ." *Where I'm Coming From,* p. 68.

Dissociation =
difference!

Lekesia distinctly calls out the (differences) in her experience from her
boss, the comically named "Mr. Ivory," a White man who despairs
that he is "always getting dumped on" by Black people and women,
arguing that he is not responsible for "everything," while Lekesia
argues that Mr. Ivory needs to face his own prejudice and complic-
ity or "stay away from the mirror." In this sequence, Brandon-Croft
breaks apart assumptions and challenges White, cis-male privilege,
using dissociation to hasten "a more or less profound change in the
conceptual data that are used as the basis of argument. It is then no
more a question of breaking the links that join independent elements,
but of modifying the very structure of these elements" (Perelman and
Olbrechts-Tyteca 412). Brandon-Croft points to the difference and
seeks to modify the reader's understanding of these subject positions,
not simply dismantling Mr. Ivory's opinion, one that might be shared
by readers, but seeking to transform it by calling out its inadequacy,
for the visages of White men loom over the specters of racism, sexism, the economy, and war.

Brandon-Croft's use of association and dissociation simultaneously creates a connection even as it disassembles stereotypes, a
fitting response to an exigent rhetorical situation. However, some

Both / And

members of the audience of readers, much like Mr. Ivory, strongly rejected *Where I'm Coming From*'s rhetorical appeal. And, in studying these responses it becomes clear, as Carolyn Miller determines, that "studying the typical uses of rhetoric, and the forms it takes in those uses, tells us less about the art of individual rhetors or the excellence of particular texts than it does about the character of a culture or an historical period" (158). The reactions of some readers indicate a culture unable to "look in the mirror" and acknowledge racism, as evidenced in a "Letter to the Editor" by Clifford Morris from Lithonia:

> This is about Barbara Brandon, a woman whose comic strip, *"Where I'm Coming From"* was given national syndication a while back. She joined the ranks of all the wonderful people who earn good money creating comic strips with characters and thoughts mostly meant to amuse the reader. While reading her comic strip Monday, Nov. 8, about a complaining white boss who is worried to death about being blamed for all of the social troubles of today. I was highly amused. She named the boss Mr. Ivory-oh, how brilliant! And then she really cut him down at the end. Wow! She showed him! Letting off your own personal steam at the expense of further separating the races seems to be the popular thing to do these days. Let's just go ahead and let a comic strip do it too while we're at it. Hey, why not? I think I'll create a comic strip of my own about a woman whose comic strip is so bad that she finally gives it up and goes on to more worthwhile endeavors. (A12)

Morris begins his missive with a personal attack on the creator, implying her luck at becoming one of the "wonderful people who earn good money" creating comic strips that are meant to "amuse" rather than, say, educate. Morris plays heavily on a sense of irony here, as he does throughout the letter, suggesting he is savvy and intelligent enough to imply the opposite—that Brandon-Croft is not worthy to join her compatriots on the comics page. He continues, noting he was "highly amused" by her play on the name "Mr. Ivory" as well his appreciation with how she "cut him down" with the use of frequent exclamation points. Morris argues that the creator is "letting off your own personal steam" while "further separating the races," using an argument dependent on negatives couched as positives. The sarcasm is cutting, suggesting Brandon-Croft deserves neither the company of fellow "wonderful" creators, nor the excellent salary she is earning. Morris's letter takes a turn when he insinuates he might just fashion his own comic strip, implying this is an easy task, but his comic strip, once again taking the form of a very personal, very direct attack, will focus on a female whose "strip is so bad that she finally gives it up." The letter writer invokes *antiphrasis* in his disdain for Brandon-Croft, implying a patronizing tone that seeks to identify her as an unworthy outsider and racist, causing additional fissures between races.

strip reception

Where I'm Coming From elicited a similar reaction from Mrs. Gary Crow, who voiced her thoughts in a letter to the *Atlanta Journal and Constitution* on April 1, 1992:

> The March 23 cartoon, *"Where I'm Coming From"* is sending mixed messages. When African-Americans, blacks, or whatever they call themselves in 1992 complain about their equal share of the American pie, the subject of segregation is always used as an excuse for their present status in life. Now that segregation is illegal, is not being taught and is constantly fought via "equal opportunity," Barbara Brandon uses the subject as her cartoon theme. This depicts the narrow-mindedness and negativism that keeps a person from succeeding. What is the value of portraying a character who would accentuate the negative? (A12)

The strip, originally published March 23, 1992, once again features Lekesia directly addressing the audience in a series of six faces, divided not by panels or lines but text, residing just to the right of Lekesia's face (see figure 6.5). Lekesia explains:

> My boss said to me at lunch today, "Is that your nose in another history book? I thought that black thing was last month." I said, "Yes, Black History Month has passed, but March happens to be Women's History Month." Then I heard him mutter, "Black History, Women's History, whatever happened to good old American history?" I said, "Excuse me. I don't think I heard what you said." He said, "Why do you people always have to separate yourselves?" I said, "I guess we had good teachers; the idea of segregation wasn't something **we** invented."

FIGURE 6.5. Barbara Brandon-Croft. "My Boss Said to Me . . ." *Where I'm Coming From*, p. 17. Originally published March 23, 1992.

Lekesia moves little from image to image, her eyes remaining downcast, although they widen when she confronts her boss on his mumblings, not allowing him to escape without confrontation of his prejudices. Her arms and hands support her face, then gesture, and ultimately cross in front of her, framing her visage. In the sequence, Lekesia indicates her support of both Black History Month and Women's History Month through reading historical books during her lunch break, a stance her boss simply doesn't understand, as he indicates his mumbled desire for a return to "good old American history," presumably a history of White, cis-males that ignores women and people of color. But when Lekesia calls out this disrespect and ignorance, her boss doubles-down on his position, asking why "you people," presumably people of color and women, choose to set themselves apart from the dominant narrative, not participating in the glory of American history. In a scathing retort, Lekesia delivers the back-handed compliment to the "good teachers," otherwise known as the White men who invented segregation, who chose from the onset to define themselves as dominant, and all others unworthy to participate.

Of course, the argument that it is, in fact, a direct result of men like Lekesia's boss and the myopic focus on White men as presented in historical narratives that has forced marginalized people to create new histories that challenge and intersect the grand narratives greatly upset some readers, such as Mrs. Crow, who appears to utterly misinterpret Brandon-Croft's strip as, once again, contributing to racial divides, even as Mrs. Crow aligns herself with Lekesia's boss. In her letter, Mrs. Crow struggles with terminology, unsure whether to use "African-Americans, blacks, or whatever they call themselves in 1992," pointing to what she sees as a capricious and changeable identity. Additionally, in a letter that purportedly challenges divisions, Mrs. Crow notably uses "they," as opposed to "us" or "we." Mrs. Crow also perceives the strip as representative as one of "them," i.e., non-White Americans, or, as Lekesia's boss prefers, "you people," whining about not getting an "equal share" as a result of segregation, a position Mrs. Crow steadfastly counters with the fact that segregation is now illegal and is being "constantly" offset by "equal opportunity," which is marked by rather ironic quotation marks, implying that these opportunities are not actually equal but rather a special gift or unearned reward.

reception

It is quite fascinating to observe the leaps in logic maintained by Mrs. Crow in her conjecture that equal opportunity is capable of forever and always counterbalancing years of slavery, segregation, and racial prejudice. In her continued confusion, Mrs. Crow laments Brandon-Croft's "narrow-mindedness and negativity," completely missing the strip's larger cultural critique, ultimately concluding that Lekesia's attitude will result in personal failure, something neither the character nor the creator Brandon-Croft have cause to fear. But fear is an undercurrent in the letter, for in her willful misinterpretation, Mrs. Crow clearly demonstrates her fear of "them," of the creator, and of acknowledging the racism pervasive in American society, as voiced by Lekesia's boss, and, of course, the letter writer herself. For her part, Brandon-Croft seemed unbothered by the letters, in an interview with Hariette Cole reflecting ruefully on the writers, who told her, "'We don't want black people on our page'. . . . I got a letter saying that I should go back to Africa and take Jesse Jackson." But Brandon-Croft's editor Marty Claus remarked that despite a few critics, *Where I'm Coming From* "can appeal across all lines. And a lot of her mail points out she does" (Farley 4D). Brandon-Croft's work inspired heated conversation, bringing to fore a conversation about race many feared to have.

Constraints and Community

good summary of argument

Clearly, *Where I'm Coming From* struck a chord with readers, as Brandon-Croft worked to address this moment of historical exigence by associating and developing points of connection, even as she disassociated with racism and essentialism, indicating intersections of difference. Although her work represents an important intervention, as a comic strip it was marked by important constraints that limited its reach. Initially the strip struggled to find a home and was "rejected by every major syndicate except Universal Press Syndicate" (Bentley 1E). Brandon-Croft explained that editors "would say, 'We're not going to be able to sell this because it's about black women, written by a black woman, it has no mass appeal.' . . . But I say, we're here, we're not going anywhere so you might as well get to know us" (Bentley 1E). Brandon-Croft faced "double" discrimination, as she recounted to Keith Loria: "I get it double duty. . . . I'm told, 'We already have a black comic strip and we have "Cathy" (a "woman's strip").' It's ignorant, but it happens." Once it was nationally syndicated, the strip had to contend with its small size and, although it was the distinct choice of the creator, its "outsider" position on the lifestyle or editorial pages, along with its once-a-week delivery, which may have made it more difficult to forge a connection with readers.

Yet Brandon-Croft argued that her strip had a wide appeal, despite the concerns of editors, and indeed, echoing Harper, we are "all here together," and despite the angry letters, *Where I'm Coming From* flourished for sixteen years, marking a physical place in the newspaper as well as a place and positionality in public conversation, the subject position of diverse Black women that needed to be represented in everyday discourse. Patricia Collins remarks on the importance of acknowledging the standpoints of Black women, noting that "the overarching theme of finding a voice to express a collective, self-defined Black women's standpoint remains a core theme in Black feminist thought" (110). *Where I'm Coming From* pointed out commonalities through association, addressing problems with work, relationships, money, bosses, and beauty, thus developing a sense of community and connection, yet she also used dissociation to dismantle stereotypes and indicate differences, representing the diversity of Black women through multiple characters and perspectives. Audre Lorde argued:

> As women, we have been taught either to ignore our differences, or to view them as causes for separation and suspicion rather than as forces for change. Without community there is no liberation, only the most vulnerable and temporary armistice between an individual and her oppression. But community must not mean a shedding of our differences, nor the pathetic pretense that these differences do not exist. (112)

Brandon-Croft answered Lorde's call, building community while acknowledging difference.

Where I'm Coming From was a nationally syndicated comic strip that appeared each week on the editorial pages. That is, in fact, its location—where it came from. Yet it also represented a meta-cognitive position, addressing the exigence of a pressing rhetorical situation, a public conversation that lacked Black female voices. Brandon-Croft developed what Michael J. Hyde describes as an "ethos of rhetoric," which can be seen

> to refer to the way discourse is used to transform space and time into "dwelling places," where people can deliberate about and "know together," (con-scientia) some matter of interest. Such dwelling places define the grounds, the abodes or habitants, where a person's ethos and moral character take form and develop. (xiii)

Where I'm Coming From presented such a dwelling place where readers were able to think and learn, adapting and growing, and this "abode" was established within the tradition of the White, male newspaper comic strips. And it was in this space that *Where I'm Coming From* challenged stereotypes, through its heteroglossia, establishing a presence, a situatedness that argued for a community marked by diversity. Brandon-Croft takes advantage of the rhetorical situation, acknowledging the exigence of the moment to draw upon association and dissociation, and illustrate intersectionality as well as points of connection, developing cooperation and conversation. Lekesia can be Black and a feminist and American—she can be more than one thing. And a comic can reach out and build a community through the newspaper and into the larger world. In her study of Frances Watkins Harper, Shirley Logan suggests Harper's importance as a "public intellectual . . . one who participates in public discourse that has as its purpose the application of ideas to the understanding and possible modification of social and political phenomena" (127), and like Harper, Brandon-Croft acted as such a public intellectual, a figure occupying a space in the newspaper and offering a point-of-view that educated, informed, and confronted the readership, inviting them to connect and challenging them to truly see her place and position, summoning a sense of harmony and accord that recognized and celebrated multiplicity.

CHAPTER 7

SOMETHING FROM NOTHING

The Inductive Argument of *Stone Soup*

Mom, are you a feminist?

—Jan Eliot

WHEN I WAS a girl in 1984 I awaited the arrival of the newspaper eagerly, pulling back the yellowing curtains of our large front window and surveying the street, impatiently anticipating delivery. I was the youngest in my family, and therefore by all rights the last to receive the paper, but I often got up early to sneak a peek before the rest of the family. I still do. Sometimes I wonder if I'm one of the last of the newspaper readers who cherishes the walk down the driveway each morning, the ritual of turning the crinkly pages while drinking my coffee. But for me and many others, the newspaper was a constant, reassuring presence in my life, and the comics in particular undoubtedly shaped my perceptions of self and society. For Lynda Barry, *Family Circus* was a window into another world where happy families played with sunbeams and took naps with the family dog. For me, the comics offered a sense of the wider world for an awkward tomboy in a small, conservative town. I didn't understand a lot of the strips, but I read them anyway. Once again, although I've moved and grown and I'm no longer so young, I still read the comics every morning.

personal anecdote

[handwritten margin note: (lack) of change in newspaper comics from 1984 – 2014]

In fact, when I recently compared the comics pages from the *Oregonian* from December 5, 1984, to the pages from December 5, 2014, precisely thirty years later, very little had changed at all. While the total number of strips dropped from thirty-six to twenty-nine, there were still only three strips authored or coauthored by women—the number had not risen at all. The year 1984 featured the work of Lynn Johnston, Nicole Hollander, and Cathy Guisewite, while 2014 included *Luann,* coauthored by Karen Evans along with her father Greg Evans; *Rhymes with Orange* by Hilary Price; and *Stone Soup* by Jan Eliot. Thus, female creators continued to be utterly underrepresented. Creators of color also remained absent. While several Black creators were active during this thirty-year period, such as Ray Billingsley with *Curtis,* Aaron McGruder with *The Boondocks,* Robb Armstrong with *Jump Start,* Morrie Turner with *Wee Pals,* Brumsic Brandon Jr. with *Luther,* and Brumsic's daughter, Barbara Brandon-Croft, with *Where I'm Coming From,* none of these comics appeared in the *Oregonian* in 1984 *or* in 2014. Furthermore, while it would be inappropriate to make presumptions regarding the backgrounds of comics creators, it is clear that creators of color, including those of Asian, Hispanic, Pacific Islander, and Native American descent, are lacking, to say the least. Once again, it would be inaccurate to draw conclusions about creators' LGBTQ+ status, but it can be said that the comics themselves did not feature LGBTQ+ characters or themes in 1984 or 2014, at least in the mainstream papers.

And, indeed, a closer look at the characters and themes demonstrates, once again, how little changed over those thirty years. On the pages from December 5, 2014, I identified twelve animal characters, seventeen women, and thirty-eight men.[1] There was only one Black character, Phil, a police officer and the boyfriend/fiancée of Val Stone from *Stone Soup.* No other characters of color were represented. By 2014 the action comics had largely been phased out, with the focus fixed squarely on domestic strips, while a few others revolved around work or gags. Men are pictured working, driving, drinking, raging, and pondering their careers. The men in these strips are out and about in the world, with the exception of Dagwood, who takes a bath in honor of "Bathtub Party Day." Women cook, wonder whether

[handwritten margin note: still gender stereotypes]

---

1. I did not count individual characters in crowd scenes, due to the difficulty of discerning distinct people. I also did not guess the genders of animals or babies.

their clothing makes them look fat (and no, it's not *Cathy* but *Bizarro*), chat and argue with friends, and discuss relationships. The women are mothers, caretakers, parents, and the keepers of the family. Only Val Stone appears to be at work. In fact, although several of the strips have been traded out since 1984, these pages bear an uncanny resemblance to the pages from thirty years prior, with White, cis-gendered men dominating the pages, both as creators and characters.

However, one newer strip that appears in 2014 and didn't feature thirty years prior bears additional attention for its approach in depicting women, men, and families, and in doing so, positing an evolving legacy of feminism: *Stone Soup.* On this particular day in 2014, *Stone Soup* features main character Val Stone sitting at her desk in her office, speaking to her boyfriend, Phil Jackson (see figure 7.1). In the three-panel strip, Phil and Val discuss a conversational gaffe in which Phil's aunt referred to Val as his fiancée. The first panel features a split screen introducing the two characters speaking on the phone, divided by a jagged vertical line. The split screen panel is followed by two subsequent panels, one featuring Val sitting at her computer screen speaking on a phone, querying Phil regarding his feelings about the faux pas, asking, "Well . . . When your aunt misspoke and said I was your fiancée . . . How did that **make** you **feel?**" The final panel focuses on Phil, his face contorted with anxiety as evidenced by his wide eyes, raised eyebrows, and his mouth pulled into a rictus of a toothy grimace as his thought balloon screeches, "Danger! Danger! Danger!" The strip illustrates a key moment in the couple's development, as, despite Phil's misgivings, the couple do become engaged, eventually marrying in July 2015, only a few months before Eliot decided to cease publishing daily strips, although she published a Sunday strip until July 2020, even after the final daily was published in October 2015. Moreover, the strip features Val, a single mother, clearly working in her office, rather than cleaning house or looking after the children. Additionally, Phil is a Black police officer, defying the disturbing historical trend of erasing Black characters or, alternately, depicting them as criminals or comic relief. *Stone Soup* showed readers another point-of-view, another powerfully persuasive perspective on family, gender, and feminism.

In fact, *Stone Soup* represents the theme of making "something from nothing," in this case a feminist community, invoking *phronesis* through *epagoge,* or inductive argument. In her book, *An Aristotelian Account of Induction: Creating Something Out of Nothing,* Louise

STONE SOUP JAN ELIOT

FIGURE 7.1. Jan Eliot. *Stone Soup. Oregonian.* December 5, 2014.

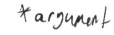

Groarke explains that although she is arguing for "a kind of 'creation of something from nothing,' this is not to make any kind of metaphysical claim about existent things somehow springing out of non-existence. It is to claim, more modestly, that induction produces more knowledge from less" (4). Thus, through its daily accounts of the Stone family, Eliot develops an accretion of images, a layering of impressions and moments that conjure up a practical, identifiable, relatable feminist community, one that breaks the fourth wall and reaches out to other comic strips and, ultimately, to the readers. This chapter explores *Stone Soup* and its impact as one of the few female-created comic strips that continued in syndication until July 2020, considering what has changed on the comics pages since 1975 and speculating about what might be next.

Inductive Reasoning: From the Ground Up

Philosophers argue passionately about Aristotle's intentions regarding *epagoge* as inductive reasoning or argument, and they have been doing so for quite some time. However, an extended evaluation of the long-running quarrel is beyond the scope of this particular analysis.[2] Despite any philosophical wrangling, the idea of developing a position through the accrual of small details bears special

2. Louise Groarke's *An Aristotelian Account of Induction: Creating Something Out of Nothing* usefully outlines the history of this discussion before introducing her own "reclamation" of the term, which bears significantly on my use of the term in this chapter.

consideration in regards to newspapers strips. A comic strip that appears daily over many years makes an ampliative argument—it enlarges thought and understanding through the very accumulation of moments. Groarke clarifies that "whenever we engage in induction, we end up with more than what we started with. We begin with sense perception and are somehow able to transform our experience into a larger understanding. We begin with a few examples and are somehow able to know something about the universal case" (4). Furthermore, "the mental process that precipitates induction operates by a radical leap of creativity that closely resembles artistic inspiration" (Groake 38). Regular readers of newspaper comics thus build up a bigger picture, a "larger understanding," of an idea or concept or community, bringing their own creative thinking and insights to bear as they consume the content and reflect on the insights inherent in each small comic strip.

Comics & inductive reasoning or epa-joge

And in that way, attentive readers of *Stone Soup* had the opportunity to gradually build an informed position on a community rarely depicted in the comics prior to the strip's publication—a thriving matriarchal family with no husbands or fathers (at least until much later in the history of the strip). What is more, the everyday strips were marked by another rhetorical concept *phronesis* the sort of practical, real-world information that resonates widely. While Aristotle lauded the value of theoretical wisdom *sophia* to address higher, universal truths *phronesis* is embedded in everyday interactions. David Blockley contends that "*phronesis* was an intellectual virtue of perceiving and understanding in effective ways and acting benevolently and beneficently." Likewise, Blockley notes that "the intellectual faculties required were *phronesis* for *praxis*," arguing that practical wisdom is necessary to guide our actions in the real world, apart from any erudite theories or philosophies. Christopher Long reasons, "*Phronesis* recognizes that truth must always be critically engaged, for it does not lie in ultimates but rather in the give and take between actually existing beings" (54). And although the members of the Stone family do not actually exist, they do dwell in tangible form in the newspaper, and they depict the normal give-and-take of family and friends who truly care for one another. This is not a bitter or caustic strip. It is not biting or sarcastic, but full of flawed and relatable people interacting on a daily basis and through small moments, ultimately establishing a feminist community.

Phronesis & stone soup

In fact, Eliot's path to building this comic strip family was a long biography one, marked by numerous fits and starts along the way as she worked toward syndication. Born September 27, 1950, in San Jose, California, Eliot found herself, according to an interview with Tom Zucco, "a single mom with two young daughters living in Eugene, Ore. In the midst of the late 1970s recession. But at least she could always find a job. She waited tables, sold cars and worked in a library. Well, actually, she drove a bookmobile" (1F). According to Randi Bjornstad, as the creator launched her comics career, she felt she needed a new name, for "her surname at birth had been Buell, and her married name was Graveline, but as she prepared to begin a new life she really didn't want to be either one." Eliot chose her pseudonym in honor of George Eliot, and remembered on a blog entry on September 9th, 2009, that she

> began cartooning as creative therapy shortly after a divorce, when I was a working mom of two young girls. The stress of making ends meet, managing my dear daughters and their school, daycare and my own work schedule, left me a bit drained and overwhelmed. And of course, feeling guilty about all I couldn't do. Cartooning was a perfect outlet, one I could afford, among other things.

Ethos magazine recounts:

> In 1979, a close friend suggested Eliot try cartooning. Intrigued by the idea, she bought a handful of how-to cartooning manuals from Eugene-based Smith Family Bookstore. Following the instructions, she started experimenting with characters and storylines. . . . To develop her own personal style, Eliot studied the work of other cartoonists. In the process, she fell in love with the art form. Her day job in graphic design and advertising permitted a bit of artistic freedom when drawing up visuals for projects, but nothing compared to making comic strips. ("Funny Business")

Her first strip, titled *Patience and Sarah,* appeared in the *Willamette Valley Observer* and eventually about ten weekly and monthly papers. It ran from 1980 to 1982 and featured a single mother and her daughter. Eliot found encouragement from Nicole Hollander, with whom she'd been corresponding, and when Hollander "invited Eliot to attend the

1982 National Cartoonist Guild annual weekend in New York" (Yackley F3), Eliot raised money to attend by selling her original art. At the time Eliot was considering a syndication offer from United Feature Syndicate, but at the conference, legendary cartoonist Mort Walker advised her that it was "a terrible contract, and the deal fell through" (Yackley F3). Discouraged, Eliot quit cartooning for several years. According to an interview with Randi Bjornstad, it was only after Eliot married "corporate trainer" Ted Lay that she "had the emotional strength to begin cartooning again." Encouraged by her good friend Val Brooks, Eliot began the weekly strip *Sister City* in 1990, which "ran regionally in the *Register Guard,* the *Cottage Grove Sentinel* and the *Vancouver Columbian*" (Bjornstad) and featured the characters "Val and Joan, sisters and working moms, one divorced and one widowed (Val) . . . their three kids Holly, Alix and Max, and their mother who came to live with Val. Joan showed up on Val's doorstep after her husband Leon went out for milk and ended up in the Virgin Islands" (Tobin). In later years Eliot added neighbor Wally, who later marries Joan, and Officer Phil Jackson, Val's love interest, and Andy, Wally's nephew.

Eliot worked hard on the strip, honing her craft, pursuing national syndication relentlessly, and "in 1995, after 16 years of trying, she convinced Universal Press to pick up one of her strips" (Zucco 1F). It was a long and arduous journey, and one beset by sexism. In an online interview with Suzanne Tobin of the *Washington Post,* Eliot remembered, "When I first started breaking in, a syndicate said to me, 'We have Cathy, we have Lynn (FBOFW), why do we need you?' There's a perception that you only need a sampling of women to get the woman's viewpoint. Aren't we just cartoonists, with a cartoonists [*sic*] viewpoint?" Even once Eliot had broken through and received the contract offer, Rachel Baruch Yackley noted that Universal Syndicate was concerned about the strip being perceived as "too feminist": "Viewing the name 'Sister City' as possibly off-putting to the wider audience, Universal asked Eliot to come up with a new name, and 'Stone Soup' hit the ground running" (F3). Actually, Eliot further clarified to Randi Bjornstad, "They said the name 'Sister City' might be perceived as too ardently feminist in the South. . . . I had chosen it because it had two sets of sisters—Val and Joan, and Holly and Alix—but I didn't mind the change. I actually like the reference to the 'stone soup' fable, which is making something out of nothing."

With syndication Eliot committed fully and unequivocally to the strip. In an interview with Cara Roberts Murez, Eliot remembered, "I quit my job as soon as the strip was launched. . . . It was only launched in about 25 papers. I think my first paycheck was $700. I was 45 by the time the strip got launched and I wasn't going to risk not giving it my full attention." *Stone Soup*'s popularity rose steadily over the years, and, "At the comic strip's peak, 'Stone Soup' was in 300 newspapers seven days a week" (Murez). In 2015, after many successful years in syndication, Eliot decided to semi-retire, cutting her strip down to Sundays only. The strip appeared once-a-week on Sundays until 2020, giving her loyal readers continued snapshots into the lives of the Stone family before the final strips were published in the summer of 2020.

Eliot drew on her family and friends for inspiration for the Stone family. In a "Meet the Creator" blog entry for GoComics, Eliot stated:

> My characters were originally created from the raw material of my own family and friends. I have two daughters, just like Val, and while Holly and Alix are not 'like' my daughters, my years as a mom inform who they are and what they do. Because I did not get syndicated until my daughters were nearly grown, I decided to freeze Holly and Alix at ages that are fun for me to write for.

And even though the characters didn't age, over the years of the strip new cast members have been added, joining the Stone family in spirit, if not in name. Indeed, the surname "Stone" is significant, not only for its resonance with the "Stone Soup" myth, but the name also points to Eliot's feminist intentions, although it is likely that most readers wouldn't make the connection between the family and historical feminist Lucy Stone. Eliot explained in an online blog post from January 9, 2009:

> Val and Joan are both "Lucy Stoners." Lucy Stone was a feminist from the 1800s, and she and her husband attempted to challenge the marriage laws of the day. Their two main issues were inheritance (women didn't get any) and maiden names. Lucy Stone believed that a woman should be able to keep her maiden name in marriage. This practice was again promoted by Jane Grant, a co-founder of the *New Yorker* magazine. She created the "Lucy Stone Society" in New York in the 1920s, an organization to encourage women to

keep their maiden names in marriage, as a way of asserting their independence. A woman who kept her maiden name was dubbed a "Lucy Stoner." So, the family name is "Stone" in *Stone Soup,* and both women have kept it. When Joan had a baby last year, I finally had the opportunity to include the name Lucy Stone in my strip by naming her daughter "Luci Stone Weinstein."

Thus, Eliot incorporated her own feminist heroes into her strip, although the naming likely went unnoticed by mainstream fans. For Eliot feminism was always important, as Eliot told *Ms.* magazine in a 1997 interview, her "purpose in doing the strip is to portray women in a feminist light. . . . My women are central characters who don't depend on men and aren't props in someone else's story" ("Jan Eliot" 72). However, the article continues on, noting that Eliot "is cautious about how far she can push her politics," for, according to Eliot, "cartooning is a very conservative field," and she "can't be too radical because right now the strip can't survive the crisis of an uproar" (72). Thus, particularly in the early days of the strip, Eliot maintained feminist intentions, but aware of her audience and the context of cartoons and daily newspaper strips, chose to be surreptitious, positing a feminist community through the lives and experiences of her characters, but doing so "cautiously" so as not to overly unsettle her syndicate or her readers.

Style and the Family Stone: Process, Theme, and Technique

In her long journey to syndication, Eliot continually endeavored to improve her drawing and writing skills. Eliot studied English and Women's Studies at the University of Oregon's Honors College, and also worked for many years drawing and writing technical manuals. By the time she was syndicated, Eliot had developed a process that has worked for her over the years, as she explained to GoComics:

> I still draw with an old-fashioned dip pen on archival paper. I work on a light table, scan the finished drawing, then fix my mistakes and add shading in Photoshop. I have a colorist, Olivia, who has been coloring Sundays for me since she was in her teens, and now she also colors the dailies for online distribution. I need quiet when I

FIGURE 7.2. Jan Eliot. "Sarah Resents." *Patience and Sarah.* 1981. From Jan Eliot's blog entry, "Beginnings."

write, rock and roll when I draw, and Comedy Central or a long phone conversation when I scan. While I'm very happy with the development of *Stone Soup,* I still think I have a lot to learn about drawing and writing.

Stone Soup generally has three or four panels for the dailies, with occasional divergences into single panels or a greater number of panels, particularly on Sundays. The focus of this analysis rests primarily on the daily comics, with an occasional study of a Sunday strip. The Sunday strips vary little in theme or tone from the dailies, but they tend to represent a pause in the unfolding narrative, instead providing a comment or respite, with the characters resting to enjoy the seasons, such as the yearly "You Gotta Love August" series in which the Stone family is pictured enjoying swimming, rafting, and cooking out in the backyard.

Over time, Eliot's artistic style evolved and become more polished. Although the themes remained much the same, in very early examples of *Patience and Sarah* the characters were rougher and the backgrounds consisted primarily of empty space (see figure 7.2), as evidenced in examples Eliot shared on her blog ("Beginnings"). Throughout the run of the strip, there has been no extradiegetic narrator or narrative text, and the strip largely maintains fixed internal focalization, a point-of-view that focuses on the characters and is guided by their actions. The style became more confident over the years, landing somewhere between abstract and realistic. It is a soft, comfortable style, and by the time the strip evolved into *Stone Soup,* Eliot used an accumulation of small details such as dirty dishes and rumpled clothing to help tell her stories. Eliot likes to play with speech balloons, using them, along with variations in the weight of the text, to convey emotion, although she always preserves a clear, legible style with her uppercase lettering. Eliot called the strip

FIGURE 7.3. Jan Eliot. "Don't Worry." *Stone Soup: The First Collection.* Kansas City: Andrews McMeel, 1997, p. 36.

"heartfelt" in an interview with Eric Alan, and the drawing style reflects that; it feels approachable, comforting, and warm.

On a daily basis, the strip depicts a community of women working together, beginning with the two sisters, extending to their family, and moving beyond their circle to the larger community that supports them. The locus of the action is the Stone household, anchored by Val. Val serves as the steady center of the family, supporting her sister, mother, and children. The strip shows, in a gentle and generous light, the struggles of the mothers to support their families, as seen in an early comic strip from the first collection of strips, published in 1997 by Andrews McMeel (see figure 7.3).

The strip follows a very similar format to an earlier strip from *Patience and Sarah,* although the characters and situation have altered slightly. In this four-panel sequence, Val attempts to comfort her sister Joan, as they both try to leave for work. The first panel features Val, clearly dressed in her work clothes, putting a comforting hand on her sister's shoulder, as Joan is pulled by her crying toddler Max, who screams "Ma! Ma! Ma!" Their mother Evelyn is bisected by the right panel border, but can be seen holding Max's hand. Val encourages her sibling, explaining "Don't worry, Joan. Max will be fine with Mom while you work." But Joan worries, "But I feel so bad! He looks pitiful." In the second panel, Joan sits at a desk, surrounded by papers, a lamp, and her computer, while Val stands behind her, again soothing, "Comes with the territory. Holly and Alix still dream up ways to make me feel guilty. You get used to it." The third panel serves to prove Val's point, as she is pictured, half bisected by the left panel border, startling back and crying, "What's this?!" as her two daughters, Holly and Alix are pictured to the right of the panel, Alix taking a picture of her mother as Holly coaxes her forward, stating, "Hurry, Alix, before she leaves for work again." Joan is absent from this third panel, with only Val confronted by her two daughters, the door separating them literally and figuratively. The smiles of the two young girls suggest delight in this prank, as in the final panel Joan peeks out of the door to her office to see the two girls singing sweetly, as demonstrated by the musical notes in the speech balloon, "Just a little something to remember you by." Val watches her daughters with a dark storm cloud over her head and a sour expression on her face, her hand resting on the door between work and home. Joan, new to this guilt and these performances, peeks out from her office and stares at the girls in alarm, as if just realizing the future of guilt she is now assuming. The girls both look up to the sky in angelic poses. Alix still clutches the camera, and their smiles and eyes display their giddiness.

The strip exhibits the guilt of the working mother. Joan shows her sadness at being separated from her crying son, and although Val clearly has more experience in this realm, her children have learned to adapt as well, provoking guilt by taking a photo, a clever statement about their mother's absence in their lives. They need an image to hold onto, they suggest, given her time away. Joan is new to this and looks worried. Val, however, initially appears calm and unflappable, but later, when confronted by her daughters, shows her annoyance in the form of the small, dark cloud hovering over her. Despite the very real angst of the situation that many working parents can relate to, there is also a suggestion that the girls, with their teasing smiles and singsong voices, are absolutely fine. Working together to guilt trip their mother, the daughters are clearly not tortured or unhappy—the kids are, in fact, alright.

The gag was adapted from an earlier incarnation in Eliot's strip, *Patience and Sarah* (see figure 7.2.). Comparing the two versions of the anecdote, it is evident that Eliot's style evolved, and in the later version the characters are drawn in a more fluid style. Similarly, the backgrounds have developed in the later iteration, becoming much more polished. Small details like the camera, a telephone, and even the clothing are sharper, adding specificity to the domestic scenes. The focus has now shifted to the larger family. The grandmother provides support for her daughters and grandchildren. Val comforts Joan. And the two younger sisters torment their mother. The family dynamics gain more importance, stressing the relationships between various figures, rather than just the mother/daughter bond of *Patience and Sarah*. *Stone Soup* is a community marked by collaboration rather than isolation.

FIGURE 7.4. Jan Eliot. "Ms. Stone." *Stone Soup: The First Collection.* Kansas City: Andrews McMeel, 1997, p. 123.

Unfortunately, not all in the community are understanding of working mothers, as evidenced in an early strip concentrating on the erosion of "family values" (see figure 7.4). In the first panel of the four-panel strip, Val's boss, Mr. Mabey (a clever play on the man's indecision and ineptitude), stands at the left of the panel, his emphatic speech balloon hovering above him, as, with his arms crossed and his eyebrow arched, he declares, "Ms. Stone, this country is falling apart! It was built on family values that are now **eroding**!" To his right, Val sits at her computer, with a light over her desk and file cabinets in the background, separating the two figures. Val looks up at her boss, a quizzical expression on her face. Mr. Mabey's rant continues in the second panel, with the point of view shifting slightly to show the computer and phone on Val's desk. Mr. Mabey has become even more emphatic, his face tilts upward, his eyes squeezed shut, his finger points upward to the sky, and his mouth is wide open as he yells, "We need to **recapture** strong family values!!" Val, still sitting at her desk, holds her hands in front of her, palms upturned in confusion, querying "What exactly does that mean?" The perspective shifts again in the third panel, with Mr. Mabey, still standing, but now on the left, jabbing at his palm, explaining, "You know— Focus on the family. Care for the family. Support the family." Val, in her chair, looks past her boss, her eyes frozen in confusion. The focus shifts once more in the final panel, centering on Val, still seated at her desk, pulling the telephone and its cord toward her, her eyes downward commas indicating dismay, as a jagged speech balloon radiates a message from the office staff: "Ms. Stone, your daughter is on line 2." Mr. Mabey, now cut in half by the right-side panel with only his face and shoulder visible, looms over Val, his eyes scrunched in anger as he argues, "Your kids call **way** too much." The sequence sends up the buffoonery of a blowhard of a man lecturing on the importance of family, then denigrating an employee when an actual family situation arises.

In the sequence Mr. Mabey is a dark and looming presence, his business jacket, tie, hair, and striped pants taking up too much space. He seems to hang over Val, cornering her in her chair. Val, in contrast, though also dressed in a work-appropriate blazer, wears much lighter colors and seems anchored to her desk as her boss circles around her. She is trapped by his presence and his words. The juxtaposition of the final two panels, in which Mr. Mabey rants about the need to "Focus on family. Care for the family. Support the family," followed by his angry dismissal of Val's family, points to the awful contradiction of this working mother and the privilege of the boss who pays lip service to "family values," while dismissing them in practice. Eliot makes a bold yet clever move in arousing the emotions of the reader in support of Val and a new sort of "family values" that supports working mothers, even as she invokes the logic or, in this case, lack of logic of Mr. Mabey, who is unable to see his specious position. In this case, the comic strip, often considered a lesser form of communication, takes advantage of its positioning to make a powerful argument. Robert Hariman notes, "As rhetoric is marginal, it also is a reservoir of power—a zone of those potencies suppressed in society" (48), and so, too, does this strip act as a "zone" or *agora* of rhetoric, inviting the readers to witness another sort of attack on family values.

Val frequently struggles with the sexism of her boss and colleagues, recalling Cathy's challenges with Mr. Pinkley, but throughout her battles Val radiates a calm confidence in her abilities, not doubting her worth. Unlike Cathy or even the women of *Where I'm Coming From*, Val appears actively opposed to dating men until much, much later days. At one point, Val explains her preference to her sister over coffee (see figure 7.5). The two sisters move very little in the four-panel sequence. They are both seated, drinking coffee, with the table in the foreground. The coffee pot rests in the center of the table, mooring the homey scene from panel to panel. Throughout the conversation Val holds a newspaper in front of her, only briefly glancing up at her sister in the second panel. Otherwise her gaze looks down at the paper (within the actual paper!). Joan sits at the table, also with her coffee mug, and her son Max rests in her lap, a bowl of food on the table in front of him. Max provides the movement and motion in the scene, offering a subtle,

FIGURE 7.5. Jan Eliot. "Do You Ever Think?" *Stone Soup: The First Collection.* Kansas City: Andrews McMeel, 1997, p. 12.

wordless secondary narrative as he initially stares at his food in the first panel, uses his spoon to lift food to his mouth in the second, drops the food into his lap in the third, and eventually buries his head in his lap in search of the aforementioned food in the final panel. Max's struggle emphasizes the domestic nature of the scene while delivering a humorous element to a strip that seems rather serious until the final panel.

The conversation presented in the speech balloons carries the action of the strip, with Joan querying whether her sister, a widow, would ever want to find a man and remarry. Val, uninterested and unconcerned wonders, "You mean when I can't open a jar or something?" alluding to an insignificant household task that might prove to be annoying, and could, conceivably be handled by a male counterpart (in the context of the daily newspaper, a female partner is inconceivable). Joan argues that Val is unromantic, but Val retorts that her sister "has a terrible track record when it comes to men," and, indeed, Joan's husband did leave her and her young son without warning. Yet Joan has not become jaded by her experience, asking, "Don't you miss waking up to that reassuring warmth and strength everyday?" a statement fully ironic in light of Joan's own husband, who was neither reassuring in his flightiness nor strong in character. Val responds, once more thoroughly disinterested, with a "nope," but Joan presses, asking "Why not?" Val, still focusing on the paper, suggests just how little she cares for this conversation, offering, "I bought a coffeemaker with a timer," which she implies give her all the "reassuring warmth" and "strength" she requires on a daily basis. Val equates a husband with a coffeemaker, an utterly domestic object and one which, in the form of the coffee pot, permeates every panel of the strip. Thus, Val ultimately concludes that the coffee maker, in its reliability and comfort, is superior to any male companion.

FIGURE 7.6. Jan Eliot. "If You'd Buy Polyester." *Stone Soup: The First Collection.* Kansas City: Andrews McMeel, 1997, p. 114.

While some readers might have balked at Val's dismissal of male companionship, unlike other comic strips in mainstream newspapers, *Stone Soup* worked, subtly in early days and more overtly in later years, to espouse feminist principles. In fact, in 1997 *Ms.* magazine declared, "Jan Eliot is one creative woman: she managed to bring the word 'feminism' into the lives of millions of readers in approximately 100 daily newspapers in the United States, Canada, and the Philippines without a peep from conservatives" ("Jan Eliot" 72). Of course, this is not entirely true as Eliot received her share of hate mail, such as the criticism from reader Ann Whelihan, who argued that the strip was "the ramblings of a person who only sees the dark side of life," and outrage from another reader, Bob Shackelford, who argued that he wanted "entertainment not politics on the cartoon page," after the strip supported universal healthcare, not to mention the offensive commentary on her website after the marriage of Val and Phil, a multiracial couple. In particular, Val is not afraid to take a stand, even as she continues her domestic duties, as she does in an encounter with her mother, Evelyn (see figure 7.6).

The four-panel strip begins with Evelyn facing the reader, mug of tea in hand, her daughter positioned behind her, smiling while ironing. Evelyn argues that if her daughter purchased polyester garments, she wouldn't need to iron, but Val responds, "I use the time to daydream." The point of view shifts in the second panel, closing in on Val, who raises a shirt with enthusiasm, exclaiming, "I pretend that each garment is an ultra-conservative. This could be Jesse Helms. This one Rush Limbaugh." Evelyn looks on in profile from the left side of the panel. The third panel features a tight shot of Val alone at the ironing board, one hand holding a pair of pants while the other hand sprays steam from the iron. She cries out, the speech balloon absent, "Oooh look! Mr. Buchanan! Crank this baby up to linen! Turn on the **steam!**" In the final panel, Evelyn, once more featured in a disapproving profile on the left of the scene, wonders, "Is this what happens when you let feminism into the home?" Meanwhile, Val, positioned on the other side of the ironing board, leans back, eyes closed, and calls out "How do **you** like the heat, Pat?" This strip takes a particularly political slant, not only naming Val as a feminist but also calling out several prominent conservative politicians. Yet, interestingly enough, the scene plays out between two women, one drinking tea and the other ironing, two domestic tasks associated with women. Val remakes this female-identified household chore into an act of rebellion, scorching the men of Capitol Hill, all the while erasing the rumples and the mess. Evelyn, an older generation, suggests Val simply give up the gendered task of ironing in favor of new technologies, but Val has found another purpose, a feminist repurposing, in the act of using heat and imagination to smooth out the creases, the literal wrinkles as represented by the sexist men who would stifle and stereotype her.

And in a fascinating twist which breaks the fourth wall, or panel, as the case may be, Val of *Stone Soup* brings together her own feminist community drawn (quite literally) from the daily comics. In a series of comic strips from 2004 (later reprinted in the anthology *Not So Picture Perfect: Book Five of the Syndicated Cartoon Stone Soup* by Four Panel Press), Val begins a book group comprised of female characters from other daily strips. In a post on her website, Eliot explained that the idea was inspired by her friend Lynn Johnston, who encouraged her work early on. While she was working toward a syndication contract, Eliot wrote to Johnston praising Lawrence's coming out storyline and including some of her own work. Johnston responded with a phone call, saying that "she appreciated my letter, and to say she liked my stuff, and that she thought I'd 'make it.'" In fact, Eliot received her contract "about a year later," and the two cartoonists became friends. Thus, when Eliot got the idea for Val to begin a book club, Elly from *For Better or For Worse*, was "the first character" she thought to include. And in that way the real-world community of female comic strip creators was reflected in the daily strips, although Eliot expanded her group to include a number of female characters from strips not created by women, including Connie from *Zits*, Rose from *Rose Is Rose*, and Alice from *Dilbert.* In the initial story arc, Val starts a book club with fellow female comic strip characters, providing a meta-commentary on female creators and female cre-

FIGURE 7.7. Jan Eliot. "How'd Your Book Club Go?" *Not So Picture Perfect: Book Five of the Syndicated Cartoon Stone Soup.* Eugene: Four Panel Press, 2005, p. 191.

ations in the newspaper strips. However, there was one noticeable absence in that first appearance of the book club—Cathy. When Val asks about Cathy's whereabouts Elly responds, "She said she'd join us right after she loses ten pounds and finds the perfect guy." To which Alice responds, "So . . . that's a 'never.'" Although Cathy later joins the group, her absence in the first gathering is noticeable as she was (and remains) one of the most popular, most recognizable female characters in comics created by a woman.

During the first meeting, the group discusses the book choice, at which point Rose transforms into her alter-ego, Vicky the biker, startling the other book club members, and though the metamorphosis is played as a gag, it also highlights the duality of these figures. While Rose shifts dramatically from dowdy mother to glamorous motorcycle rider, Elly is also portrayed as wilder than her wholesome image in the comics. The series suggests that these characters are an illusion of womanhood that never truly existed, for these characters hold depths long-hidden from readers.

As the group disbands for the night, daughter Alix enters the kitchen holding a bowl and queries her mother, Val, "How'd book club go, Mom?" (see figure 7.7). In the second panel of three, Alix wonders, "Where'd you meet those women, anyway?" Val responds, "Through work. I see most of them every day. But we never get a chance to socialize," a humorous commentary on the fact that all of these characters "work" with one another on the pages of the comics, but they never intermingle across the boundaries of their individual strips. The final panel switches to an exterior scene, with Vicky and Alice in the foreground of the Stone household driving away on her motorcycle. A speech balloon emerges from the house, indicating Val's commentary, "You never know what friendships will grow out of a book club," the unlikely pairing of Vicky and Alice underscoring the friendships and the differences of the female characters on the comics pages. And though this meeting of the book group has come to an end, the group would meet again several more times, most notably for Joan's baby shower—this time with Cathy in attendance.

Not only do the book club sequences reflect the multifarious nature of the female characters and the depths hidden from view, they also mirror the real-life community of female comic strips creators. Archived materials from the Billy Ireland Museum of Comics and Cartoon Art reveal various letters from one cartoonist to another, demonstrating the ways in which female comics creators supported one another. In one archived letter, Jan Eliot encouraged Nicole Hollander to pursue self-syndication, and in other letters between Nicole Hollander and Lynda Barry, Barry discussed Hollander's problems with rights and permissions. Hollander also exchanged epistles with Alison Bechdel, commenting on syndication and success. Thus, these women who also worked in the same field forged a connection like their comic strip counterparts, even though they, too, rarely had the chance to socialize in the "real world."

The Past as Future

Eliot frequently praised her connections with other creators, commending Lynn Johnston and Cathy Guisewite for inspiration, particularly as she worked toward syndication. Once she'd received her contract, Eliot commented that she remained cautious of being perceived as overly feminist, although over the years as the strip became more popular, it also became more directly political and overtly feminist, as in this later strip from September 2017, which demonstrates *Stone Soup*'s declaration as fully feminist. The argument for gender equality, long simmering with each addition, was unabashedly in evidence (see figure 7.8).

In the Sunday strip, Alix and Val are seated at the breakfast table. Val wears her robe and is drinking coffee while reading the newspaper. Alix, seated opposite, has a bowl of cereal in front of her as she poses a question to her mother: "Mom, are you a feminist?" The extended Sunday format allows room for six wider panels, three in each row, creating a structure that is both regular and repetitive. This is a cozy, stable domestic scene, most likely reflecting back the environment in which the comic itself is (optimistically) being read—the

FIGURE 7.8. Jan Eliot. "Mom, Are You a Feminist?" *The Oregonian*. September 24, 2017.

tradition of gathering at the breakfast table on a Sunday morning. Val responds to her daughter, "Absolutely," and in the second panel Alix asks, "Does Phil know?" Val, utterly nonplussed, barely looks up from her newspaper to respond, "Of course, Alix!" The third panel shifts the point of view behind Alix and Val and introduces the entrance of older sister Holly, who walks behind the table holding the cereal box. Holly watches the interaction as Val explains that her husband Phil is "a feminist too." Alix exclaims, "But he's a guy!" The fourth panel once again shifts point of view, this time focusing on the two sisters without their mother, emphasizing the next generation of women, and hopefully, feminists, as Holly leans down to her sister and explains, "Anyone who believes that a person's gender should not restrict access to success and happiness is a feminist." The fifth panel, which still focuses on the two girls, shows Alix asking, "So you're a feminist, Holly?" to which her sister, one hand raised in frustration, the other still clutching the cereal box, responds, "Who wouldn't be?" The final panel depicts the three females from the front, Alix to the left, quietly and contemplatively eating her cereal, while Holly on the right pours herself a bowl. Mother Val, at the center, pauses, clutching her coffee cup. Her smile is a tilted line indicating bemusement or perhaps bewilderment, and her eyebrows frame the dots of her eyes, suggesting surprise as a thought balloon rises up, pondering, "Omigosh. I did something right." Holly, like the strip, accepts feminism easily and casually, as being accessible to all and utterly logical. For Holly, feminism is as ordinary and accepted as breakfast cereal, a fact reinforced by strip after strip in Eliot's exploration of this feminist, female-led family. The humor comes from the wry and happy understanding of a mother comprehending that her work in educating her daughter has been realized. And Val and the Stone family did, indeed, instruct readers, more and more explicitly over the years, in the rightness of feminism.

Eliot decided to go into semi-retirement in 2015, choosing to publish *Stone Soup* only on Sundays. But in the flurry of concern over her leaving the funny pages, many paused to ask—who will take her place in the comics pages? Interviewer Eric Alan asked Eliot, "Who will pick up feminist, matriarchal issues?" to which Eliot responded, "There is no one doing what I do." And, indeed, *Cathy, For Better or For Worse,* and *Sylvia* have ended in the mainstream papers, as have *Where I'm Coming From, Dykes to Watch Out For,* and *Ernie Pook's Comeek. Stone Soup* itself retired officially in 2020. For years Eliot made an increasingly direct argument for a feminism through an inductive accumulation of small moments in the Stone household. Louise Groarke contends, "Induction is not an exercise in free creativity, but in representational creativity. . . . Induction is a power of making that also supplies an accurate account of something" (360), and thus *Stone Soup* offers this "accurate account" which came to represent feminism. Through their conversations, interactions, and problems, a feminism marked by equality and care was represented as the only logical choice—the accretion of humorous details served to demonstrate a feminism of connection and compassion that brought people together, rather than, as was frequently suggested in mainstream media, a strident feminism that pulled communities apart. Thomas Farrell notes that "the whole point of the *Rhetoric* is not its monism, but its circumstantiality and its eclecticism. That is what the practical ideal of *phronesis* really is all about" (188). Circumstantiality, as understood in psychological circles, is the notion of speech that might diverge and circle around the subject but eventually makes its point, while eclecticism, both in psychology and philosophy, points to incorporating many schools of thought and many points of view, and thus *Stone Soup* makes a phronetic argument for feminism that is sprawling and meandering and that brings in many characters and subject positions. Nedra Reynolds maintains, "Agency is not simply about finding one's own voice but also about intervening in discourses of the everyday and cultivating rhetorical tactics that make interruption and resistance an important part of any conversation" (59). *Stone Soup* intervenes in the "discourses of the everyday" disrupting and rescripting the conversation. These small moments come together, as in the folk tale of "Stone Soup," to make something larger. *Stone Soup* has, as Groarke notes of inductive argument, brought "something more out of something that is less" (429), invoking induction, which is, in her way of thinking, "more than an argument form, more than an indicative syllogism. It is the expression of a creative capacity to discern universal concepts and principles in the raw data of particular sense experience. First principles come into existence by a stroke of cognitive insight" (429). *Stone Soup* demonstrates the daily lives and moments of the Stone family, a shared "sense experience" that encouraged the reader to come to a larger conclusion, as Holly did, that feminism is the natural and sound state of the world and the family.

inductive reasoning

As Eliot's strip has come to an end, I find myself reflecting on what has and hasn't changed since *Cathy* appeared in 1976. Of course, there are the obvious changes wrought by technology. As people turn to the internet for news, actual newspaper readership is dwindling. And within the pages, the number of comics is decreasing, and perhaps even more alarmingly, the size of comic strips themselves is shrinking. However, technology has brought about some pleasing changes, with web comics growing in popularity and democratizing the publishing landscape, providing a platform for more diverse voices to share their work. And even within the narrowly circumscribed world of print, there are some exciting improvements, as many newspapers have switched to color even for the dailies. Yet a keen examination of the pages reveals that, unfortunately, much has stayed the same. As previously indicated, there are very few strips by women, and people of color remain largely absent, a fact not lost on Jan Eliot, who, in an interview with the *Washington Post*, commented that "it still feels like a boys club. Mostly you hear comments like women's humor is too 'soft' or not 'edgy enough' or, my favorite, not 'universal.' Or that we're just not funny. Well, that's bunk," but this misconception seems to ring true, for the number of female-created comic strips is in no way a reflection of society at large (Tobin). Furthermore, female characters, characters of color, and the LGBTQ+ community remain similarly underrepresented. When they are pictured, women in the comics continue to reflect stereotypes of gen-

not much has changed in print

dered behavior—tending children, cleaning house, and chatting, and they are overwhelming White, straight, and middle class. Sadly, there is no vision of intersectional feminism in the comics pages, and though many look to the internet for comics and new voices, the staid pages of the newspaper remain a stalwart bulwark against change. Despite the efforts of creators like Barry, Eliot, Johnston, Guisewite, Hollander, Brandon-Croft, and Bechdel, to look in the newspaper today, even the alternative weeklies, is to see a vision of gendered stereotypes that seems curiously resistant to change, reflecting a simulacrum of a conservative, homogenous society that has never truly existed. Unfortunately, I fear it is not only comic strips that remain relatively unchanged in depicting women, but society itself remains mired in sexism, misogyny, racism, and homophobia. Cathy's experience with Mr. Pinkley mirrors numerous accounts of the #MeToo movement. Elly's struggle to balance work and home looks like the lives of women today. And simply change the names of a few politicians in *Sylvia,* and the cartoons still resonate. Comics have endured for many years, but if newspaper comics are to continue, I would think that they would have to adapt to reflect culture and argue for change. What, I wonder, will I see in another thirty years? Will the comics remain largely insulated from actual society or will they shift and embrace diversity? As a girl I looked to the comics to help shape my identity, and as a woman I will continue walking down my driveway, collecting the paper, and looking for the Vals, Cathys, Ellys, Lekesias, Sylvias, and Mos. For in them I see connection and community, a wider world of women and the possibilities represented therein.

WORKS CITED

Alan, Eric. "Jan Eliot Retires from Daily *Stone Soup* Cartooning." 8 October 2015. Available online at: https://www.klcc.org/post/jan-eliot-retires-daily-stone-soup-cartooning.

Alexander, Jonathan and Jackie Rhodes. "Queer Rhetoric and the Pleasures of the Archive." *Enculturation* (2012). Available online at: http://enculturation.net/queerrhetoric-and the-pleasures-of-the-archive.

Alley, Patricia Williams. "Hokinson and Hollander: Female Cartoonists and American Culture." *Women's Comic Visions.* Ed. June Sochen. Detroit: Wayne State UP, 1991, pp. 115–40.

Appelo, Tim. "The Curator's Eye: Counterculture Comix." 1 September 2010. *City Arts Magazine*. Available online at: https://www.cityartsmagazine.com/issues-scattle-2010-09-curators-eye-counterculture-comix/.

Aristotle. *Nicomachean Ethics.* Available online at: http://classics.mit.edu/Aristotle/nicomachaen.1.i.html.

Aron, Nina Renata. "Lesbians Battled for Their Place in 1960s Feminism." 19 January 2017. Available online at: https://timeline.com/lesbians-battled-for-their-place-in-1960s-feminism-25082853be90.

Astor, Dave. "End Is Near for Groundbreaking 'Where I'm Coming From.'" 8 March 2005. *Editor and Publisher.* Available online at: https://www.editorandpublisher.com/news.end-is-near-for-grouwndbreaking-where-i-m-coming-from/.

Barry, Lynda. *Big Ideas.* Seattle: Real Comet Press, 1983.

——. *Blabber Blabber Blabber: Volume 1 of Everything.* Montreal: Drawn & Quarterly, 2011.

——. *Cruddy: An Illustrated Novel.* New York: Scribner's, 2000.

——. Email communication. 9 July 2007.

——. *The Freddie Stories.* New York: Harper Perennial, 1999.

——. *The Fun House.* New York: Harper and Row, 1987.

——. *Girls and Boys.* Seattle: Real Comet Press, 1981.

——. *The Good Times Are Killing Me.* New York: Harper Perennial, 1988.

——. *The! Greatest! of! Marlys!* Seattle: Sasquatch Books, 2000.

——. "The Home Front/Modern Romance." *Esquire Magazine.* August 1983–December 1988.

——. *One Hundred Demons.* Seattle: Sasquatch Books, 2002.

——. Personal interview with Susan Kirtley. Rhinebeck, NY. 19 July 2006.

——. *Picture This: The Near-Sighted Monkey Book.* Edmonton: Drawn & Quarterly, 2010.

——. *Syllabus: Notes of an Accidental Professor.* Montreal: Drawn & Quarterly, 2014.

——. *What It Is.* Edmonton: Drawn & Quarterly, 2008.

Bechdel, Alison. *Are You My Mother?: A Comic Drama.* New York: Houghton Mifflin, 2012.

——. *Dykes to Watch Out For.* Ithaca: Firebrand Books, 1986.

——. *Dykes to Watch Out For: The Sequel.* New York: Alyson Books, 1992.

——. *The Essential Dykes to Watch Out For.* New York: Houghton Mifflin, 2008.

——. *Fun Home.* New York: Houghton Mifflin, 2006.

——. *The Indelible Alison Bechdel: Confessions, Comix, and Miscellaneous Dykes to Watch Out For.* Ithaca, NY: Firebrand Books, 1998.

——. *More Dykes to Watch Out For.* New York: Alyson Books, 1998.

——. *New, Improved! Dykes to Watch Out For.* Ithaca, NY: Firebrand Books, 1990.

Bentley, Rosalind, "Cartoonist Brandon Knows Just Where She's Coming From." *Minneapolis Star Tribune.* 23 August 1993, p. 1E.

Berger, Arthur Asa. *Li'l Abner: A Study in American Satire.* Jackson: University Press of Mississippi, 1994.

Berinstein, Paula. "Black and White and Dead All Over: Are Newspapers Headed 6 Feet Under?" *Searcher,* vol. 13, no. 10, November 2005, p. 46.

Berkeley, Kathleen C. *The Women's Liberation Movement in America.* Westport: Greenwood Press, 1999.

Bernstein, Robin. "'I'm Very Happy to Be in the Bernstein Reality-Based Community'": Alison Bechdel's *Fun Home,* Digital Photography, and George W. Bush." *American Literature,* vol. 89, no. 1, March 2017, pp. 121–54.

Beyerstein, Lindsay. "Cathy Was Not a Feminist Trailblazer." *BigThink.* Available online at: http://bigthink.com/focal-point/cathy-was-not-a-feminist-trailblazer.

Beyette, Beverly. "Politics in Comic Strips: It's No Funny Business." *LA Times.* 2 November 1988. Available online at: https://www.latimes.com/archives/la-xpm-1988-11-02-vw-701-story.html.

Bitzer, Lloyd. "The Rhetorical Situation." *Philosophy & Rhetoric,* vol. 1, no. 1, 1968, pp. 1–14.

Bjornstad, Randi. "Comic Relief." *Eugene Register Guard.* 11 October 2015. Available online at: https://www.registerguard.com/article/20151011/LIFESTYLE/310119954.

Blake, Meredith. "The Demise of 'Cathy.'" *New Yorker.* 12 August 2010. Available online at: http://www.newyorker.com/books/page-turner/the-demise-of-cathy.

Blockley, David. "Practical Wisdom and Why We Need to Value It." 11 July 2014. Available online at: https://blog.oup.com/2014/07/practical-wisdom-vsi/.

Borrelli, Christopher. "Being Lynda Barry." 8 March 2009. *Chicago Tribune.* Available online at: https://www.chicagotribune.com/news/ct-xpm-2009-03-08-0903030596-story.html.

Brandon-Croft, Barbara. *Where I'm Coming From.* Kansas City: Andrews McMeel Publishers, 1993.

———. *Where I'm Still Coming From.* Kansas City: Andrews McMeel Publishers, 1994.

Breines, Winifred. *The Trouble Between Us: An Uneasy History of Black and White Women in the Feminist Movement.* New York: Oxford UP, 2006.

Brooke, Robert, and Charlotte Hogg. "Open to Change: Ethos, Identification, and Critical Ethnography in Composition Studies." In *Ethnography Unbound: From Theory Shock to Critical Praxis,* eds. Stephen Dobrin and Sidney Brown, Albany: SUNY Press, 2004, pp. 115–30.

Brunner, Edward. "'Shuh! Ain't nothin' to it': The Dynamics of Success in Jackie Ormes's *Torchy Brown.*" *MELUS,* vol. 32, no. 3, Fall 2007, pp. 23–49.

Buchanan, Lindal. *Rhetorics of Motherhood.* Carbondale: Southern Illinois UP, 2013.

Burke, Kenneth. *Attitudes Toward History.* Los Altos: Hermes Publications, 1959.

———. *A Rhetoric of Motives.* Berkeley: U of California P, 1969.

Campbell, Karlyn Kohrs. *The Rhetorical Act,* Belmont, CA: Wadsworth, 1982.

Carlson, A. Cheree. "Ghandi and the Comic Frame: Ad Bellum Purificandum." *Quarterly Journal of Speech*, vol. 72, no. 4, 2009, pp. 446–55.

Carrier, David. *The Aesthetics of Comics.* University Park, PA: Pennsylvania State UP, 2002.

Charland, Maurice. "Constitutive Rhetoric: The Case of the *Peuple Québécois.*" *Quarterly Journal of Speech*, vol. 72, no. 2, 1987, pp. 133–50.

Chávez, K. R., and C. L. Griffin. "Introduction." *Standing in the Intersection: Feminist Voices, Feminist Practices in Communication.* Albany, NY: SUNY Press, 2012.

Chute, Hillary. *Graphic Women.* New York: Columbia, 2010.

———. "Interview with Lynda Barry." *Believer,* vol. 6, no. 9, November/December 2006, pp. 47–58.

Cole, Harriette. "Dreamleapers with Harriette Cole." 23 December 2018. Available online at: http://harriettecole.com/Barbara-brandon-croft-dreamleapers-with-harriette-cole-onwbai/ 01.

Collins, Gail. *When Everything Changed: The Amazing Journey of American Women from 1960 to the Present.* New York: Little, Brown, and Co., 2009.

Collins, Patricia. *Black Feminist Thought. Knowledge, Consciousness, and the Politics of Empowerment.* New York: Routledge, 2000.

Comic Book Legal Defense Fund. "Barbara Brandon-Croft." 23 February 2016. Available online at: http://cbldf.org/2016/02/profiles-in-black-cartooning-barbara-brandon-croft/.

Crenshaw, Kimberlé. "Demarginalizing the Intersection of Race and Sex: A Black Feminist Critique of Antidiscrimination Doctrine, Feminist Theory and Antiracist Politics." *University of Chicago Legal Forum,* 1989, pp. 139–67.

Crow, Mrs. Gary. "Letter to the Editor." 1 April 1992. *Atlanta Constitution,* p. A12.

"Crusaders with Pen and Ink." *Ebony,* January 1993, p. 36.

Cvetkovich, Ann. "Drawing the Archive in Alison Bechdel's *Fun Home.*" *WSQ: Women's Studies Quarterly,* vol. 36, nos. 1–2, 2008, pp. 111–28.

Dean, Gabrielle. "The 'Phallacies' of Dyke Comic Strips." *The Gay 90s: Disciplinary and Interdisciplinary Formations of Queer Studies,* edited by Thomas Foster et al. New York: New York UP, 1997, p. 203.

Dean, Michael. "Lynda Barry Interview." *Comics Journal,* vol. 296, February 2009, pp. 34–51.

de Jesús, Melinda. "Liminality and Mestiza Consciousness in Lynda Barry's *One Hundred Demons.*" *MELUS,* vol. 29, no. 1, Spring 2004, pp. 219–52.

———. "Of Monsters and Mothers: Filipina American Identity and Maternal Legacies in Lynda Barry's *One Hundred Demons.*" *Meridians: Feminism, Race, Transnationalism,* vol. 5, no. 1, 2004, pp. 1–26.

Dworkin, Andrea. *Right Wing Women.* New York: Tarcher Perigee, 1983.

Eco, Umberto. *In The Name of the Rose.* Harcourt Brace: San Diego, 1983. First published 1980. Paperback repr. (New York: Warner Books, 1984).

Egendorf, Laura. *Satire.* Farmington Hills, MI: Greenhaven Press, 2002.

El Refaie, Elisabeth. "Visual Modality Versus Authenticity: The Example of Autobiographical Comics," *Visual Studies,* vol. 25, no. 2, 2010, pp. 162–74.

Eliot, Jan. "The Amazing Cathy Guisewite." 12 August 2010. Available online at: https://www.stonesoupcartoons.com/2010/08/the-amazing-cathy-guisewite.html.

———. "Back in the Studio." 9 January 2009. Available online at: https://www.stonesoupcartoons.com/2009/01/back-in-the-studio-after-holidays-and-snow-storms.html.

———. "Beginnings. 9 September 2009. Available online at: https://www.stonesoupcartoons.com/2009/09/beginnings.html.

———. "Blog for Go Comics." 16 August 2013. Available online at: https://www.gocomics.com/blog/3368/jan-eliot-stone-soup.

———. *Not So Picture Perfect: Book Five of the Syndicated Cartoon Stone Soup.* Eugene: Four Panel Press, 2005.

———. *Stone Soup: The First Collection of the Syndicated Cartoon.* Eugene: Four Panel Press, 1997.

Emmert, Lynn. "Life Drawing: An Interview with Alison Bechdel." *The Comics Journal,* vol. 82, 2007, pp. 34–52. Available online at: http://www.tcj.com/the-alison-bechdel-interview/.

Farley, Christopher John. "Black Women Find a Voice on the Comics Page." *USA Today*. 13 October 1991, p. 4D.

Farrell, Thomas. "Practicing the Arts of Rhetoric: Tradition and Invention." *Philosophy & Rhetoric*, vol, 24, no. 3, 1991, pp. 183–212.

Franzen, Monika, and Nancy Ethiel. *Make Way: 200 Years of American Women in Cartoons*. Chicago: Chicago Review Press, 1987.

Freedman, Ariela. "Drawing on Modernism in Alison Bechdel's *Fun Home*," *Journal of Modern Literature*, vol. 32, no. 4, 2009, pp. 125–40.

Frye, Northrop. *Anatomy of Criticism*. New Jersey: Princeton University Press, 2000.

"A Funny Business." *Ethos*. Available online at: https://issuu.com/ethosmag/docs/summer2012/23.

Galvan, Margaret. "Feminism Underground: The Comics Rhetoric of Lee Marrs and Roberta Gregory." *WSQ: Women's Studies Quarterly*, vol. 43, nos. 3–4, Fall/Winter 2015, pp. 203–22.

Garden, Joe. "Interview." 8 December 1999. Available online at: http://www.avclub.com/content/node/24257.

Gardiner, Judith Kegan. "Queering Genre: Alison Bechdel's *Fun Home*: A Family Tragicomic and *The Essential Dykes to Watch Out For*." *Contemporary Women's Writing*, vol. 5, no. 3, 2011, pp. 188–207.

Gardner, Jared. "Storylines." *SubStance*, vol. 40, no. 124, 2011, pp. 53–69.

Gill, Miranda. *Eccentricity and the Cultural Imagination in Nineteenth-Century Paris*. Oxford: Oxford UP, 2009.

Glaubitz, Nicola. "Playbooks as Imaginary Theatre: Visuality and Description in Early Modern English Drama." *Literary Visualities: Visual Descriptions, Readerly Visualisations, Textual Visibilities*. Ed. Guido Isekenmeier, et al., Berlin: De Gruyter, Inc., 2017, pp. 21–78.

Goldstein, Kalman. "Al Capp and Walt Kelly: Pioneers of Political and Social Satire in the Comics." *Journal of Popular Culture*, vol. 25, no. 4, Spring 1992, pp. 81–96.

Gordon, Ian. *Comic Strips and Consumer Culture, 1890–1945*. Washington, DC: Smithsonian Institution Press, 1998.

Grant, Pat. "Lynda Barry . . ." *Guardian*. 1 November 2016. Available online at: https://www.theguardian.com/books/2016/nov/02/lynda-barry-on-comics-creativity-and-matt-groening-we-both-disdain-each-others-lives.

Gray, Louise. "Aartsetc: Just an Everyday Story of Lesbian Folk at Home: What Makes *Dykes to Watch Out For* Such a Hit Cartoon Strip," *Independent on Sunday*, 19 October 2003, Features 8.

Green, Constance M. "Barbara Brandon." Available online at: https://www.encyclopedia.com/education/news-wires-white-papers-and-books/brandonbarbara-1960.

Groarke, Louise. *An Aristotelian Account of Induction: Creating Something Out of Nothing*. Montreal: Queens UP, 2009.

Grossberg, Lawrence. "Is There Rock after Punk?" *Critical Studies in Mass Communication*, vol. 3, no. 1, 1986, pp. 50–74.

Grossman, Pamela. "Barefoot on the Shag." Salon.com. May 18, 1999. Available online at: http://www.salon.com/books/int/1999/05/18/barry/index.html.

Guisewite, Cathy. *The Cathy Chronicles.* Kansas City: Sheed Andrews and McMeel, 1978.

———. *Cathy Twentieth Anniversary Collection.* Kansas City: Andrews McMeel Publishers, 1996.

———. 1994 Commencement Address. University of Michigan. LSA Magazine. Fall 1994, pp. 31–33.

———. Interview with Makers. 21 September 2012. Available online at: https://www.youtube.com/watch?v=V9Bn62E5Z9g.

———. *Reflections: A Fifteenth Anniversary Collection.* Kansas City: Andrews McMeel Publishers, 1991.

Hambly, Mary. "An Interview with Lynda Barry." *Backbone 4: Humor by Northwest Women.* Ed Barbara Wilson and Rachel Da Silva. Emeryville: Seal Press, 1982.

Harding, Sandra. "Introduction: Is There a Feminist Method?" *Feminism and Methodology.* Ed. Sandra Harding. Bloomington: Indiana UP, 1987, pp. 1–14.

Hariman, Robert. "Status, Marginality, and Rhetorical Theory." *Quarterly Journal of Speech,* vol. 72, no. 1, 1986, pp. 38–54.

Harper, Frances Ellen Watkins. "Address to the Eleventh National Women's Rights Convention." May 1866. Available online at: https://www.blackpast.org/african-american-history/speeches-african-american-history/1866-frances-ellen-watkins-harper-we-are-all-bound-together/.

Harris, Miriam. "Cartoonists as Matchmakers: The Vibrant Relationship of Text and Image in the Work of Lynda Barry." *Elective Affinities: Testing Word and Image Relationships,* edited by C. MacLeod and V. Plesch. Amsterdam: Rodopi Press, 2009, pp. 129–43.

Harvey, R. C. *The Art of the Comic Book.* Jackson: U of Mississippi P, 1996.

———. *The Art of the Funnies: An Aesthetic History.* Jackson: U of Mississippi P, 1994.

———. "Chic's Blondie." *Comics Journal.* 13 September 2012. Available online at: http://www.tcj.com/chics-blondie/.

Hatfield, Charles. *Alternative Comics: An Emerging Literature.* Jackson: U of Mississippi P, 2005.

Heer, Jeet, and Kent Worcester, eds. *Arguing Comics: Literary Masters on a Popular Medium.* Jackson: U of Mississippi P, 2004.

———. *A Comics Studies Reader.* Jackson: U of Mississippi P, 2009.

Heintjes, Tom. "The Cathy Guisewite Interview." *Hogan's Alley: The Magazine of the Cartoon Arts.* Available online at: https://www.hoganmag.com/blog/cathy-guisewite-the-goodbye-girl.

———. "The Lynn Johnston Interview." *Hogans Alley #1.* Available online at: https://www.hoganmag.com/blog/the-lynn-johnston-interview.

Hendley, W. Clark. "The Horatian Satire of Trudeau's Doonesbury." *Journal of Popular Culture,* vol. 16, no. 4, Spring 1983, pp.103–15.

Hester, Sam. "Crossovers and Changeovers: Reading Lynn Johnston through Margaret Mahy." *ImageText,* vol. 3, no. 3. Available online at: http://imagetext.english.ufl.edu/archives/v3_3/hester/.

Hewitt, Annie. "Universal Justice and Epieikeia in Aristotle." *POLIS,* vol. 25, no. 1, 2008, pp. 115–30.

Hickey, Elisabeth. "Black Woman Cartoonist Is First to Hit Syndication." *Washington Times.* 17 September 1991, p. E1.

Hodgart, Matthew. *Satire: Origins and Principles.* New York: Routledge, 2017.

Hollander, Nicole. *I'm Training to Be Tall and Blonde.* New York: St. Martin's Press, 1979.

———. Journal. January 1983. *The Nicole Hollander Archives.* The Ohio State University. Billy Ireland Cartoon Museum and Library. NH 3. Folder 28.

———. *Ma, Can I Be a Feminist and Still Like Men?: Lyrics from Life.* New York: St. Martin's, 1980.

———. *The Sylvia Chronicles: 30 Years of Graphic Misbehavior from Reagan to Obama.* New York: New Press, 2010.

———. *Tales of Graceful Aging from the Planet Denial.* New York: Broadway Books, 2007.

———. *That Woman Must Be on Drugs: A Sylvia Collection.* New York: St. Martin's, 1981.

———. *The Whole Enchilada: A Spicy Collection of Sylvia's Best.* New York: St. Martin's Griffin, 1986.

Horn, Maurice. *Women in the Comics.* Philadelphia: Chelsea House Publishers, 2002.

Hughes, Judy. "Cathy Isn't Comic." Letter to the Editor. *Washington Post.* 5 November 1988, p. A21.

Hyde, Michael J., ed. *The Ethos of Rhetoric.* Columbia: U of South Carolina P, 2004.

Inge, M. Thomas. "Comics as Culture." *What's So Funny: Humor in American Culture.* Ed. Nancy Walker. Wilmington: Scholarly Resources Inc., 1998, pp. 185–92.

"Jan Eliot." *Ms.,* January/February, 1997, p. 72.

Jewish Women's Archive. "Nicole Hollander." Available online at: https://jwa.org/feminism/hollander-nicole.

Johnston, Lynn. "Blog." *GoComics.* Available online at: https://www.gocomics.com/blog/3161/lynn-johnston-for-better-or-for-worse.

———. *It's the Thought That Counts: For Better or For Worse 15th Anniversary Collection.* Kansas City: Andrews McNeel Publishing, 1994.

———. *I've Got the One-More-Washload Blues.* Kansas City: Andrews McNeel Publishing, 1981.

———. *A Look Inside: 10th Anniversary Collection.* Kansas City: Andrews McNeel Publishing, 1999.

———. *Suddenly Silver: Celebrating 25 Years of For Better or For Worse.* Kansas City: Andrews McNeel Publishing, 2004.

Jones, Steven Loring. "From 'Under Cork' to Overcoming: Black Images in the Comics." Available online at: https://www.ferris.edu/HTMLS/news/jimcrow/links/essays/comics.htm.

Joseph, Sister Miriam. *Shakespeare's Use of the Arts of Language.* New York: Columbia UP, 1947.

Kahn, Juliet. "On Hating Cathy." *Comics Journal.* 10 April 2018. Available online at: http://www.tcj.com/on-hating-cathy/.

Laughlin, Kathleen, Julie Gallagher, Dorothy Sue Cobble, Eileen Boris, Premilla Nadasen, Stephanie Gilmore, and Leandra Zarnow. "Is It Time to Jump Ship?

Historians Rethink the Waves Metaphor." *Feminist Formations,* vol. 22, no. 1, Spring 2010, pp. 76–135.

Leff, Michael, and Ebony A. Utley. "Instrumental and Constitutive Rhetoric in Martin Luther King Jr.'s 'Letter from Birmingham Jail.'" *Rhetoric and Public Affairs,* vol. 7, no. 1, Spring 2004, pp. 37–51.

Lemberg, Jennifer. "Closing the Gap in Alison Bechdel's *Fun Home." WSQ: Women's Studies Quarterly,* vol. 36, nos. 1–2, 2008, pp. 129–40.

Levine, Judith. "The Dykes Next Door." *Ms.,* vol. 11, no. 6, October–November 2001, pp. 52–58.

Lipsky, Jessica. "Erasing the Establishment: Wimmen's Comix Gets Its Due." *San Francisco Weekly.* 6 July 2016. Available online at: http://www.sfweekly.com/news/erasingthe-establishment-wimmens-comix-getsitsdue/.

Litton, Claire. "No Girls Allowed!: Crumb and the Comix Counterculture." PopMatters. 23 January 2007. Available online at: https://www.popmatters.com/no-girls-allowedcrumb-andthe-comix-counterculture-2495784021.html.

Logan, Shirley Wilson. *We Are Coming: The Persuasive Discourse of Nineteenth-Century Black Women.* Carbondale: Southern Illinois UP, 1999.

London, Lisa. "Review of *Dykes to Watch Out For," Women's Review of Books,* vol. 21, no. 3, December 2003, p. 10.

Long, Christopher P. "The Ontological Reappropriation of Phronesis," *Continental Philosophy Review,* vol. 35, no. 1, 2002, pp. 35–60.

Lorde, Audre. *Sister Outsider: Essays and Speeches.* Trumansburg, NY: Crossing, 1984.

Loria, Keith. "Cover Story: A Comic Strip Is a Comic Strip." *Associated Press.* 8 October 1993.

Lucas, J. R. "The Lesbian Rule." *Philosophy,* vol. 30, no. 114, July 1955, pp. 195–213.

Markstein, Don. "Friday Foster." Available online at: http://www.webring.org/l/rd?ring=comics;id=1;url=http%3A%2F%2Fwww%2Etoonoedia%2Ecom%2Ffriday%2Ehtm.

Mautner, Chris. "Interview with Lynn Johnston." 14 August 2007. Available online at: http://panelsandpixels.blogspot.com/2007/08/lynn-johnston-part-two.html.

McKinnon, Sara L. "Essentialism, Intersectionality and Recognition: A Feminist Rhetorical Approach to the Audience." *Standing in the Intersection: Feminist Voices, Feminist Practices in Communication,* edited by K. R. Chávez and C. L. Griffin. Albany, NY: SUNY Press, 2012, pp. 189–210.

McNulty, Timothy. "'Cathy' Broke Glass Ceiling for Comics: Strip About Single Woman Had 34-year Run." *Pittsburgh Post-Gazette.* 14 August 2010, p. A–1.

Medjesky, Christopher. "The Logic of Ironic Appropriation: Constitutive Rhetoric in the Stewart/Colbert Universe." Dissertation. August 2012. Bowling Green State University.

Miller, Ann. *Reading Bande Desineé: Approaches to French-Language Comic Strip.* Chicago: U of Chicago P, 2007.

Miller, Carolyn. "Genre as Social Action." *Quarterly Journal of Speech,* vol. 70, 1984, pp. 151–67.

Montresor, Jaye Berman. "Comic Strip-Tease: A Revealing Look at Women Cartoon Artists." *Look Who's Laughing: Gender and Comedy,* edited by Gail Finney. Langhorn, PA: Gordon and Breach Science Publishers, 1994, pp. 335–47.

Moore, Anne Elizabeth. "The Rumpus Interview." 22 April 2012. Available online at: https://therumpus.net/2012/04/the-rumpus-interview-with-lynda-barry/.

Moore, Ryan. "Postmodernism and Punk Subculture: Cultures of Authenticity and Deconstruction." *Communication Review,* vol. 7, 2004, pp. 305–27.

Moraga, Cherrie, and Gloria Anzaldúa, eds. *This Bridge Called My Back: Writings by Radical Women of Color.* New York: Kitchen Table/Women of Color Press, 1983.

Morgan, Marcyliena. *Language, Discourse and Power in African American Culture.* Cambridge: Cambridge UP, 2002.

Morris, Clifford. "Letter to the Editor." 25 November 1993. *Atlanta Journal and Constitution,* p. A12.

Muñoz, José Esteban. *Disidentifications: Queers of Color and the Performance of Politics.* Minneapolis: U of Minnesota P, 1999.

Murez, Cara Robert. "Enduring Friendship Supports Structure, Sympathy and Cheerleading." *Eugene Register Guard.* 21 October 2018. Available online at: https://www.registerguard.com/entertainmentlife/20181021/enduring-friendship-supports-structure-sympathy-and-cheerleading.

Murray, Steve. "A Woman's Work is Finally Done: Cathy is Retiring, Having Taught Me All I Know About the Fairer Sex." 27 August 2010. *National Post.* Available online at: https://www.pressreader.com/canada/national-post-latest-edition/20100827/284614598852733.

Musgrave, David. *Grotesque Anatomies: Menippean Satire Since the Renaissance.* Cambridge: Cambridge Scholars Publishing, 2014.

Olson, Valerie Voigt. "Garry Trudeau's Treatment of Women's Liberation in *Doonesbury.*" Master's Thesis. Michigan State University, 1982.

O'Sullivan, Judith. *The Great American Comic Strip: One Hundred Years of Cartoon Art.* Boston: Little, Brown, and Co., 1990.

Peck, Harry Thurston. *American Edition of Petronius. The Bookman: An Illustrated Magazine of Literature and Life,* vol. 17, March–April 1903, pp. 86–92.

Perelman, Chaïm, and L. Olbrechts-Tyteca. *The New Rhetoric: A Treatise on Argumentation.* Notre Dame: U Notre Dame P, 1969.

Perry, Elizabeth Israels. "Introduction." Alice Sheppard's *Cartooning for Suffrage.* Albuquerque: U of New Mexico P, 1994, pp. 3–19.

Pew Research Center. "Newspapers Fact Sheet." 9 July 2019. Available online at: https://www.journalism.org/fact-sheet/newspapers/.

Pomerleau, Clark A. "Consorting with the Enemy?: Women's Liberation Rhetoric About Sexuality." In *Sexual Rhetorics: Methods, Identities, Publics.* Edited by Jonathan Alexander and Jacqueline Rhodes. New York: Routledge, Taylor & Francis Group, 2016, pp. 188–202.

Powers, Thom. "Lynda Barry." *Comics Journal,* vol. 132, 1989, pp. 60–75.

Quintero, Ruben, ed. *A Companion to Satire: Ancient and Modern.* Malden: Blackwell, 2007.

Rand, Erin J. "An Appetite for Activism: The Lesbian Avengers and the Queer Politics of Visibility." *Women's Studies in Communication* vol. 36, no. 2, 2013, pp. 121–41.

Reynolds, Nedra. "Interrupting Our Way to Agency: Feminist Cultural Studies and Composition." *Feminism and Composition Studies: In Other Words,* edited by Susan Jarratt and Lynn Worsham. New York: MLA, 1998, pp. 58–73.

Rich, Adrienne. *Of Woman Born: Motherhood as Experience.* New York: Norton Inc., 1995.

Robbins, Trina. "Desperate Housemates." *Women's Review of Books,* vol. 26, no. 3, 2009, p. 11.

———. *From Girls to Grrlz: A History of Women's Comics from Teens to Zines.* San Francisco: Chronicle Books, 1999.

———. *The Great Women Superheroes.* Northampton: Kitchen Sink Press, 1997.

———. *Pretty in Ink: North American Women Cartoonists 1896–2013.* Seattle: Fantagraphics, 2013.

Rogers, Sean. "A Conversation with Lynda Barry." *Walrus Magazine.* 17 November 2008. Available online at: http://www.walrusmagazine.com/blogs/2008/11/17/a-conversation-with-lynda-barry/.

Rohy, Valerie. "In the Queer Archive: *Fun Home," GLQ: A Journal of Lesbian and Gay Studies,* vol. 16, no. 3, 2010, pp. 341–61.

Roth, Benita. *Separate Roads to Feminism: Black, Chicana, and White Feminist Movements in American's Second Wave.* Cambridge: Cambridge UP, 2003.

Round, Julia. "Visual Perspective and Narrative Voice in Comics: Redefining Literary Terminology." *International Journal of Comic Art* 9.2 (2007): 316–29.

Rule, Sheila. "Popular Culture; The 'Girls' Talking, With a Black Perspective." 19 July 1992. *The New York Times.*

Saguisag, Lara. *Incorrigibles and Innocents: Constructing Childhood and Citizenship in Progressive Era Comics.* New Brunswick: Rutgers UP, 2018.

Samanci, Özge. "Lynda Barry's Humor: At the Juncture of Private and Public, Invitation and Dissemination, Childish and Professional." *IJOCA,* vol. 8, no. 2, Fall 2006, pp. 181–99.

Schlafly, Phyllis. "What's Wrong with Equal Rights for Women." Originally published 1972. Available online at: https://awpc.cattcenter.iastate.edu/2016/02/02/whats-wrong-with-equal-rights-for-women-1972/.

Shaw, Adrienne. "Women on Women: Lesbian Identity, Lesbian Community, and Lesbian Comics," *Journal of Lesbian Studies,* vol. 13, 2009, p. 93.

Shafer, Jack. "A Eulogy for the Alt-Weekly." *Politico Magazine.* 20 December 2017. Available online at: https://www.politico.com/magazine/story/2017/12/20/a-eulogy-for-the-alt-weekly-216124.

Sheppard, Alice. *Cartooning for Suffrage.* Albuquerque: U of New Mexico P, 1994.

Sherman, Bill. "Interview with Trina Robbins: The First Lady of Underground Comix." *Comics Journal,* vol. 53, 1980, pp. 46–54, 56–58.

Shimanoff, Susan B. "The Portrayal of Conversation in 'Cathy' Cartoons: A Heuristic Tool for Rules Research." *Communication Yearbook,* vol. 10, no. 1, 1987, pp. 788–807.

Snyder, R. C. "What Is Third Wave Feminism? A New Direction Essay." *Signs*, vol. 34, no. 1, Autumn 2008, pp. 175–196.

Soper, Kerry D. *Garry Trudeau: Doonesbury and the Aesthetics of Satire.* Jackson: UP of Mississippi, 2007.

———. *We Go Pogo: Walt Kelly, Politics, and American Satire.* Jackson: UP of Mississippi, 2012.

Spacks, Patricia Meyer. "Some Reflections on Satire." *Satire: Modern Essays in Criticism,* edited by Ronald Paulson. Englewood Cliffs, NJ: Prentice Hall, 1971, pp. 360–78.

Stallcup, Jackie. "'The Feast of Misrule': *Captain Underpants,* Satire, and the Literary Establishment." *Genre,* vol. 41, Spring/Summer 2008, pp. 171–202.

Stansell, Christine. *The Feminist Promise: 1792 to the Present.* New York: Modern Library, 2010.

Sweeney, Louise. "When Life Becomes a Comic Strip." *Christian Science Monitor.* 13 March 1980. Available online at: https://www.csmonitor.com/1980/0313/031358.html.

Syme, Rachel. "The Feminist Paradox of Cathy Guisewite." *Cut.* 19 March 2019. Available online at: https://www.thecut.com/2019/03/the-feminist-paradox-of-cathy-guisewite.html.

Tesher, Ellie. "Witty New Strip Joins Cartoon Lineup." *Toronto Star.* 5 January 1992, p. A2.

Thomas, Keith. "Homegirls in 'Toon Town.'" *Atlanta Journal and Constitution.* 13 January 1992, p. B1.

Thorpe, Martha Elizabeth. "Making American: Constitutive Rhetoric in the Cold War." Dissertation. August 2011. Texas A & M University.

Tinker, Emma. "Selfhood and Trauma in Lynda Barry's 'Autobifictionalography.'" *Identity and Form in Alternative Comics, 1967–2007.* Unpublished Thesis 2008. Available online at: http://emmatinker.oxalto.co.uk/.

Tobin, Suzanne. "Stone Soup." *Washington Post.* 24 October 2003. Available online at: http://washingtonpost.com.

The Toronto Star. "Was Cathy a Voice of Female Progress or Stereotyped Neurosis?: Character was No Blondie, But Feminists are Happy to See Her Go." 22 August 2010. IN 1. Available online at: <http://www.pressreader.com/canada/toronto-star/20100822/282166467489466>. Accessed 10 April 2017.

Trove. "Barbara Brandon." Available online at: https://inthetrove.com/barbarabrandoncroft.

Tyree, Tia C. M. "Contemporary Representations of Black Females in Newspaper Comic Strips." *Black Comics: Politics of Race and Representation,* edited by Sheena C. Howard and Ronald L. Jackson II. New York: Bloomsbury, 2013, pp. 45–64.

Walker, Nancy A. *A Very Serious Thing: Women's Humor and American Culture.* Minneapolis: U of Minnesota P, 1988.

Wander, Philip. "The Third Persona: An Ideological Turn in Rhetorical Theory." *Central States Speech Journal,* vol. 35, no. 4, 1984, pp. 197–216.

Wandering Schmuck. "Why All the Hate for Cathy?" 25 May 2013. Available online at: http://www.wanderingschmuck.com/the-wandering-schmuck-blog/why-all-the-hate-for-cathy.

Wanzo, Rebecca. *The Blacker the Ink*. New Brunswick: Rutgers, 2015.

Warner, Judith. *Perfect Madness: Motherhood in the Age of Anxiety*. New York: Riverhead Books, 2007.

"Was Cathy a Voice of Female Progress or Stereotyped Neurosis?: Character was No Blondie, But Feminists are Happy to See Her Go." *Toronto Star*. 22 August 2010, p. IN 1.

Watson, Julia. "Autographic Disclosures and Genealogies of Desire in Alison Bechdel's *Fun Home*." *Biography*, vol. 31, no. 1, 2008, pp. 27–58.

Westerband, Yamissette. "Lesbian in the 20th Century." Available online at: http://outhistory.org/exhibits/show/lesbians-20th-century/lesbian-feminism.

White, James Boyd. "Law as Rhetoric, Rhetoric as Law: The Arts of Cultural and Communal Life." *University of Chicago Law Review*, vol. 52, no. 3, Summer 1985, pp. 684–702.

Williams, Mary Elizabeth. "Goodbye, Cathy, Feminist Trailblazer." 13 August 2010. Available online at: https://www.salon.com/2010/08/13/requiem_for_cathy/.

Witek, Joseph. *Comic Books as History: The Narrative Art of Jack Jackson, Art Spiegelman, and Harvey Pekar*. Studies in Popular Culture. Jackson: UP of Mississippi, 1989.

Wolk, Douglas. "Dreams of Youth: Lynda Barry's *Blabber, Blabber, Blabber* and More." 13 April 2012. *New York Times*. Available online at: https://www.nytimes.com/2012/04/15/books/review/lynda-barrys-blabber-blabber-blabber-and-more.html.

Worcester, David. *The Art of Satire*. Cambridge, MA: Harvard UP, 1940.

Yackley, Rachel Baruch. "Enjoy a Little 'Stone Soup' What's Funny About Single Parenthood? Cartoonist from St. Charles Knows." *Chicago Daily Herald*, 12 March 2003, p. F3.

Yonker, Madeline. "The Rhetoric of Mom Blogs: A Study of Mothering Made Public." Dissertation. Syracuse University, 2012.

Zerbisias, Antonia. "Ack! Cartoonists and Feminists Quarrel Over Demise of Cathy." *Star*. 20 August 2010. Available online at: https://www.thestar.com/news/insight/2010/08/20/ack_cartoonists_and_feminists_quarrel_over_demise_of_cathy.html.

Zucco, Tom. "Stone Soup: Making Something Out of Nothing." *St. Petersburg Times*, 26 January 2003, p. 1F.

INDEX

STUDIES IN COMICS AND CARTOONS

Jared Gardner and Charles Hatfield, Series Editors
Lucy Shelton Caswell, Founding Editor Emerita

Books published in Studies in Comics and Cartoons focus exclusively on comics and graphic literature, highlighting their relation to literary studies. The series includes monographs and edited collections that cover the history of comics and cartoons from the editorial cartoon and early sequential comics of the nineteenth century through webcomics of the twenty-first. Studies that focus on international comics are also considered.